Internet Searches for Vetting, Investigations, and Open-Source Intelligence

Internet Searches for Vetting, Investigations, and Open-Source Intelligence

Edward J. Appel

CRC Press
Taylor & Francis Group
Boca Raton London New York

CRC Press is an imprint of the
Taylor & Francis Group, an **informa** business

CRC Press
Taylor & Francis Group
6000 Broken Sound Parkway NW, Suite 300
Boca Raton, FL 33487-2742

First issued in paperback 2017

© 2011 by Taylor and Francis Group, LLC
CRC Press is an imprint of Taylor & Francis Group, an Informa business

No claim to original U.S. Government works

ISBN-13: 978-1-4398-2751-2 (hbk)
ISBN-13: 978-1-138-11223-0 (pbk)

Library of Congress Cataloging-in-Publication Data

Appel, Edward J.
　　Internet searches for vetting, investigations, and open-source intelligence / Edward J. Appel.
　　　　p. cm.
　　Includes bibliographical references and index.
　　ISBN 978-1-4398-2751-2 (hardcover : alk. paper)
　　1. Information technology--Social aspects. 2. Social change. 3. Internet searching. 4. Computer crimes--Prevention. I. Title.

HM851.A727 2011
303.48'33--dc22
　　　　　　　　　　　　　　　　　　　　　　　　　　　　　　　　　2010044424

Visit the Taylor & Francis Web site at
http://www.taylorandfrancis.com

and the CRC Press Web site at
http://www.crcpress.com

To my wife, Nancy,
without whose loving editing
my life would be illiterate.

CONTENTS

SECTION II   *Legal and Policy Context*

SECTION III   Framework for Internet Searching

SECTION IV *Internet Search Methodology*

INTRODUCTION

The design, mode of use, and nature of a shared infrastructure create vulnerabilities for all users.[1]

At the core of the information infrastructure upon which we depend is the Internet, a system originally designed to share unclassified research among scientists who were assumed to be uninterested in abusing the network. It is that same Internet that today connects millions of other computer networks making most of the nation's essential services and infrastructures work.[2]

Perhaps nothing better symbolizes the information age transformation of the world than the changes that the Internet is bringing about in social, business, and government life. From communications and commerce to games, dating, and blogging, the World Wide Web of networks is a host of increasing importance to human activities of all kinds. For public and private enterprises, information technology (IT) has enabled improved efficiencies, but has introduced increased levels of complexity and vulnerability that—at least twenty-five years into widely networked computing—still present a daunting challenge for enterprise and personal security.

This book is dedicated to intelligence, investigative, and research professionals who must utilize the Internet in their duties. Today's changes in technology, human activities, and global connectivity are taking place so rapidly that we must anticipate, and continually update, what is available, in order to learn what we can online. Some institutions, businesses, and other organizations may adapt more slowly than others. The law (statute, litigation, regulation) is also deliberate in addressing technological and social change. Because this book is about the intersection of Internet technology, investigative, or intelligence methodology and legal frameworks, it is also about how to approach changes. Therefore, every effort has been made to keep this text forward looking, timely, useful, and adaptable to likely outcomes.

The Internet and the *World Wide Web*, or *Web* and *Net*, are often used synonymously, but in fact they are different. Excellent histories of the Internet have been written, as well as texts about the basics of operating systems, applications, and other personal computer attributes (some of which are listed in the bibliography of this book). Here, the focus is on how to use a computer and the Internet (with the Web riding on it) for intelligence, information, and investigation, assuming that the reader has a basic knowledge of browsing, research, and analysis. Yet it is valuable to see this resource in historical context, because, since it was created by scientific researchers for researchers, the Internet has offered a unique capability of finding and accessing data quickly and accurately over distance. Suffice it to say that the creation of the Web in 1991 enabled the Internet to function more efficiently for searching, accessing, transmitting, and analyzing information. As the Internet and Web mature, the evolutionary drive toward providing ever more useful and timely information should allow users continuously to improve in online research.

To an intelligence analyst, the Internet has become vital because of the capabilities of browsers, search engines, Web sites, databases, indexing, searching, and analytical applications. A competent user need not understand that the Internet, through Web protocols and applications, enables the transmission of packets reassembled in a browser or application to view a replica of data hosted elsewhere. By the mid-1990s, this ability to "teleport" the information sought at near light speed from remote systems to a user had become a vital part of business, government, academia, and the investigative community. Since the 1990s, the investigative community itself has grown rapidly, as corporate, law enforcement, intelligence, and academic uses of computer systems updated their methods. What data aggregation, computer analysis, and visualization did for science in the two generations before the twenty-first century, networking through the Internet allowed the rest of us to exploit in the 2000s. Without the capabilities of a mathematician, computer programmer, database specialist, statistician, or philosopher-logician, the ordinary user can leverage the capabilities of networked systems on the Internet to find critically important data on a timely basis. Spurred by 9/11, intelligence, law enforcement, and security personnel have accelerated the use of the Internet to help paint a much more complete and up-to-date picture of people, entities, and activities. Meanwhile, vendors of data—exploiting the unprecedented opportunity to aggregate identifiable information on any topic—have taken the achievements of the LexisNexis, ChoicePoint, and Accurint types of data aggregation products to the next level. Now all three are one company, and LexisNexis is a prime example of how valuable data can be monetized through Internet services provided to subscribers for a fee.

The most remarkable aspect of the expansion of Internet data services is that most are free. Huge quantities of information are housed in databases accessible at no charge over the Internet, if one knows where to look. As the competition for browser popularity was won at the end of the 1990s by Internet Explorer (IE), most users took it for granted that IE, Netscape, Safari, FireFox, and several others will provide quick, graphically rich, relatively secure connections to any Web site sought in seconds. To find those Web sites, of which there were over 200 million by about 2003, Google and its competitors were indexing over 3 billion pages. By 2004, weblogs were very popular, as were social sites that began to make MySpace, Facebook, and a raft of others an increasing part of the daily lives of tens of millions of users worldwide. By 2005, over 50% of Americans (and higher percentages of other countries' populations) had high-speed, broadband connections and relied on the Internet for emails, instant messaging, and daily information queries. By the end of 2009, the plethora of personal Internet applications became available on computers, mobile platforms including cell phones, and media-like electronic books.

The two most significant trends of the past twenty years' Internet development are high-speed connection, anytime, anywhere, and the ability to use the connection to find and use the information you need, when you need it. Another trend is that connection to the Internet may be a very risky endeavor.

It may appear odd that IT security is still such a major issue after about thirty years of personal computers. However, it is natural for several reasons, the least of which is that people, not machines, commit the deliberate and erroneous acts that breach security. IT architecture still struggles to incorporate comprehensive safeguards. Enterprise philosophy often fails to include the simple fact that in any sizable group of workers, some will always steal or otherwise harm the organization's interests. The malevolent and error-prone users, coupled with many varieties of malicious codes, more than ever before have automation at their disposal, magnifying the potential harm they cause, and the difficulty of protection.

Inevitably, crime has migrated onto the Internet along with all other types of human activities. Socially unacceptable behavior has found its happy place in Web sites, blogs, and communities of all kinds, from child exploitation to frauds, extremism, harassment, slander, identity theft, and anonymous leaks. Identity theft and trafficking in illegally copied films, TV shows, music, software, and hardware designs are good examples of how the Internet has magnified the impact of crime. When terrorists want to ensure the widest impact of a bloody attack, or gather greater support, they use the Internet to disseminate news, propaganda, and proselytizing messages. Once, dozens of instances of illegal online acts were documented. Now, tens of millions of victims or perpetrators may be involved in a single act or enterprise, and criminal gangs reside, seemingly untouchable, all over the World Wide Web.

When the President's Critical Infrastructure Protection Board was set up in the mid-1990s with my participation on the NSC staff, I suffered along with many others from a remarkable form of myopia: We knew that telecommunications, IT, transportation, utilities, financial services, etc., were all critical infrastructures. However, as the headlong plunge into an online world engulfed the on- and off-duty workforce, we did not include people—the lifeblood of the enterprise—as a separately identifiable critical infrastructure. In an age that has rapidly progressed from looking at personnel as human resources to human capital, and in which more workers have been displaced by layoffs, outsourcing, robotics, and downsizing than ever before, how can we not look at people as the most critical part of the critical infrastructure?

As a majority of people embraced the Internet for all sorts of activities and have made it a part of their lives at work and at leisure, records of their lives have been embedded in the public, semipublic, and deep Internet. On social sites like MySpace and Facebook, sales sites like eBay and Craigslist, thousands of blog sites and more, hundreds of millions of individuals have painted self-portraits online. In a pre-Internet world, a background investigation would seek out the education, prior employment, residences, references, and records that verified the candidate's eligibility and qualifications. Today, when a significant part of a candidate's life takes place online, and a substantial body of Web-based data may provide key insights into past behavior, an investigation must include Internet vetting to be complete and successful. Yet most employers do not include Internet vetting in background investigations.

While the examples above are about employment background vetting, all types of investigations require comprehensive, professional Internet checking. Today, online investigations have become vital for tracking criminal enterprises using the Internet, including drug dealers, gangs, spammers, crackers, pirates, sexual predators, fraudsters, identity thieves, and contraband traffickers of all types. Computer crime and digital evidence are growing by orders of magnitude that are as yet unmeasured except by occasional surveys. Law enforcement and private security lack precise metrics to demonstrate the extent, incidence, growth, and impact of computer-related crime, but perceive its expansion. IT security lacks firm benchmarks for cost-benefit ratios for network, software, and hardware security options. Monumental growth in the quantity of digital evidence mirrors the rapid expansion and dropping cost of digital storage and data creation. The digital footprints of cybercriminals are now essential for tracking the perpetrators of illicit acts.

Similarly, open-source intelligence increasingly relies on fusion of all-source collection and analysis by computer, with Internet data included. Such intelligence is a vital part of national security, competitive intelligence, brand protection, marketing research, benchmarking, and even data mining within the enterprise. Without items posted online, a research report on any topic may not be timely, complete, or include the basis for reliable predictions and trends, visualization, geolocation, and statistical analysis.

In the information age, it is critical that we understand the implications of the activities and data documented on the Internet. It is equally important that we study and adopt the privacy principles necessary to keep any Internet searches legal, fair, equitable, and transparent.

This book was written to advocate improved security and investigative measures, and establish guidelines for adopting new methods to improve the profession: Internet searching conducted as part of investigations and intelligence collection. To master Internet searching, enterprises and investigators must adopt legal, policy, and procedural principles and methods suitable to the purpose. As a relatively new technique, it is important that Internet searching be used carefully and appropriately. The guidance here should help both government and private sector enterprises, lawyers, and investigators of all kinds to apply the right techniques and thereby significantly improve their practices.

Likewise, this book is meant to help investigative professionals develop the core skills and techniques to exploit the huge and quickly growing resources available on the Web on every topic imaginable, and to place these methods in the context of analytical processes that are useful in academic, professional, and personal life.

NOTES

1. Dam, Kenneth W., and Lin, Herbert S., eds., *Cryptography's Role in Securing the Information Society* (Washington, DC: National Research Council, The National Academies Press, 1996).
2. Schneider, Fred B., ed., *Trust in Cyberspace* (Washington, DC: National Research Council, National Academies Press, 1999).

3. Lewis, James A., *Securing Cyberspace for the 44th Presidency, A Report of the CSIS Commission on Cybersecurity for the 44th Presidency* (Washington, DC: Center for Strategic and International Studies, 2008).
4. Berners-Lee, Tim, *Weaving the Web* (New York: HarperCollins, 1999).
5. O'Harrow, Robert, Jr., *No Place to Hide* (New York: Free Press, 2005).

Section I

Behavior and Technology

> When I took office, only high energy physicists had ever heard of what is called the World Wide Web.... Now even my cat has its own page.[1]

Since the early 1990s, profound changes have taken place in the Internet, sociological patterns of behavior involving information systems, and the quantity and availability of data online. Meanwhile, enterprise and information security pose as serious a challenge to agencies and businesses today as ever. Among the personnel security and counterintelligence implications of these changes is the need to prevent, detect, and respond to illegal behavior on an employer's system and on personal systems that implicate an employer, pose a threat to people, assets, or information, or threaten the employer's reputation. Evidence of illicit and illegal behavior on the public Internet by employees could expose an employer to significant and unforeseen liabilities and damages.[2] While the world seems to agree that the employer has the right to monitor and control enterprise systems, which are, after all, the employer's property, users are able to compromise enterprises using not only their employer's but also their personal computers, and have been known to do so on the public Internet. Failure to consider online behavior by employees, candidates, and others connected with an enterprise (e.g., contractors, partners, and customers) can result in serious vulnerabilities. Similar implications apply to any person or entity that is of concern to decision makers, such as executives, competitors, products, and the latest developments.[3] For investigators, intelligence analysts, and researchers, the

Internet has reached the stage where it is more likely than not to provide valuable information on any topic.

In this section, the need for Internet searching for investigations, including vetting and intelligence, will be explored.

NOTES

1. Clinton, Bill, "Excerpts from Transcribed Remarks by the President and the Vice President to the People of Knoxville on Internet for Schools," The White House, Office of the Press Secretary, October 10, 1996, http://govinfo.library.unt.edu/npr/library/speeches/101096.html (accessed August 6, 2010).
2. SANS on Internet security, http://www.sans.org/reading_room/; NIST Computer Security Resource Center, http://csrc.nist.gov/; U.S. Department of Justice, Computer Crime and Intellectual Property Section Internet Security resource list, http://www.cybercrime.gov/links1.htm#ISSRb.
3. Dam, Kenneth W., and Lin, Herbert S., eds., *Cryptography's Role in Securing the Information Society*, Washington, DC: National Research Council, National Academies Press, 1996); Schneider, Fred B., ed., *Trust in Cyberspace*, National Research Council (Washington, DC: The National Academy Press, 1999; Lewis, James A., Project Director, *Securing Cyberspace for the 44th Presidency, A Report of the CSIS Commission on Cybersecurity for the 44th Presidency* (Washington, DC: Center for Strategic and International Studies, December 2008); O'Harrow, Robert, Jr., *No Place to Hide* (New York: Free Press, 2005).

1

The Internet's Potential for Investigators and Intelligence Officers

According to Merriam-Webster, the Internet is an electronic communications network that connects computer networks and organizational computer facilities around the world.[1] While the World Wide Web is defined differently, the words *Web* and *Net* have become more or less synonymous with the Internet. By design, the Internet is "public." Incredible quantities of data on the Internet are available to anyone with a computer and a browser. Some Web sites limit access to hosted data in various ways, and some allow the individual posting information to invoke privacy restrictions on unauthorized access. If no limitations apply, posted information is open to the public. Some Web sites require users to register to gain access to data, but registered users are not restricted in their use of the site's data, within its authorized use policy (AUP) and applicable copyright and trademark law. Therefore, on a great number of sites, the posted information could be deemed public even with access limitations. AUPs on some sites prohibit certain uses of hosted information, such as for commercial purposes or marketing (e.g., spam, unsolicited commercial email). Users agree to abide by AUPs to gain access to these sites, but enforcement of AUP violations is rare and ineffectual.

PEOPLE, PLACES, ORGANIZATIONS, AND TOPICS

The Internet and World Wide Web were created to facilitate communications and exchange of government and private sector research information.[2] Starting in the early 1990s, the Internet began a process of rapid expansion, in terms of linked computers, users, and activities taking place online. The global network of networks has continued to grow, and with the addition of wireless connectivity in cell phones and portable devices, the Internet has permeated every facet of society—the "information society" in global parlance.[3] Studies of American Internet usage by the Pew Internet and American Life Project chronicle the fact that living life online has rapidly become a habit for about 80% of the U.S. population.[4] Internetworldstats.com reports that of the 6.7 billion world population in 2008, about 23.8% (1.6 billion) used the Internet, and usage has grown 342% between 2000 and 2008.[5]

In the charts in Figures 1.1 to 1.3, which should be interpreted as high-level estimates, recent and projected Internet growth are shown.[6]

Key attributes of American Internet use include growing dependence on the communications, social interaction, and data storage "in the cloud" offered by computing devices, and the ability to use mobile devices such as a cell phone to interact in real time with other people and online systems.

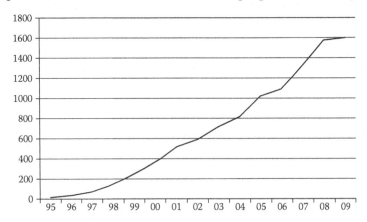

Figure 1.1 Millions of users. Fifteen years of growth have driven worldwide Internet users from 16 million to over 1.6 billion (as of January 2008). (From InternetWorldStats.com, Miniwatts Marketing Group, January 2008, http://www.internetworldstats.com/emarketing.htm [accessed May 5, 2010].)

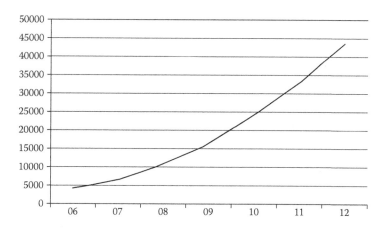

Figure 1.2 Petabytes per month. Cisco's report and estimate of Internet Protocol traffic in petabytes per month (including both Internet and non-Internet traffic, i.e., including private networks) from 2006 to 2012. (From Cisco Internet and network traffic estimates, http://www.cisco.com/en/US/netsol/ns827/networking_solutions_white_papers_list.html [accessed April 10, 2010].)

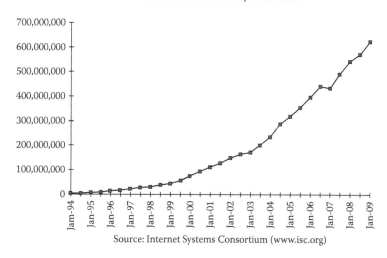

Figure 1.3 The Internet Systems Consortium Internet Survey Host Count shows Web site growth since the explosive expansion began in the mid-1990s. (From Internet Survey Host Count, The Internet Systems Consortium, http://www.isc.org/solutions/survey [accessed May 5, 2010].)

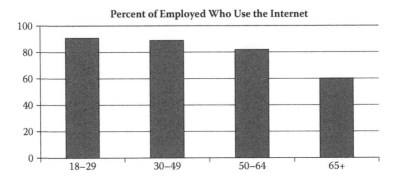

Figure 1.4 Pew Internet study of wired workers.

The Pew Internet and American Life Project (www.pewinternet.org) presents some of the richest and most useful data on the meaning of the Internet in American life, its growth, and trends. Pew's study of networked workers reveals some interesting trends in American workplaces and homes, among which are that government workers are more likely to use the Internet or email daily at work (72%), while 62% of all workers do. About 42% of workers do some work at home, but 56% of networked workers do some work at home. This poses obvious security concerns.

It appears that besides business, the vast majority of Internet users enjoy legal activities, from communications and commerce to games, dating, and blogging. Increasingly, people are looking to the Internet for entertainment, including films, videos, music, TV, and applications that they can access for free or at low cost. Declining revenues at television networks, newspapers, and publishing houses testify to the shift from TV and print to online media. But while enjoying the virtual world, a large-scale change in society's views about creative intellectual property rights has occurred. Copyrighted movies, music, publications, and software are traded openly over Internet sites specifically designed to deter criminal investigations and to facilitate transfer of goods without royalty to producers, such as by peer-to-peer networks.[7] Are users of fee-free films, music, and software more likely to misappropriate their employer's digital intellectual property for their own use?

One of the more fascinating aspects of the Internet from a behavioral point of view is whether the use of this technology has changed how people act, and if so, the implications. In just two areas, child exploitation and fantasy games, disturbing trends have become visible (if not yet fully understood). For almost twenty years, child pornography, solicitation of minors by predators, and illicit group activities centered on sexual exploitation of children have dominated the computer crime and digital evidence efforts of federal, state, and local U.S. law enforcement. "Massively multiplayer online role-playing games" and other fantasy games, like *Second Life*, have begun to allow players to live an alternate existence, complete with the option to commit virtual and actual criminal acts with no real-world consequences. Not surprisingly, crimes like money laundering have already invaded virtual reality games. Even some video games focused on crime (*Grand Theft Auto*) and warfare (*Fantasy Wars*, the *Halo* series) may encourage players to act out violently or criminally. The wide popularity of child porn and even wider popularity of fantasy may or may not portend new neuroses or inclinations to physical criminal acts, but some psychologists and psychiatrists have expressed concerns. One of the world's oldest professions, prostitution, occupies its place in e-commerce. Police, perplexed, see the trends and are inundated with cases. Victimization starts in front of a computer screen.[8]

Internet crime has been growing while computer evidence (including that found in digital devices like cell phones) has spiked for all sorts of crimes.[9] Digital evidence is not confined to the devices used in criminal acts (which are instruments of the crime) but often can be found in the network logs of Internet service providers (ISPs), telecommunications companies, and computer systems hosts. Internet-based digital evidence can be transient and remote, including data stored abroad, where records unavailable to U.S. law enforcement may protect international cybercriminals. International cybercrime agreements have recently been strengthened to attack such problems. At this writing, only a small minority of Internet criminals are being identified and prosecuted. Cybercriminals therefore pose a new threat to society in the form of potential insiders, working in government, business, or academia while committing crimes anonymously on the Internet.

As previously stated, most Internet users are well within legal bounds. Yet recent expansion of Internet use and the quantity and types of data available have created an opportunity and a necessity for background vetting, investigations, and open-source intelligence of all types.

An interesting phenomenon accelerating the popularity of the Internet is the emergence of search engines, with Google dominating the field over rivals including Yahoo!, Microsoft's search engine Bing, AOL, and Ask. Consolidation of search engines is inevitable, and is ongoing (e.g., Microsoft's search/marketing agreement with Yahoo! and the evolution of Live Search to Bing). The usefulness of Internet search is aptly measured in the billions of dollars of Google stock value, as well as Google's expansion into offering applications, online storage, email, etc. "The ultimate search engine would basically understand everything in the world, and it would always give you the right thing. And we're a long, long ways from that," said Google cofounder Larry Page.[10] Yet search has become essential to those online. Internet users, including investigators, human resources staff, attorneys, and everyone else involved in assessing people in the workplace, are apt to conduct searches when they believe it is potentially useful. Today, that includes Googling applicants, coworkers, superiors, subordinates, and just about anyone else interesting. While most organizations wait to consider the right (fair, effective) way to include Internet vetting in personnel processes, the staff has already adopted their own policies, procedures, and methods for inquiring into individuals' online presence.[11]

Many employers use the Internet as a part of the application process, requiring candidates to fill in online application forms and communicate at least in part online during the preemployment processing. Automation not only makes the process potentially more efficient, accurate, and timely, but it also can allow candidates a greater measure of control and understanding of the various stages (e.g., declaration of interest, formal request to be considered, presentation of credentials, competitive evaluation, interview, conditional offer of employment, background investigation, adjudication).[12] The personally identifying information exchanged in the process is sensitive and should be protected, to ensure applicants' privacy.

Employers conduct background investigations to determine the eligibility, qualifications, and trustworthiness of prospective employees, existing employees, and candidates for clearance or promotion. Traditionally (within federal and state laws) employers either in-house or through background investigation firms verify the facts on a resume and application, including checks of identity, residences, education, prior employment, arrests, convictions, civil suits, bankruptcies, legal sanctions, and similar indicators of past behavior. Because past behavior is the single most reliable indicator of future behavior, a candidate's track record often provides the most convincing evidence of the likelihood of success in his or her new position. Likewise, a record of past misbehavior may indicate that the candidate would be likely to fail, to cause a loss to the new employer, or to pose a threat to people, assets, and information in the workplace.

Internet activities have become a new "neighborhood," where people are likely to have posted information, to be recorded in directories and other online databases, and to have been the subject of postings by other people. Scores of federal, state, and local records are available online, including criminal and civil court records, residence and telephone directories, employer Web sites, business directories, professional associations, and similar files accessible from the Internet. Some of the data available from the public Internet include text, photographs, video, audio, and media records that chronicle serious misbehavior by individuals.[13]

Past investigations for government clearances often included "neighborhood investigations," where those living near a candidate were canvassed for information relating to factors used to determine eligibility and establish knowledge, skills, and abilities, to add to evidence needed to offer employment, grant clearances, and document suitability for the job. Over the past several decades, the neighborhood investigation (though still carried out) has produced less information of value than before. Not only are neighbors less likely to share derogatory observations about the candidate, but fewer neighbors are likely these days to even know the person. This is particularly true since many people move frequently and reside in multi-family structures or neighborhoods where social contact is minimal.[14]

Today, an individual's social circle may not be defined as much by geography as it is by electronic connectivity. Using social Web sites, instant messaging, cell phones, and similar networking, people are likely to exchange information about themselves by posting it online or sending it (illustrated with photos, video, and sound) to a list of friends and acquaintances. The profiles created often include peccadilloes, problems, and misbehavior unlikely to have been communicated or documented electronically in a previous era.[15] In order to address this opportunity, about 45% of employers told a 2009 CareerBuilder.com survey (up 20% from the previous year) that they search the Internet for social postings by applicants, to see if what they find may impact a hiring decision. About 35% reported that social Web site postings and similar online data resulted in "no hire" decisions. Among the reasons cited to the CareerBuilder survey were provocative/inappropriate photos or information, drinking or drug use, bad-mouthing previous employers, coworkers, or clients, poor communications skills, discriminatory comments, misrepresentation of qualifications, and shared confidential information from a previous employer.[16]

A PRACTITIONER'S PERSPECTIVE

In over four years of systematic Internet searches on individuals under investigation, the author's company has found a wide variety of types of derogatory information, some exclusively found online and some found through multiple sources. The vast majority of the information found supports subjects' candidacies, verifies their background, shows the subjects in a good light, or is otherwise positive in nature. In our experience, about 6% or less of those being screened for employment have had Internet references online significant enough to warrant doubt about their eligibility. During investigations and collection of open-source information about suspected individuals (those believed to have committed wrongdoing), we have found documentation of illegal, illicit, or socially unacceptable behavior considerably more often than not. The bottom line is that the Internet is a valuable source of information on individuals.

Beyond people who often appear in Internet files, we found that businesses, organizations of all kinds, groups, entities, and topics are profiled more efficiently when Internet sources are used, in addition to any other research methods. By experimenting with the timing and nature of the searches used, we found that often descriptive information can be found and a "dossier" started literally within a few minutes, on virtually any topic. This can enable more rapid, accurate, complete, and sophisticated planning of the sources to be used and steps to be taken in collecting and analyzing required information. Among the uses for these kinds of searches are due diligence, mergers and acquisitions, litigation support, marketing, brand protection, competitive intelligence, counterintelligence, counterterrorism, identifying groups for and against an issue, scoping out the extent of a particular illegal or illicit activity online, following comments and postings about a current topic (e.g., a trial or dispute), and contractor surveys prior to a request for proposals. We found an astonishing array of different types of data, which can enable a much better analysis of available information on any topic when Internet search results are included.

Besides intelligence, investigator, and security exploitation of the Internet, professionals in many different areas have come to rely on information available over the Internet. Two examples are clinicians and librarians, based on recent articles and books illustrating how important reference materials online have become to efficiency in their practices.[17]

10

THE SEARCH

Creation and innovation in Internet search tools have provided the opportunity for both Internet advertising and research to grow quickly. Finding open-source information on virtually any topic has been made easier, while all types of data available on the public Internet continuously expand. A 2003 University of California at Berkeley study[18] estimated the quantity of data available on the Internet at about 533,000 terabytes as of 2002, and growing rapidly. One measure found that 95% of the worldwide Internet audience conducted 61 billion searches in August 2007. Over 10.5 billion searches using the five most popular search engines were conducted in January 2008.[19] In 2008, Google said its search engine had "crawled" (collected and indexed material) from 1 trillion unique URLs, or Web addresses.[20] While these statistics are provided to give a sense of the volume of Internet searches conducted, their most important meaning is that Internet search is popular with users, and even more popular with advertisers and e-commerce sites that depend on search engines for much of their revenue. Just as we should be a bit skeptical about the statistics, we should also understand that search engines exist primarily to sell, and as Google's multi-billion-dollar income illustrates, the audience is huge.

Both data growth and data mining are related to the uses made of the Internet, and its usefulness to researchers. Dramatic growth of Internet-accessible data is documented and forecast to continue.[21] One conclusion haunting security and counterintelligence officers is that finding the information needed (on or off the Internet) and information assurance will become more challenging and important with time.

Investigators, security officers, adjudicators, intelligence personnel, and other authorities all use the Internet to find facts quickly. Because they utilize common search engines like Google (along with perhaps 60%+, 71%, or 87% of the population, depending on which market share statistics you believe),[22] they often find references that are instructive, informative, and useful about people, organizations, and topics of interest. There are few guidelines for random Internet searches conducted out of curiosity, for a business purpose or research. Many people have adopted their own approach to searching, with more or less skill depending on their level of interest, training, or experience.

The ubiquity of Internet searching and lack of guidelines can create issues. When is it appropriate or inappropriate to use Internet searching to collect information about an individual? The answer depends

11

on interpretation of a variety of current laws, regulations, and standards, among which are the Fair Credit Reporting Act (as amended), Privacy Act (as amended), and state employment laws. Several laws, including the Health Insurance Portability and Accountability Act, Gramm–Leach–Bliley, and Sarbanes–Oxley Act, control the protection of personally identifying information in certain industries. In a nutshell, information collected for an investigative purpose that creates a record containing personally identifying information may be subject to U.S. laws and regulations. It is potentially problematic if casually searched, individual-specific information is handled inappropriately. U.S. government laws and regulations require that if a federal employee acquires Internet search data to be used or retained, it must be placed in an authorized records repository. While it is not forbidden to look for, find, and record such data, possession of Internet search results imposes both declared and implied responsibilities on persons, depending on what they do with the data.

The ethics of Internet searching and use of the results thereof are another challenge. Is it appropriate (legal and ethical) to use a highly personal item posted on a social site to share with friends and family in an employment adjudication? Some argue that the intent of the one posting personal information should be respected by others, yet anything posted publicly is by its nature made available to anyone and everyone.

In the absence of policies or procedures (or adherence to them), a person in authority may selectively conduct Internet searches on some, but not all, individuals of interest. Search methods may vary. Analysis of search results may be disciplined and effective, or not. Depending on the searcher, the search itself and analysis of the results may be incomplete, ineffective, and inaccurate. Information gleaned may be correct or incorrect. The subject of the search may be aware of it, or not. Casual searching can therefore raise issues of fairness, competence, proper handling and analysis of data, secure storage, privacy protection, redress, and perhaps other questions.

There is nothing wrong with using the Internet as a telephone directory, method of connecting with someone else, or reminder of facts about an individual of interest. Profiles with photos online make it easy for two new acquaintances to meet in a crowded public place, because each recognizes the other from their pictures. It is when an inquiry begins to delve into the personal profiles of others with potentially adverse consequences that questions arise. After all, the information is posted on the Internet in a manner that makes it available to anyone inquiring—so it hardly can be said to enjoy privacy protection. However, depending on the role and intentions of the searcher, Internet data that may impact a decision assumes another character, and must be approached according to some basic principles. The alternative could result in unfair, arbitrary, or prejudicial treatment.

INTERNET POSTS AND THE PEOPLE THEY PROFILE

"On the Internet, nobody knows you're a dog," said a famous *New Yorker* cartoon in which a dog at a keyboard was speaking to another dog.[23] Even when the name, nickname, "handle," or other identifier of the person of interest appears on a Web page, one may not know who actually posted it. Essentially, there are many ways to post material anonymously or falsely in another's name. Current social norms include the use of nicknames for many types of social networking profiles, as well as game sites, interest group pages, sales sites like eBay and Craigslist, blogs, Internet Relay Chat (IRC), and free email accounts. Such nicknames are in fact aliases, and some would suggest that it is proper to conceal the true (or full) identity of the person by use of the nickname. This may help protect the individual against unwelcome contacts from strangers. Ironically, it creates a situation in which almost everyone fails to list their "virtual identities" (i.e., those used on the Internet) as aliases when filling out application forms. In addition, it is common for users to have their formal email address (e.g., John.Doe@gmail.com) as well as their recreational, more personal email address (e.g., BigJD123@yahoo.com). Identifying individuals online is rendered more difficult when they use multiple identities for different Internet activities and communications. However, if one can find out all or most of such nicknames, each one can be used as a search term, to find instances where the individual appears online. Analysis of the results must always include the caveat that the individual found may not really be identifiable with the person of interest, since multiple individuals can use the same nickname, people can pretend to be someone else, and users can share the same computer with the same virtual identities (e.g., spouses using the same email address).

While those who post information can provide a treasure trove of useful facts about themselves, it is also true that people often upload items about other individuals as well. Many personal profiles carry a fairly large body of information, including blogs, messages posted (e.g., MySpace friends' comments), photos, and links to the personal profiles of a social circle. By reading not only the postings of one individual but also those of his or her connections, it is often possible to develop a more complete impression of the subject's behavior, characteristics, and suitability. As indicated above, most often a person's online profile results in a positive impression of the subject, because most people behave well in the virtual presence of others, including their social circle. However, it also occurs relatively frequently that misbehavior can be seen where the person has that proclivity. Even though more mature people all should know that postings without privacy controls can be seen by anyone, it is not unusual to find postings that are scandalous, embarrassing, and likely to result in denial of employment by any employer made aware of them.

As with caveats about postings ostensibly attributable to a known individual, postings by a person about someone else may suffer from several defects, including lack of attribution (i.e., an anonymous poster), untrue or unverifiable allegations, and practical jokes or slander. The questions that must be asked about such postings include: Who said what about whom? Are there any other indications of similar allegations? Are the statements, photos, videos, audio recordings, etc., believable?

Despite the care that must be exercised with postings by one person about another, examples abound of useful information found online. A son revealed his father's illegal activities and hatred for his employer. A man's social profile contained a link to his ex-wife's blog, which detailed his many years of misbehavior, including domestic abuse. A woman and her friends posted stories and photos of their drunken partying, complete with sexual content and ample examples of faulty judgment. Another woman recounted her history of drug abuse and sales in postings on a friend's blog. A police officer posted his photo in neo-Nazi regalia.

A key example of third-party postings is the ever-widening variety of records that appear online. All records may include errors. However, records are especially useful because they are kept in the normal course of business and are apt to be accurate, on the whole. Records not only include public government databases, but also media reports, directories, and cross-references such as telephone numbers and Internet identifiers like Internet Protocol addresses, profiles, and lists of links. All of these provide information by one person or entity about another, and while each should be viewed as requiring verification, they are an excellent way to amass facts, suspicions, and leads for an investigation about a subject.

FINDING THE NEEDLES

Those familiar with database administration will no doubt understand that the "data density" and unstructured formatting of Internet data add complex problems to the task of thorough searching. Since society has gotten used to using Google as its overwhelming choice for most Internet searching, it may come as a shock that Google provides neither complete nor unbiased results. While the results page may show millions of "hits," the site will most likely provide only up to one thousand results, one page of ten at a time, unless you adjust the settings. Google (and similar search engines) use elegantly designed algorithms to find and rank references to the search term entered. Rather than searching the Internet that exists at the moment the search is launched, search engines refer to mammoth databases of information collected and indexed by "spiders" that systematically record Web site content continuously, month by month. Not all Web sites, and not all pages or Web site-accessible databases, allow spiders to record their contents. Therefore, even in the best of circumstances, a search engine can only deliver a small portion of available information to the searcher.[24]

A key challenge is finding information identifiable with a person, entity, or topic of interest. The volume of data available on the Internet is such that there will most likely be many references to any search term, and filtering out the irrelevant information is necessary. What's more, finding references and links that lead to more useful, detailed, or relevant information (based on the purpose of the search) is at times a difficult task. Many researchers get so bogged down in "hits" from search engines that they fail to utilize the wide variety of sites where databases with more useful information resides such as professional associations and publications, social networking, business or organizational Web sites, and activity group sites like blogs, calendars, and chat. Mining data that could more likely provide accurate, detailed results requires insightful analysis of the subject of inquiry, based on his or her known profile, and exploiting Internet sites likely to provide nonindexed (but richer) information. In short, nothing can substitute for knowledge and experience of the Internet (not even Google!).[25]

THE NEED FOR SPEED

Because of the large volumes of data available on the Internet, the rapidity of collection, filtering, and analysis comprise an important aspect of searching. If they take too long, Internet searching and analysis become counterproductive as investigative methods. Fortunately, search and analysis tools enable much greater efficiencies. A forty-hour search and analysis project can be reduced to less than two hours for experienced analysts, provided that they have the right systems, processes, training, and experience. Several years' experience have proved two insights: The human analyst remains a key processor in Internet search, and two competent analysts will most often come up with better results if they work as a team. This phenomenon is related to the facts that individuality causes online profiles to differ, no one analyst knows (or thinks of) all the possible Internet sources to use, and two or more heads are inevitably better than one. A corollary is that by pursuing linked people and terms, a fuller profile of the subject may emerge than if one confines the search to the first set of references that are presented by a search engine.

When appropriate technology and methodology are applied, Internet searching can be a great equalizer, producing a relatively complete profile of a subject in a short time.

WHAT WE CAN'T DO WITHOUT

Because the oceans of data available on the Internet contain valuable facts on many topics, structured and thorough searching has become necessary for complete investigations and intelligence production. For individuals, businesses, and government agencies, an Internet presence is critical for networking, information dissemination, marketing, recruiting, and customer fulfillment. Large-scale efforts to make data of all kinds accessible online are paying off, as reference materials, government records, media reports, books, and profiles of people have been added. Along with records, social, fantasy, recreational, and gaming data have been added for hundreds of millions of users. Both the benign and the derogatory appear in large quantities of references on people, enterprises, and topics. It follows that business and government should require searching for numerous purposes, to ensure that one has the facts needed to make timely, valid decisions.

Over the past several years, extensive Internet research has demonstrated that unique and valuable information can be found on the Internet, benefitting investigations, open-source intelligence, and vetting. Unfortunately, many firms, agencies, and organizations lack a policy, procedures, or a thoughtful approach to Internet searching. This does not mean that searches are not conducted. Quite the contrary: Searches are done incompletely or poorly, and results are not always used as they should be. If the approach outlined in the following chapters is used, an enterprise can structure its approach to Internet searching so that results are not only useful, but also lawful, fair, and fully within national and international standards.

NOTES

1. Merriam-Webster, Internet definition, http://www.merriam-webster.com/netdict/internet.
2. Berners-Lee, Tim, *Weaving the Web* (New York: HarperCollins, 1999).
3. OECD resources on policy issues related to internet governance, Information Society studies, http://www.oecd.org/document/56/0,3343,en_21571361_34590630_34647416_1_1_1_1,00.html (accessed June 1, 2010).
4. Pew Internet and American Life Project (Surveys), http://www.pewinternet.org.
5. Internet Survey Host Count, The Internet Systems Consortium, http://www.isc.org/solutions/survey.
6. Figure 1.1: InternetWorldStats.com, Miniwatts Marketing Group, January 2008, http://www.internetworldstats.com/emarketing.htm (accessed May 5, 2010); Figure 1.2: Cisco Internet and network traffic estimates, http://www.cisco.com/en/US/netsol/ns827/networking_solutions_white_papers_list.html (accessed April 10, 2010); Figure 1.3: Internet Survey Host Count, The Internet Systems Consortium, http://www.isc.org/solutions/survey (accessed May 5, 2010).
7. Meetings of Computer Crime and Digital Evidence Ad-Hoc Committee, International Association of Chiefs of Police, 2005–2010, in which briefings were received from law enforcement on computer crime and digital evidence trends seen by law enforcement and private sector investigators.
8. Ibid.
9. Ibid.
10. Page, Larry, "Google's Goal: 'Understand Everything,'" *Business Week*, May 3, 2004, http://www.businessweek.com/magazine/content/04_18/b3881010_mz001.htm (accessed August 6, 2010).
11. American Management Association, 2007 Electronic Monitoring & Surveillance Survey, http://press.amanet.org/press-releases/177/2007-electronic-monitoring-surveillance-survey/ (accessed May 5, 2010).
12. Nixon, W. Barry, and Kerr, Kim M., *Background Screening and Investigations, Managing Risk from HR and Security Perspectives* (Burlington, MA: Elsevier, 2008).

13. Madden, Mary, and Jones, Sydney, *Networked Workers*, Pew Internet & American Life Project, September 24, 2008, http://www.pewinternet.org/Reports/2008/Networked-Workers.aspx. Instances of scandalous behavior posted online by an individual about himself of herself have been seen by the writer in five years of open-source intelligence and investigations services for numerous clients.

14. Security Policy Reviews, Intelligence Office, National Security Council, The White House, Washington, DC, January 1995–May 1997, by the author as Director, Security and Counterintelligence Programs, Personnel Security Working Group, et al., *Evaluation of DCID 1/14 Investigative Requirements* (Washington, DC: Director of Central Intelligence, April 1991): "The least productive sources include neighborhood interviews, which are also the most expensive and time consuming." PERSEREC, *SSBI Source Yield: An Examination of Sources Contacted during the SSBI*, TR 96-01, March 1996, explored the net value of sources used in background investigations, http://www.dhra.mil/perserec/index.html.

15. Madden, Mary, Fox, Susannah, Smith, Aaron, and Vitak, Jessica, *Digital Footprints, Online Identity Management and Search in the Age of Transparency*, Pew Internet and American Life Project, December 16, 2007, http://pewresearch.org/pubs/663/digital-footprints (accessed June 24, 2010).

16. CareerBuilder.com survey, August 20, 2009, http://thehiringsite.careerbuilder.com/2009/08/20/nearly-half-of-employers-use-social-networking-sites-to-screen-job-candidates/ (accessed March 30, 2010).

17. Beyea, Suzanne, "Finding Internet Resources to Support Evidence-Based Practice," *AORN Journal*, September 2000; Cassell, Kay Ann, and Hiremath, Uma, *Reference and Information Services in the 21st Century, An Introduction*, 2nd ed. (New York: Neal-Schuman Publishers, 2009), www.neal-schuman.com/reference21st2nd.

18. "How Much Information? 2003—Internet," University of California at Berkeley Study, http://www2.sims.berkeley.edu/research/projects/how-much-info-2003/internet.htm (accessed June 1, 2010).

19. comScore, Inc., Google, Yahoo, Microsoft, AOL, and Ask, February 2008, http://www.comscore.com/press/release.asp?press=2068 (accessed June 1, 2010). Additional search statistics appear at http://www.newsfactor.com/story.xhtml?story_id=0110010E9FHI&full_skip=1, http://www.seoconsultants.com/search-engines/, http://www.hitwise.com/datacenter/main/dashboard-10133.html. comScore, in its first comprehensive study of worldwide search activity, from the top fifty worldwide Internet properties where search activity is observed, found that more than 750 million people age fifteen and older—or 95% of the worldwide Internet audience—conducted 61 billion searches worldwide in August, 2007, an average of more than eighty searches per searcher; October 10, 2007, http://www.comscore.com/Press_Events/Press_Releases/2007/10/Worldwide_Searches_Reach_61_Billion/(language)/eng-US (accessed June 1, 2010).

20. Lardinois, Frederic, "Google Now Knows about 1 Trillion Pages," *ReadWriteWeb*, July 25, 2008, http://www.readwriteweb.com/archives/google_hits_one_trillion_pages.php (accessed August 6, 2010).
21. IDC Research, *The Expanding Digital Universe: A Forecast of Worldwide Information Growth through 2010*, EMC, http://www.emc.com/collateral/analyst-reports/pund-it-review-digital-universe.pdf. In 2006, 161 exabytes (161 billion gigabytes) were created and copied; in 2008, 281 exabytes, growing 60% annually, according to Judy Motti, "Enterprises Face Data Growth Explosion," *Enterprise IT Planet*, March 13, 2008, http://www.enterpriseit-planet.com/storage/news/article.php/3733916 (accessed August 6, 2010).
22. comScore, U.S. Search engine rankings, 2009, http://www.didiknow.com/2009/03/search-engine-usage-of-february-2009-us.html (accessed August 6, 2010). Statistics consistently show Google retaining over a 60% share of search traffic.
23. Steiner, Peter, "On the Internet, nobody knows you're a dog." *The New Yorker*, 69, No. 20 (July 5, 1993): 61.
24. Google Guide, http://www.googleguide.com/advanced_operators_reference.html (accessed June 1, 2010).
25. Stross, Randall, "World's Largest Social Network: The Open Web," *New York Times*, "Digital Domain," May 16, 2010.

2

Social and Technological Change

INTERNET USE GROWTH

Hundreds of millions of people worldwide, including nearly 80% of adult Americans, with higher percentages of those who are younger, more affluent, and better educated, use the Internet for all types of commercial, social, recreational, communications, and information exchanges. The Internet has become an essential element of life for government, industry, organizations, and individuals. As constructive Internet uses have enriched American life dramatically, an equally dramatic increase has occurred in the use of the Internet for illegal, illicit, and inappropriate purposes.

Susannah Fox of Pew's Internet and American Life Project said in 2008, "Our research finds that many Americans are jumping into the participatory Web without considering all the implications. If nothing really bad has happened to someone, they tend neither to worry about their personal information nor to take steps to limit the amount of information that can be found about them online. On the other hand, if someone has had a bad experience with embarrassing or inaccurate information being posted online, they are more likely to take steps to limit the availability of personal information."[1] The phenomenon of Americans revealing a little too much about themselves, including documenting their own misbehavior, suggests that employers should be concerned about what is online. If no "bad news" about a candidate or employee can be found on the Internet, so much the better—that will be the case for the vast majority of individuals. If there is derogatory information, it will either have a bearing on the job or not, and will either be of sufficient seriousness (e.g., an arrest or conviction) or not (e.g., party photos). As with all other aspects of a person's background, when handled correctly, online postings can help determine eligibility and qualifications, and can be strong indicators of an individual's trustworthiness in using an employer's IT systems.

Adoption of Internet services delivered over high-speed Internet connections at work and at home has spurred massive Internet usage both during and after work hours. For example, recent statistics show that over 400 million users subscribe to Facebook and 200 million are daily users.[2] Previously larger, MySpace has slipped to about 60 million frequenters, including 57 million unique U.S. users.[3] These sites facilitate information sharing in many different ways. Many people use Twitter (the instant messaging Web site), Facebook, and MySpace for both work and personal networking. LinkedIn, Plaxo, and other professional networking sites facilitate work contacts and often interlink with social sites. Of course, these are only a few of many similar networking sites.

Diversion by "tweet," daily social site profile updates, and scanning friends' sites alone represents a challenge to an organization's systems security, productivity, bandwidth use, and authorized use policy, and opportunities for inadvertent disclosures of sensitive information. Browsing, playing games, stock trading, shopping, gambling, and other personal online activities at work are common. Many employers, including military bases abroad, have responded by limiting employees' ability to use devices and applications on enterprise systems, and block access to certain Web sites and online activities. Among concerns are exposure to malicious code, intellectual property theft, and diversion from duties.[4] However, at a higher level, a variety of security vulnerabilities have been introduced by Internet use habits, among which are industrial espionage, competitive intelligence, infiltration, social engineering, fraud, and misuse of IT systems, including unauthorized "parking" of illicit data or applications on enterprise systems. A malicious outsider now has many more ways to survey, case, and penetrate a targeted business, agency, or organization. Recruiting the assistance of a complicit or unwitting insider accomplice just got much easier. A core vulnerability in a time of greater Internet exposure by an enterprise's employees is that it only takes one compromised insider account to do grave damage, due to the very IT infrastructure created to make the enterprise more efficient.

While innocent Internet uses surge, a wide variety of serious crimes and misbehaviors are being committed on the Internet, as many people and sites dedicated to illegal and illicit activities have appeared.[5] Surprisingly, many individuals take part in illegal and illicit activities using the virtual identities (email addresses, user identities) issued by their business and government employers. Many others use virtual identities freely available through Internet service and email service providers like Hotmail, Google, Yahoo, AOL, and others. Because a user can create a virtual identity that contains no reference to a true name or other valid contact information, a high degree of anonymity can be employed in Internet activities. Given the amount of commercial email (spam), phishing (fraudulent spam), and other threats based on a user's virtual identity, it is normal to use an email address or nickname that does not include one's true name online.

As the types of Internet sites appealing to all types of users have expanded, naturally more Web sites with a criminal purpose have also come online. Some illicit Internet activities are readily found on public sites that anyone can encounter, while others take place on sites that have a degree of exclusivity, such as requiring a user to sign in with a password. Even on such password-protected sites (e.g., Facebook, MySpace), it may be possible to find misuse by searching on true names and email addresses on the public Internet, because the Web sites themselves facilitate search engine indexing of names (so that one can find one's friends). Some Web sites employing user passwords (such as MySpace and Facebook), with tens of millions of simultaneous users are, therefore, quite "public," since the only practical function of the sign-on is to facilitate counting users (for advertising), and not to prevent widespread exposure of postings. Note that sites' authorized use policies (AUPs) may forbid certain uses of information (e.g., collecting users' identifying data for commercial advertising purposes), but having an account allows a user to see other users' public profiles. While users can invoke privacy controls, a large number do not choose to do so.[6] This results in a large number of postings of a potentially offensive nature, such as self-admitted drug users and postings offering pornography. Employees using ostensibly innocent sites can expose the workplace to those offensive postings. Internet use habits thus bring a certain amount of unwelcome content into the workplace.

Unfortunately, improper computer use occurs both outside and inside the workplace. Increasingly, businesses monitor employees' Internet surfing, email, blogging, social networking, and other online activities on company machines. A substantial percentage of monitored employees are caught and fired or disciplined for improper systems use. Most employers told an American Management Association survey[7] that although they notify employees of the monitoring, there is an increased incidence of disciplinary action. Clearly, this indicates that the temptation to abuse employers' systems overcomes the threat of termination. Reportedly, 28% of employers surveyed fired workers for email misuse. At the root of concern is accountability for online actions. As far as we know, no correlation was measured between employers who check candidates' Internet habits before hiring and employers who monitor employees' work computers on the job. As yet, Internet vetting is not a common practice, at least not so common as to be included in the survey.

The incidence of employee criminal activities detected has grown, according to recent surveys, including studies of identity theft, retail industry losses, and applicant misrepresentation.[8] An additional concern for industry is that employers continue to lose 73% of negligent hiring cases that go to jury trials, as cited by W. Barry Nixon and Kim Kerr in their recent (excellent) book on background investigations.[9] Therefore, available information about trends suggests that employers have reason for concern about the potential incidence, impact, and security implications of illicit computer use by both candidates and employees.

EVOLUTION OF INTERNET USES

Online habits reflect the massive surge of individuals of all ages on the Internet, some allowing migration to automated versions of physical activities (email for postal mail), and some for the new forms of Internet social interaction, entertainment, education, e-commerce, news, games, fantasy, pornography, and communications offered. Moore's law, a metric reflecting rapidly advancing computing technology, could well be applied to the ways in which Internet uses have changed (morphed, evolved, and progressed in some cases). Trends in hardware and software, particularly mobile devices, along with services like low-cost, high-bandwidth, wireless telecommunications, search, and networking, have allowed large-scale growth of business, government, academic, and organizational online functions.

Frequently updated demographic data from Pew Internet and American Life surveys suggest that Internet use is much higher for those with more education, more income, dwelling in urban areas, and among non-Hispanic whites. For example, 95% of white college graduates with income over $75,000 annually are Internet users. Lower participation groups (e.g., low-income blacks, rural residents, those over fifty years old) have steadily moved online.[10] From the standpoint of a personnel security

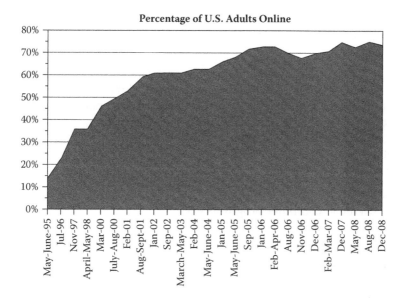

Figure 2.1 Pew Internet and American Life Project estimates of American Internet usage.

specialist, there is no demographic that now can be discounted in terms of Internet use.

The highest percentages of those online use the Internet for email, searching, directions, a hobby or interest, health, product searches, weather, travel, news, purchases, government services, entertainment, school, audio/video, "do it yourself" project help, white or yellow pages lookups, online banking, virtual tours, job searches, etc. Social networking is a highly popular Internet activity, driving many adults (not just teens) to use sites like MySpace and Facebook daily. By the end of 2008, adults with social site profiles had quadrupled in four years to 35%. As the impact on society of daily Internet use has progressed, so has the "power user" group, those who are devoted to the portions of their days that are spent online.[11]

> For 39% of the adult population, mobile and wireline access tools have a symbiotic relationship. Mobile users typically have ready access to high-speed connections at home, which likely pushes them toward deeper home high-speed use; the digital content found on the mobile device may prompt more activity on their broadband-enabled big screen at home. At the same time, the desktop internet experience migrates to "on the go"

as the handheld becomes a complementary access point to connect with people and digital content wherever a wireless network reaches.[12]

For the remaining 61% of Internet users tied primarily to wired devices, the devotion to technology may be decidedly less, but their daily use nevertheless consumes substantial portions of their day. By inference from the Pew data, one can discern that at least 40% of new job applicants "live online" for a large part of their day.[13]

A 2007 Pew study[14] of types of online activities that may be unacceptable in the workplace found the following percentage of users who frequently engage in them:

- Read online journals and blogs (39%)
- Download computer programs (39%)
- Download music files (37%)
- Upload photos (37%)

So the question every employer with employees online must consider is whether to accept the kinds of risks posed by Internet diversions (e.g., time to read blogs of personal interest), unauthorized software introduced into workplace systems, music and videos legally or illegally downloaded, occupying storage meant for business data with personal files, and usurping bandwidth for transmittal of large personal payloads. Activities increasingly more popular since 2007 include watching online videos and playing games, which can divert workers from work, be bandwidth intensive, and may even damage an employer's reputation.

Some recent examples are useful to illustrate the kinds of threats posed:

- A foreign-born engineer downloaded hardware and software designs and took them with him to a new employer months before his economic espionage was detected. He had a long history of unauthorized access to his employers' data not necessary for his work, and an examination of his computer use habits would have shown several red flags. He was convicted of economic espionage. (Meng case)[15]
- A computer security employee acted as the principal manager of a massively multiplayer online role-playing game (MMORPG) involving thousands of people under his direction in a fantasy space war. He held a live online strategy meeting in which he used racist, sexist, and other inflammatory language contrary to his employer's policies, and posted a recording of the offensive remarks online. Due to his prolific postings and newspaper

interviews, the true name and employment of the person were widely known. Upon investigation, it was shown that on numerous occasions he used company time to engage in his Internet fantasy role. Especially in view of his computer security role and his cavalier behavior in violation of his employer's code of conduct, he posed a significant security risk, and probably committed felonious theft of salary for services he did not perform while playing at work.

- A U.S. soldier deployed to Iraq posted numerous photographs of his deployment on his social site profile, with no privacy protections, using his military email address as his profile name. Among the photos were sensitive fortifications and an obscene photo of a fellow soldier. Not only could the enemy see the soldier's postings, but they blatantly violated the Military Code of Conduct.

- An employee of a defense facility posted a detailed biography, numerous photographs (including military bases and aircraft), travel itineraries of extensive global tourism, dozens of friends and acquaintances, including many from abroad, and indiscreet descriptions of herself as "an adventure junkie." The description included birth in a former Soviet bloc country, friends in nations unfriendly to the United States, plans to travel abroad in the future, and contact information, including true name, work email address, phone numbers and other personal data— all available for anyone to see. This is a classic case of a blatant security risk, an attractive candidate for hostile intelligence interest, and a possible indicator of naïve lack of security awareness by the individual.

Since Internet usage has changed, employers should pay attention to the risks that may be added by employees' online habits and by new employees whose IT systems habits are not yet known. The nature of added risks can be significant with even a small number of authorized users whose computer activities include illegal and illicit behaviors, such as copyright infringement, fraud, and harassment. Ironically, automation provides capabilities that convey what Chinese military leaders like to call a great equalizer, since it is the enemy's dependence on computers that allows an attack to have immediate, disproportionate impact. Insider attacks are particularly difficult to prevent and to detect. Even when detected, insider attacks may be so destructive that it is all but impossible to recover.

PHYSICAL WORLD, VIRTUAL ACTIVITIES

Among the activities moving online are several that can cause unanticipated problems in a virtual world, due to distinct characteristics that are different from the physical versions that they replace. For example, stolen property was previously offered for sale to pawn shops, flea markets, and in classified newspaper ads. Today, eBay and Craigslist (to name just two of many Web sites) offer the capability of selling to millions of prospective customers, while maintaining anonymity in a forest of similar ads. Information can be taken not by photocopying documents, but by searching for sensitive and valuable data, downloading and copying, printing, burning to a thumb drive or CD, or simply emailing it out of the enterprise.

One example of a physical norm that for most employers does not translate into the virtual world is the request that an applicant provide aliases on preemployment forms. Few employers require a listing of email addresses and other virtual identities, ignoring the widespread behavior of Internet users who have several online personas, including some without any indicator of their true name, several user IDs, also unlike their name, and several nicknames used for specific Web sites. It is not unusual for today's Internet user to have different user IDs for e-commerce, banking, social sites, email, music, videos, photos, games, hobbies, etc. Recorded online are activities that in most cases are, like their physical counterparts, legal and proper. However, in the minority of individuals inclined to engage in illegal, antisocial, or offensive behavior, it is likely that they have left evidence online. When this assertion is made to some employers and even investigators, they express skepticism because using anonymous virtual identities is so easy. Nevertheless, there will always be a substantial number of people who blatantly post evidence of their offensive conduct, either inadvertently or purposefully sprinkling the Internet with examples.

CONNECTION AND DISCONNECTION

An observer of the Internet scene remarked that when past generations graduated from college, they maintained contact with their eight best friends, losing track of the dozens of others whom they now only meet at reunions or by chance. Today's graduates often retain contact with "eighty best friends," who link to each other in a variety of ways, including social sites, alumni groups, and mutual interest Web sites. Today it is harder to avoid the one or two in every group who have taken a bad turn, such as drug abuse, criminal activities, and association with shady characters. Striving to be one of the "good guys" can expose an individual to people and activities that perhaps could easily have been avoided when our electronic personas did not allow us to be tracked wherever we go. Small indiscretions can become widespread news in a flash.

It would seem that discreet behavior would help protect the wired crowd from exposure through today's social networking. However, the opposite appears to be the case. Even in groups that have learned to turn on their Facebook privacy protections, it appears that blatant examples of misbehavior are posted often, if not by an individual about himself or herself, then by a friend or associate who considers the story, photos, videos, or other items amusing. Almost everyone has something in his or her background that he or she would rather not talk about. Today, it is likely that that something will appear online.

Extricating oneself from damning postings can be difficult (though not impossible). A cottage industry has grown up around removal of embarrassing materials from Web sites, either by those who regret having placed it there in the first place, or by those who feel slandered or at least "outed" by others' postings. Two unfortunate factors may impede removal of such postings: The Web sites may not respond positively in a timely manner, and the cached images of the prior postings could remain available through several search engines and archive sites for some time (years). The only way to be certain that derogatory information is not online is avoiding having it posted in the first place.

However, it may be easier said than done to keep the Internet free of material about anyone. In doing background investigations on numerous people at all levels of business and government, I have found extensive data even on those with little or no inclination to use the Internet. Among the types of data are directories (addresses, phone numbers), neighborhood maps and satellite photos, even ground-level photos of some homes, employers' Web sites, trade publications, associations, schools, genealogical records, court records, media reports, etc. Besides the free data available on the Internet, services like LexisNexis, Acurint (a Lexis service providing private and public data mined from multiple government, business, and directory sources), Intelius (which provides background data for a fee to anyone with a credit card), and other data providers can be found online for a fee.[16] Business and government leaders, those who are subjects of news stories, and many others find themselves "available" to anyone willing to inquire: Who are they? What is their background? What have they been accused of?

At first blush, it does not seem fair that even those who don't use the Internet would find themselves profiled there for almost anyone to see. Yet it is precisely this attribute of the information society, as the Europeans would say, that makes the Internet so interesting: You can probably find out about almost anyone. Of course, in Europe, Canada, and Asia, privacy regulations keep much personal information off the Web, if the subject of interest is not a public figure and does not "opt in." In the United States, one must "opt out" to protect personal data. More about privacy appears in Section II.

In several cases, executives have sought to find every Internet reference to them, and sought to expunge references that reveal too much. Whether they are subject to the chants of demonstrators outside their Manhattan condominiums, kidnapping attempts on their wives and children in Bogota, email extortion threats, letter bombs or other attacks in San Jose, some well-known individuals have found that Internet publicity has worked to their detriment. Those subjected to attacks by interest groups begin to feel that it is all too easy to learn about their private lives by Googling their names. Some corporate efforts have been focused on finding and erasing the postings that can facilitate threats, stalking, harassment, and in some cases, physical attacks. Yet millions of young people continue to build a rich, multifaceted online record of their life's trivia.

NOTES

1. Pew Internet and American Life Project, Tracking Survey, November 30–December 27, 2009, http://www.pewinternet.org/Static-Pages/Trend-Data/Whos-Online.aspx (accessed June 24, 2010).
2. Facebook provides use statistics at http://www.facebook.com/press/info.php?statistics (accessed May 26, 2010).
3. MySpace user statistics in the United States are found at http://www.web-strategist.com/blog/2010/01/19/a-collection-of-social-network-stats-for-2010/ (accessed May 26, 2010). MySpace statistics and a comparison with Facebook and Twitter are at http://mashable.com/2009/05/08/facebook-twitter-myspace-growth-april/.
4. Bourke, James, "Curbing and Battling Employee Misuse of Technology," March 24, 2008. An American Management Association survey found that approximately 75% of respondents monitor their employees' Web site visits in order to prevent inappropriate surfing. In addition, 65% of those surveyed use software

to block or filter connections to Web sites deemed off limits to employees, while about one-third (33%) track keystrokes and time spent online. Over 50% review and retain email messages sent to and from their employees. http://www.cpa2biz.com/Content/media/PRODUCER_CONTENT/Newsletters/Articles_2008/CPA/Mar/Misuse_of_Technology.jsp (viewed March 30, 2010).

5. In the past ten years, numerous surveys and the writer's personal experience have shown that crime has moved onto computers, and onto the Internet. While statistical representations of computer crime are as yet imperfect, they show that the impact (in victimization, dollars, and damage), incidence, and crime types have all moved steadily upward. While awareness of cybercrime has proved to be as difficult to measure as its incidence, there is no doubt in the author's mind that the Internet crime problem continues to increase in size and scope.

6. Fox, Susannah, Pew Internet and American Life Project, February 2008, based on Pew Digital Footprints Internet Project, December 2007.

7. Op. cit.

8. Greenemeier, Larry, Information Week Research—Accenture 10th Annual Information Security Survey, July 2007, http://www.informationweek.com/story/showArticle.jhtml?articleID=201001203 (accessed May 5, 2010).

9. Nixon, W. Barry, and Kerr, Kim M., *Background Screening and Investigations, Managing Risk from HR and Security Perspectives* (Burlington, MA: Elsevier, 2008).

10. Pew Internet and American Life Project, http://www.pewinternet.org/Static-Pages/Data-Tools/Download-Data/~/media/Infographics/Trend%20Data/January%202009%20updates/Demographics%20of%20Internet%20Users%201%206%2009.jpg.

11. Ibid.

12. "The Mobile Difference," Pew Internet and American Life Project, March 2009, http://www.pewinternet.org/~/media//Files/Reports/2009/The_Mobile_Difference.pdf.

13. Owyang, Jeremiah, "Social Network Stats," Forrester Research, January 2008, http://www.web-strategist.com/blog/2008/01/09/social-network-stats-facebook-myspace-reunion-jan-2008/ (accessed August 6, 2010).

14. Horrigan, John B., "A Typology of Information and Communication Technology Users," Pew Internet and American Life Project, May 7, 2007, http://www.pewinternet.org/~/media//Files/Reports/2007/PIP_ICT_Typology.pdf.pdf (accessed June 24, 2010).

15. U.S. Department of Justice, press release, August 2, 2007. On August 1, 2007, Xiaodong Sheldon Meng, forty-two, formerly a resident of Beijing, China, and resident of Cupertino, California, pleaded guilty to violating the Economic Espionage Act (EAA) and violating the Arms Export Control Act (AECA) and the International Traffic in Arms Regulations (ITAR); http://www.usdoj.gov/criminal/cybercrime/mengPlea.htm (accessed May 5, 2009).

16. O'Harrow, Robert, Jr., *No Place to Hide,* (New York: Free Press, 2005).

3

Use and Abuse—
Crime on the Internet

Computer-based crime (i.e., criminal acts committed using computers or where computers hold evidence of a crime) is poorly measured. Unfortunately, few if any solid metrics are available on the incidence, proportion, or impact of illegal Internet uses. Regional computer forensic laboratories run by the FBI in fifteen different U.S. regions have experienced rapid, sustained increases in the types, numbers, and quantities of data involved in all criminal activities involving computers.[1] The Internet Crime Complaint Center reported a rise of 33% in complaints in the one-year period ending in early 2009.[2] Cybercrime experts meeting in Australia in June 2009 cited growing Internet crime rates, including Internet crimes against children.[3] A *Washington Post* reporter cites some estimates that $100 billion worth of defense industry data have been compromised in the past two years.[4] Microsoft reported the rise of botnets (networks of remote-controlled computers in the thousands surreptitiously seized and used by criminals) as zombie attack platforms to launch frauds, denial of service attacks, identity and data theft, and spam.[5] McAfee, Symantec, and other computer security vendors cite rising organized online fraud as one indicator of growing Internet crime.[6]

BY THE NUMBERS?

Casing, communications, and planning are fundamental parts of many types of criminal conspiracies. Many types of criminal investigations, including Internet child exploitation, identity thefts, sale of stolen property, frauds, trafficking in pirated goods such as films, music, software, and hardware, counterfeiting, radical/terrorist activities, intellectual property theft, malicious code use, and denial of service attacks, have experienced substantial increases in the past few years. Despite various efforts, including an FBI–Computer Security Institute annual computer crime survey[7] and a U.S. Department of Justice, Bureau of Justice Statistics survey in 2005,[8] solid cybercrime statistics are elusive. Increasing numbers may be an indication of better Internet crime reporting, or may signal rises in crime online. After almost thirty-five years of association with computer crime investigators and computer forensic examiners, the author has no doubt that Internet crime has increased steadily and now has reached prodigious levels. The proof of this proposition is that wherever populations have grown, crime rates have increased—and it appears that the Internet is no exception.

Sadly, Internet crime is rarely reported, rarely investigated, and rarely results in arrests and convictions. The most notorious cybercriminals are comparatively few in number. State and local law enforcement take tens of millions of reports of identity crimes (mostly frauds), yet can address only a handful of them. Many reported thefts of databases containing private, personally identifying information go unsolved. Frauds using stolen identities estimated in the tens of millions (dollars and incidents) are unsolved for the most part. Undercover operations on the Internet pitting cops against child molesters and porn traders consistently show large volumes of activity, and may comprise half of anticybercrime efforts. Police chiefs have said that they have to limit their officers' involvement in Internet crimes against children. Many chiefs describe these cases as a "bottomless pit" of relentless crimes that are not diminished by high-profile enforcement, such as NBC's "To Catch a Predator" (where, ironically, repeat offenders were encountered, due to the insatiable drive in molesters who knew or certainly should have suspected that the "children" encountered online could easily be undercover police—again). Although law enforcement is making strides against cybercrime, it appears that the volume, seriousness, impact, and international reach all continue to grow. This means that for those entrusted with ensuring a trustworthy workforce, conducting investigations, and gathering intelligence, there are more challenges every day, and ignoring the Internet's threats and opportunities is simply naïve and ignorant.

ONLINE VENUES

Web sites, Internet Relay Chat (IRC), blogs, and hosted group sites have become online clubhouses for gangs and organized criminal groups. For example, there are over one thousand sites offering/hosting pirated movies, TV shows, music, and software globally. Web sites involved in criminal activities like piracy are run, supplied, and patronized by millions of persons who are not being arrested or charged.[9] Perpetrators' identities might be ascertained by Internet investigations. In some cases, their names and virtual identities are widely known, yet they are not brought to justice for many reasons, including locations abroad, where cybercrime laws are weak, nonexistent, or not enforced.

Given the current cybercrime situation, employers must confront their responsibilities to protect people, assets, and information against candidates for employment whose online misbehavior may be discoverable. Unfortunately, most cybercriminals have no arrest record.

As with all types of criminal activities, Internet crime runs the gamut from high-impact, violent activities like drug trafficking to annoying spam and pop-up ads. Like brick-and-mortar businesses, criminal enterprises have discovered that automation, networking, e-commerce, and Internet anonymity can facilitate efficiency, rapidly scaled marketing, quick sales growth, and customer satisfaction.[10] A good example of organized Internet crime is illicit online pharmaceutical sales. Large numbers of online pharmacies offer discounted brand name and generic drugs, ostensibly from Canada and Europe, but predominantly from China, India, Russia, East Europe, the Caribbean, and the South Pacific. The average U.S. consumer, facing high drug prices, cannot easily determine the legitimacy of the discount products or Web sites. U.S., Canadian, Russian, Chinese, and Indian organized criminals offer prescription drugs without a prescription, and ship or mail medicines to customers who will not know if the pills are poison, counterfeit, generic, or the real thing. Even repackaged, diverted products appear in Internet pharmaceutical channels. It's a classic case of the Web's ability to host black, gray, and legitimate markets, often indistinguishable from each other to customers.[11]

DIGITAL DELINQUENCY

By its nature, the Internet has spawned illegal activities that are digital. For example, trading in misappropriated content such as films, videos, music, audio, software, designs, and other intellectual property has become a lucrative business. Like a criminal form of eBay or Craigslist, Web sites host auctions and sales of stolen credit card data and purloined personal identities. New software and networking systems have been created to facilitate transfer of large digital files, such as Napster and BitTorrent (described as a "free, open source file-sharing application effective for distributing very large software and media files").[12] Old-fashioned fencing and duplication of stolen DVDs have been joined by high-speed transfer of films' data files from multiple sites distributed globally. In some cases, individual sites host no technically illegal content (e.g., by hosting only a part of a pirated film), and only a central controller's permission allows users to access, download, verify, and reassemble the whole thing. Some criminal sites' sophisticated use of authentication, encryption, compression, and high-bandwidth transmission at times exceeds the norm of commercial Internet services.

"FREE" INTELLECTUAL PROPERTY

While copyright violations are illegal, especially for commercial rather than personal use, Internet file sharing has given rise to a quasi-religious belief that information should be free. Large groups of people think that they have a God-given right to all the information to which they can gain access.

Profound changes in music, film, TV, and software production have been necessitated by technological challenges to digital property rights protection (digital rights management [DRM]). The blogosphere resounds with philosophical wars—some of which have resulted in retrenchment by entertainment companies—when digital rights are asserted and enforced using new technologies. Ironically, it is not the American NSA, British GCHQ, or Russian FSB (KGB) cryptographers who are most energized when new commercial encryption is deployed to protect movies, tunes, and software. A whole new class of "amateur" cryptographers has learned how to attack copyright protections, cooperating internationally and overcoming language, mathematical, and technical barriers to break controls on digital goods. In this context, it becomes clear that intellectual property protections and well-established legal principles are at considerable risk.

Large numbers of Internet users have been quickly mobilized to denounce DRM controls, resulting in entertainment companies like Sony choosing to rescind built-in protections.[13] While dwelling on the reasons for the failure of technology to solve the digital rights conundrum is not necessary here, to be fair, one must allocate some blame to the inadequacy of the technical solutions themselves. The subclass of attackers with large-scale, commercialized criminal operations has benefitted from the anticontrol feelings. This subclass threatens both government and business employers, as well as the companies whose goods they misappropriate.

Not only do Internet-facilitated illegal acts create risks for enterprises, but the cybercrimes themselves skew society's ability to detect, measure, assess, and respond to the types of crime problems that arise. Cybercrime is a category of security risk requiring in-depth study in its own right. For purposes of this review, it is necessary to recognize these key attributes:

- Internet crimes lack an enforcement mechanism similar to that in the physical world, since federal, state, regional, and local police are deployed jurisdictionally by venues that may not be discernible on the Web, and "Internet patrol" is not yet here.
- Rapid evolution of Internet crimes (e.g., phishing, which is the use of spam to entice victims online) often defeats enforcement by their speed, scale, geographic dispersal, and anonymity.
- Because the Internet is global, anticybercrime enforcers are often unable to bring perpetrators to prosecution.
- When prosecutions occur, the scale of violations documented (e.g., in seized computer hardware and records) often results in identified perpetrators who are not prosecuted because they are abroad, too numerous, deemed not to be leaders, or for other reasons.
- Prosecutorial choices (e.g., concentrating resources on child exploitation crimes instead of identity frauds) may result in relatively large numbers of cybercriminals who are not prosecuted, and crimes not investigated or not fully investigated.
- "White collar" crimes online at times are prioritized lower than violent crimes, and so receive fewer criminal justice resources.
- Criminal and civil cases' digital records often contain evidence of wrongdoing not ultimately resulting in recorded sanctions such as arrests and convictions.
- Corporate security investigations are an essential part of Internet criminal enforcement and vital to law enforcement success in many types of cybercrime, such as credit card fraud. Corporations

therefore are stakeholders and decision makers in many types of online crime. Only a minority of crimes detected by corporate security staffs are reported to law enforcement.

- Personnel security—heretofore relying on the criminal justice system to record prior criminal activity—faces the probability that cybercriminals have no prior criminal record. Further, private databases are more likely than public ones to hold evidence of prior misbehavior, on- or offline.

Probably a word about hackers and crackers is advisable here. Hackers are people who have made themselves familiar with the way computers and related devices work. Hackers can therefore use digital devices in more expert ways than the rest of us. Sometimes, you will hear the terms *white-hat hacker*, *gray-hat hacker*, or *black-hat hacker*, imitating the gray and black market concepts. Like the term *hacker*, these terms are used loosely, but may refer to those who dabble in risky but not illegal (gray) activities, and those who engage in illegal (black) acts online. Hacking is not illegal per se, and in fact is critical to IT security. The federal Computer Fraud and Abuse Act (among others) forbids unauthorized access to computers for an illegal purpose or with damaging impact over a certain dollar amount. Crackers are those who use computers and code to commit criminal acts—something hackers could choose to do, but for the most part do not. It is necessary to understand that among the cultural groups that have arisen in the Internet age, hackers are the group most likely to offer society the solutions needed to protect computing going forward—thus the term *white-hat hacker*. They are also the ones with the skills to subvert systems without anyone knowing it. Sometimes we refer to hackers by the more common terms *IT staff* and *programmers*.

THE INSIDER

The place of automation in an enterprise raises profound questions with regard to criminal insiders. Only one malicious employee with access to enterprise IT systems can compromise the most valuable assets, especially with privileged access such as that enjoyed by the IT systems administrators. As business and government systems over the past two decades have increasingly housed vital intellectual resources, the risk of loss from insiders has increased. Yet few agencies and firms ask detailed questions of applicants about prior Internet activities and confirm their answers by systematic checking. Most employers grant employees full IT systems access from their first day on the job, which increases the risk that people with prior online criminal behavior may threaten the enterprise. Leaving this risk unaddressed is no longer acceptable, especially where high-value data reside online.

As use of digital evidence and electronic records in investigations has grown, most large employers have faced the realization that their own data may become damaging evidence against them. An employee engaged in cybercrimes while "on duty" puts the employer in jeopardy of criminal or civil charges, while emails, true or untrue, can become powerful evidence of misbehavior attributable to the enterprise. Yet only a small percentage of employers have made a connection between the factors that correlate users' on-the-job and personal computer habits. For example, several trends are well known, but not considered in the context of risk to the enterprise:

- Indiscreet, blatant documentation of inappropriate behavior is common on social sites like MySpace and Facebook. Can someone so indiscreet maintain a professional discretion at work?
- Exchanges of copyrighted works in digital form—especially films, music, video, and software—without paying for them are rampant. Will workers with such habits choose to protect their employers' digital intellectual property?
- As Internet advertising and marketing illustrate (and the decline of print media reflects), networking through large numbers of professional contacts is key to enterprise reputation and market rank. As today's highly mobile workforce shuttles to their next employer, will they bring these connections with them digitally, or leave them with their former employer (to whom they may literally belong, if they are on a customer list)?

The above are only a few of many possible examples. When enterprises are dependent (as most are) on IT systems, networks, and data, the individual user's online choices assume greater importance. "Humorous" emails can turn into damning evidence in court. Digital evidence is long-lived, searchable, retrievable, often available to a legal adversary, and dependent on the input of every employee (even the ones with the worst sense of humor).

Despite the trend toward indiscreet (potentially self-damaging) online revelations and misbehavior, most employers do not address candidates' online habits directly. Screening, orientation, training, and monitoring can mitigate these risks, but strategic changes in personnel security are necessary to address them.

NOTES

1. Motta, Thomas G., FBI Digital Evidence Section Chief, address to Law Enforcement Information Management, International Association of Chiefs of Police (IACP) Conference, Nashville, Tennessee, May 8, 2008, and briefings to subsequent meetings of the IACP Computer Crime and Digital Evidence Ad Hoc Committee.
2. Internet Crime Complaint Center, *2008 Internet Crime Report*, http://www.fbi.gov/page2/march09/internet_033009.html. For example, "Reports of Internet scams and their financial toll continued to grow in 2008, according to the latest data by the Internet Crime Complaint Center (IC3), which operates a Web site, www.ic3.gov, to collect and refer public complaints about Internet fraud. In 2008, more than $264 million was lost in 275,284 complaints—an average of $931 for every complaint—according to the 2008 Internet Crime Report, released March 30. Almost one-third of the complaints were for non-delivery of merchandise purchased online; auction fraud accounted for one in four complaints."
3. Palan, Simon, "Cyber Crime out of Control (cybercrime conference)," Adelaide, Australia, June 9, 2009, http://www.abc.net.au/pm/content/2008/s2593539.htm (accessed August 8, 2010).
4. Nakashima, Ellen, "Defense Dept., Industry Join to Protect Data," *Washington Post*, May 25, 2009, http://www.washingtonpost.com/wp-dyn/content/article/2009/05/24/AR2009052402140.html (accessed May 5, 2010).
5. Microsoft briefings to law enforcement groups, 2007–2008, contained estimates of networks of tens of thousands of remote-controlled computers illicitly utilized by online criminals to carry out their activities through proxies.
6. Symantec cybercrime summary: http://www.symantec.com/norton/cybercrime/index.jsp (accessed August 8, 2010); Paget, Francois, "Cybercrime and Hacktivism," McAfee Labs, March 2010, http://www.mcafee.com/us/local_content/white_papers/cybercrime_20100315_en.pdf (accessed August 8, 2010).
7. Computer Security Institute–FBI Annual Computer Crime Survey, http://gocsi.com/survey (accessed August 8, 2010).
8. Bureau of Justice Statistics, "National Computer Security Survey," 2005, http://bjs.ojp.usdoj.gov/index.cfm?ty=dcdetail&iid=260 (accessed August 8, 2010).
9. Stahl, Lesley, *60 Minutes*, CBS Television, "Video Pirates, the Bane of Hollywood," November 1, 2009, http://www.cbsnews.com/stories/2009/10/30/60minutes/main5464994.shtml (accessed June 1, 2010).
10. Sarno, David, "The Internet Sure Loves Its Outlaws," *Los Angeles Times*, April 29, 2007.

11. The author's Internet investigations over the past five years have included online pharmacies' illegal sale of brand name and generic drugs to U.S. customers over the Internet with and without requiring prescriptions, mailing/shipping prescription drugs and controlled substances directly to consumers in contravention of federal and state laws and ethical medical practice.
12. BitTorrent self-description, http://www.bittorrent.com/ (accessed August 8, 2010).
13. Holahan, Catherine, "Sony BMG Plans to Drop DRM," *Business Week*, January 4, 2008, describes the decision by Sony BMG Music Entertainment to drop Digital Rights Management software included with music to prevent its download over the Internet, and compete with Apple's iTunes for sale of downloaded music. Sony was the last of the top four music labels to drop DRM. A 2005 version of Sony's DRM software included in each CD automatically installed controls on users' PCs that reportedly created vulnerabilities to viruses, which prompted a boycott and lawsuits (BusinessWeek.com, November 29, 2005).

4

Implications for the Enterprise

Surveys, media reports, and quotes from some employers suggest that because of online misbehavior, Internet searches are being added to pre-hiring background investigations.[1] However, the media reports appear to indicate that most private and public sector employers lack several key ingredients necessary for fair, legal, and appropriate use of Internet searching for hiring adjudications, including a written policy, procedures, search methodology, adjudication methods, notice to applicants, consent (as currently used for background investigation interviews with prior employers or schools), and an opportunity to correct adverse findings.[2] These and certain other procedures would insulate an employer from potential liabilities arising from Internet searching, including possible violations of the Fair Credit Reporting Act and Equal Employment Act. Without proper procedures and safeguards, an employer's human resources and other decision makers might use Internet searches and the results thereof inappropriately.

A related trend is for employers to spend considerable sums on systems to monitor their employees' use of work IT systems for online misbehavior, blocking access to certain Internet sites, filtering and archiving email, and even key logging.[3] In recent years, the costs of litigation, losses, and reputational damage to enterprises that fail to control employees' systems misuses have skyrocketed.

THE NEW USER: SOMEONE YOU WOULD TRUST?

Background investigations, combined with resumes, applications, interviews, and a "whole person" evaluation of eligibility, qualifications, experience, and compatibility with the enterprise, are the current gold standard for hiring the best candidates. Like all investigations, vetting allows an employer to consider facts and observations in making a decision. When the open position has multiple applicants, choosing among those most competitive and likely to succeed is the goal. The applicant's profile—factual, verified, and analyzed—is the basis for adjudicating whether to hire the individual. In this context, analysis of prior computer/Internet use has somehow been omitted by many employers.

Most U.S. employees (62% in 2008) use the Internet or email at work, and nearly all of those own personal cell phones and computers, according to a recent Pew Internet and American Life study. About 45% of employed Americans report doing at least some work from home.[4] In considering the impact of automation on employees, several recent trends are significant:

1. Most U.S. workers come into a job with prior online experience.
2. Most U.S. workers are granted immediate access to their new employer's IT systems.
3. The "networked worker" of today is much more likely to use computers and devices to accomplish a mix of personal and professional tasks throughout the day, whether it is a workday or day off, and whether during work hours or in off hours.

Employers have a variety of issues to address with today's workforce in relation to their computer, network, and data use, among which are:

- Ascertaining and evaluating employees' level of experience and expertise with computers, applications, and processes, especially as those relate to job tasks.
- Assessing employees' awareness of computer system security, IT hygiene, history of online safety, and potentially threatening habits (e.g., using risky Web sites or exchanging provocative content).
- Including candidates' online experiences in the background vetting process, to ascertain and evaluate eligibility for access to the employer's systems (in light of established authorized use policy) and potential need for extraordinary orientation and training, should the candidate's history suggest the need for the same. The inclusion of online history in vetting is neither trivial nor simple; hence, it will be treated in depth in later chapters.

44

In confronting the issues described above, the employer must weigh the relative criticality and value of enterprise data, computing and networking infrastructure, as well as the risks inherent in potentially allowing employees to use the employer's systems however they wish. While today's enterprises, including many small businesses (i.e., those with up to five hundred employees), have robust IT security built in, it is not unusual to find that the individual authorized user has a great deal of discretion in using work systems and interconnecting from outside the enterprise. There is a long list of potential problems and risks associated with enterprise computing. The user poses the single greatest risk, because he or she can often defeat even the best security measures. Unless the employer addresses individual users, the security of the enterprise's IT systems, networks, and data, as well as any potential for misuse, will depend on each individual user.

EMPLOYER LIABILITY

An area of criminal and civil law still in flux is the question of the due diligence required of an employer for Internet postings by employees using the employer's systems. When a tort arises due to actions of an employee, the courts have generally assessed whether the employee was acting in the capacity of an employee or (perhaps illicitly) on his or her own. The Internet has become an opportunity for such tortious acts as slander, libel, harassment, cyber bullying, defamation of character, unauthorized access to or release of confidential information, copyright violations, etc. Whether the employer could be held liable for illicit employee behavior online or not, the risk of criminal or civil charges alone has motivated some firms and agencies to step up monitoring of employees.[5] Clearly, the "deep pockets" of the employer (and perhaps an insurance company) are greater than that of the offending employee. What if the employer has ignored blatant evidence of online misbehavior?

Another motivator for employers is the potential cost in lost bandwidth, work hours, and reputation of employee Internet use for personal purposes, such as social networking, shopping, stock trading, surfing the Net, and other non-work-related activities. One case involved a government employee who was caught burning porn videos from the Internet onto DVDs all day at work, then selling the DVDs from home. It turned out that the heavy-duty DVD burner and DVD blanks were purchased through the agency supply office.

Litigation, although limited to date, has focused on personal injury, theft, domestic violence, harassment, and other issues arising from Internet use at work. When a candidate or onboard employee has a past history of misbehavior that can be carried out, or facilitated by Internet use, the employer would be well advised to consider the person's prior online behavior. Should the employee act out illegally in the physical world with potential digital evidence, a subsequent investigation would be likely to include both work and personal computers, especially if the employer does not prevent misbehavior online by using stringent controls on IT systems. With computer forensics and e-discovery increasingly involved in all types of criminal and civil investigations, the employer who is not acting to prevent misuse may find that internal security lapses are the least embarrassing and threatening aspects of risk incurred.

Introduction of digital forensic evidence is evolving along with the technologies and practices that create, retrieve, verify, and present its content. Among the challenges is to find the fit within a traditional legal context for electronic files that are readily changeable, may require expert interpretation, challenge hearsay, best evidence, and chain of custody rules, and often need systems administrators to introduce them in court. "Technospeak" may confuse the court officers, juries, and witnesses. A witness presenting what she knows may be hard to distinguish from one providing an opinion about the attribution of documentation. Judges must apply rules with limited precedent and sometimes questionable expert advice. Nevertheless, the contents of what are essentially electronic documents often are admitted into courts and play a vital and increasing role in both criminal and civil judgments.

VETTING, MONITORING, AND ACCOUNTABILITY

A somewhat controversial area of best security practices is employers' approach to employee IT systems use, including whether background vetting considers prior computer use, the degree to which enterprise systems are monitored to prevent, detect, and mitigate potential abuse, and the accountability (or lack thereof) to which authorized users are held. The issue of vetting will be handled in depth elsewhere. Monitoring of one's own IT systems has become an imperative today, if only to prevent viruses from bringing down computers vital to production. The question with which most employers struggle is what kind of monitoring is appropriate and cost-effective. Further, what will be done with employees or other authorized users (who may include vendors, partners, and customers) who violate the authorized use policy (AUP)?

Americans' acute sense of privacy and desire to be left alone by authority must be considered in any discussion of vetting, monitoring, and accountability. Since the sociological aspects of Internet use are progressing more rapidly than the law, policy, and established business practice can adapt, every employer must think carefully about not simply what security measures to employ, but what to do with information demonstrating the culpability of an authorized user. Simply because an act is against the rules is not necessarily a reason to take Draconian measures, yet failure to address bad behavior is a recipe for further, more damaging delinquency. Sometimes group behaviors online defeat the impulse to punish one person's misdeeds, because the employer cannot afford to fire the entire department. For example, a large employer found that a group of technicians were all enjoying Internet porn sites during the workday, but could not afford to fire the whole group. Further, the employer may not make the essential connection between the initial assessment of a new employee's proclivity to misbehave online in the context of the monitoring and controls that are routinely exercised in the enterprise. In any case, an employer needs to analyze security risk and countermeasures as they relate to any potential rogue user or group.

In the social contract that has evolved since automation became so much a part of our lives, new philosophical issues have arisen.[6] Can an enterprise survive and succeed if its people, systems, networks, and data are constantly at risk due to individual users' misbehavior? Will the best available workers wish to work in a place where ubiquitous surveillance is a constant in enterprise systems and physical space? Can an employer in the information age find the right mix of humanity and authority for the workplace? Cynics may point out that in the past few years, more Americans have been laid off, downsized, and fired than in many previous decades. Shedding workers is, especially in the recession under way at this writing, merely a way for firms and agencies to survive the lack of sufficient income and the overgrown structure that so many enterprises took on. One could ask whether IT systems monitoring is as big an issue when keeping the job at all is a struggle, even for the best of workers.

Addressing the social compact between employer and wired worker has the following foundational elements:

- Enterprise systems, networks, and data depend on each and every authorized user.

47

- There are limits to employers' ability to monitor and enforce all AUP rules.
- When an authorized user is documented abusing AUP rules, discipline will result.

When online misbehavior is involved, both the employer and employee realize that verification and attribution can be issues. Therefore, the following principles apply: (1) The employee will always be a party to considering the facts involved in misbehavior (usually in the form of an interview), and (2) employees will be held accountable for their behavior. These principles, coupled with those enumerated above, are more difficult to apply than it would appear (at least in this writer's experience). Often, employers decline to take meaningful action against an employee found to violate the AUP or to commit an illicit act. This is often because, however privately the case is handled, employers fear adverse reactions from other employees, and fear lawsuits from those discharged, suspended, or sanctioned for misbehavior. "A good talking to" is often the solution, with an attempt to extract a promise that "I won't do it again." This raises a question about the nature and effectiveness of accountability as the employer applies them.

At this writing, achieving precision in attribution for online misbehavior often depends on expensive and challenging enterprise computer forensics that appear to be overkill in the average case of misbehavior. In some business networks, it is reasonable to expect that someday, real-time forensic collection, analysis, and enforcement could literally prevent user error and malicious individuals from violating enterprise AUP rules. If "pop-ups" remind users of the limits of their authorized use, that can be a good thing. However, for most employers today, there is a reliance on the individual user to know and abide by the rules. Such reliance must include user accountability, or else the AUP has no impact.

Defining user accountability is an art akin to composing the enterprise's AUP. Among the key attributes of a successful user accountability policy are:

- Consistently applied rules that are provided to, discussed with, and known to all
- Supporting integrity as a core requirement for success in the workplace
- Relating the accountability required of all employees to success factors of the enterprise (such as teamwork to enable market-leading innovation, protection of intellectual property, discretion, exceeding customer expectations, and maintaining a professional reputation)

- Making every authorized insider a conscious player in enterprise security, for example:
  - Reminders in logon screens and shared data folders of data protection rules
  - Security updates with real-life examples
  - Required workstation scanning and authentication prior to enterprise connection
  - Adherence to security rules included in performance evaluations
- Interview of individuals involved in security inquiries, whenever possible, as a normal step in final resolution

THE EVOLVING PERSONNEL SECURITY MODEL

In the early 1990s, when the Internet was just starting to take off as a massively scaled platform for networking, security strategies for government and business were rethought[7] to:

1. Incorporate risk management (rather than risk avoidance)
2. Provide critical infrastructure protection (to mitigate against failure of vital resources)
3. Practice risk assessment (to allow comprehensive review of threats, vulnerabilities, and protection plans)
4. And some would add, practice security in depth, that is, a layered series of measures designed to help prevent, slow down, detect, and mitigate any malicious attack

At the same time, development of privacy protections matured, with one approach, common in Europe, Canada, and Asia, centered on a strong regime requiring "opt in" for personal data sharing, and a second approach, in the United States, centering on an "opt out" choice to protect privacy.[8] After September 11, 2001, new impetus impelled government and industry to adopt stronger critical infrastructure protections, public-private partnerships, proactive measures to prevent terrorist acts, and even more intensive risk assessments. The net result, in my view, omitted the improvement needed at this time in history in the most critical element of security: bringing personnel security up to date, to address the insider threat and networked information systems as part of workers' lives.[9]

Managing the risk from insiders (employees, contractors, vendors, etc.) means achieving the proper balance of oversight and worker autonomy.

The American worker historically has bridled at intense scrutiny. Close supervision is unwelcome. Depending on the nature of the workplace, tasks, teamwork, and review of results, it may behoove an employer to allow minor violations of security rules to promote job satisfaction, and possibly productivity. On the opposite side of the coin, employers must judge the extent to which minor security lapses lead to larger ones, and inadvertent disclosures of sensitive data lead to deliberate theft of intellectual property. It is people, not information systems, who are responsible for protecting the intellectual property (IP) that is the lifeblood of today's businesses and government agencies.[10]

In automating the enterprise, executives have made their business processes considerably more efficient, including the communication, collection, analysis, storage, retrieval, and application of information resources. For trusted IT systems users, these capabilities can create the means to exploit an employer's IP for their own purposes. Digital rights management, access controls, systems logging, and monitoring and blocking of prohibited activities have been introduced. Some IT systems have elaborate control regimes. Where the value, vulnerability, and usage of IP dictate, employers are beginning to invest more resources in IT systems security. Yet where every user can become a serious threat, a personnel security challenge remains.

The history of espionage—both national and corporate—is replete with examples of individuals who entered the enterprise in all respects innocent, as well as a select few who signed up with the intent of betraying their employer, and in some cases, their country.[11] Government agencies' and high-tech firms' background investigations are aimed at preventing the hiring and clearance of persons whose prior behavior proved that they were untrustworthy. Information age employers have not all confronted the dual challenges of initial clearance and reinvestigation. In order to establish a candidate's trustworthiness for initial hiring, employers need to consider several factors currently ignored by the vast majority of enterprises, including an applicant's history of

- Computer systems uses
- Internet uses, including social, game, and chat sites
- Penalties for computer abuse (e.g., Internet service provider and employer sanctions)
- Violations of authorized use policies belonging to employers, schools, or other hosts
- Violations of copyright or other proprietary information use restrictions (e.g., software, films, video, music, IP)

- Cracking, malware creation or use, and other malicious code experiences
- Anonymous Internet activities and avoidance of IT systems controls

Admitting prior misbehavior of some types cited above may not be sufficient reason to deny employment to a candidate. As with adjudication of other types of derogatory background investigative results, the employer should consider the seriousness, dates, frequency, repetition, likelihood of recurrence, and willingness to avoid future misbehavior of the same type. Today's employer depends on IT systems and knows (or should know) about the damage that only one malicious insider can do. Therefore, employers should upgrade their hiring processes to include prior IT systems and Internet use in evaluations and investigations. Most employers are unable to answer the questions about the orientation and training needed by new IT systems users, especially those relating to security. For the new employee who is immediately granted IT systems access, the level of employer risk assumed is proportional to the proclivity to misuse systems, networks, and data, and the employer's information assurance effort. Unless the individual insider is evaluated for trustworthiness with access to IT systems, the employer could be said to be negligent in IT security practice.

Beyond hiring, the lessons of insider crime suggest that there is always a danger of "good employees going bad." Mitigating this risk is essential but difficult. The individual's online behavior should be reevaluated periodically, and perhaps randomly, in much the same way as employers have required random and prescheduled drug testing. One potentially successful strategy is continuous monitoring of insider actions to prevent, detect, and mitigate IT systems abuse. Another is to conduct follow-up vetting. Since computer misuse at home may impact an employer's systems, data, and reputation (among other things), checking employees' recent online activities (i.e., those that are public) can help find the few insiders who pose a threat to the employer. The employer may discover behavior of concern that can be addressed soon enough to deter the insider from more damaging acts. Where serious wrongdoing is uncovered, it is better to address such problems sooner rather than later.

An example of the insider as traitor is Robert Hanssen, who pled guilty to espionage against his employer, the FBI, and against other agencies of the intelligence community, which he conducted over a twenty-plus-year period. Hanssen (a hacker who became a cracker) was adept at programming computers and, over the years, exploited his knowledge of FBI systems to provide the Russian intelligence services with voluminous, highly damaging data. His betrayal contributed to the deaths of ten sources of U.S. intelligence, who risked their lives as agents in place, and his disclosures led to the compromise of top secret U.S. collection systems worth billions of dollars.[12] As with all highly damaging spies, the Hanssen case led to personnel security and counterintelligence reforms designed to help prevent such betrayal and discover moles. One key lesson is that computers helped Hanssen to wreak severe damage on the United States' national security in much greater proportion than would have occurred without automation. A corollary is that monitoring and security assessment of the computer systems Hanssen used for his spying could have prevented or mitigated at least some of the damage. Press reports suggest that not only the FBI but also other intelligence community agencies have strengthened their systems to prevent similar spying in the future.[13]

To be successful, today's personnel security model must incorporate an evaluation of authorized users' past computer systems abuse, if any, and include periodic reinvestigations and monitoring to verify that insiders continue to protect the proprietary systems and data with which they are entrusted. Where the IP protected is highly valuable or priceless, "trust but verify" must be the mantra.

NOTES

1. Rosen, Jeffrey, "The Web Means the End of Forgetting," *New York Times Magazine*, July 25, 2010, http://www.nytimes.com/2010/07/25/magazine/25privacy-t2.html?_r=1&ref=magazine&pagewanted=print (accessed July 25, 2010), quotes a recent Microsoft survey saying 75% of U.S. recruiters and human resource professionals report that their companies require them to do online research about candidates, and many use a range of sites when scrutinizing applicants, including search engines, social networking sites, photo- and video-sharing sites, personal Web sites and blogs, Twitter, and online gaming sites. Seventy percent of U.S. recruiters report that they have rejected candidates because of information found online, like photos and discussion board conversations and membership in controversial groups.
2. Ody, Elizabeth, "Keeping Your Profile Clean," *Washington Post*, May 18, 2008: "A recent survey by ExecuNet, a networking organization for business leaders, found that 83% of executives and corporate recruiters research job candidates online, and 43% have eliminated a candidate based on search results." Bigam, Kate, "Employers May Be Eyeing Students' Facebook Accounts," related an October 2006 report by CareerBuilder.com saying that 26% of employers searched candidates online, including one in ten hiring managers,

and 63% of employers chose not to hire based on discoveries, key facets of which included lying about job qualifications, poor communications skills, and engaging in criminal behavior.

Peacock, Louisa, "Social Networking Sites Used to Check Out Job Applicants," March 17, 2009, http://www.personneltoday.com/articles/article.aspx?liarticleid=49844&printerfriendly=true, said 25% of employers worldwide check social networking sites such as Facebook and MySpace for information about job candidates. A study by Development Dimension International, Inc. (DDI) found 52% of those that did look up prospective employee profiles used the information in making hiring decisions.

Hechinger, John, "College Applicants Beware: Your Facebook Page Is Showing," *Wall Street Journal* online, September 18, 2008, http://online.wsj.com/article/SB122170459104151023.html. Ten percent of admissions officers in a survey of five hundred top colleges admitted checking social networking sites to evaluate applicants, and 38% said that what they saw "negatively affected" their views of the applicant.

3. American Management Association, Electronic Monitoring and Surveillance Survey, 2007, http://press.amanet.org/press-releases/177/2007-electronic-monitoring-surveillance-survey/.

4. Madden, Mary, and Jones, Sydney, *Networked Workers*, Pew Internet and American Life Project, September 24, 2008, http://www.pewinternet.org/Reports/2008/Networked-Workers.aspx.

5. For an example of monitoring file use and protecting data at work, see Verdasys, http://www.verdasys.com/ (a former client of the author).

6. Hall, George M., *The Age of Automation* (New York: Praeger Publishers, 1995).

7. Joint Security Commission, *Redefining Security*, Report to the Secretary of Defense and the Director of Central Intelligence, February 1994.

8. Bouckaert, Jan, and Degryse, Hans, "Opt in Versus Opt out: A Free-Entry Analysis of Privacy Policies," December 2005, http://weis2006.econinfosec.org/docs/34.pdf (accessed June 1, 2010).

9. Shaw, Eric, Ruby, Keven G., and Post, Jerrold M., "The Insider Threat to Information Systems," Political Psychology Associates, Ltd., 1999, http://www.pol-psych.com/sab.pdf (accessed August 9, 2010).

10. Computer Science and Telecommunications Board, National Research Council, *The Digital Dilemma, Intellectual Property in the Information Age* (Washington, DC: National Academies Press, 2000).

11. Fischer, Lynn F., "Espionage: Why Does It Happen" (DoD Security Institute, October 2000), http://www.hanford.gov/oci/maindocs/ci_r_docs/whyhappens.pdf (accessed September 21, 2010).

12. Rowan, J. Patrick, Deputy Assistant Attorney General, U.S. Department of Justice, "Enforcement of Federal Espionage Laws," Statement before the Subcommittee on Crime, Terrorism, and Homeland Security, Committee on the Judiciary, U.S. House of Representatives, January 29, 2008.

Herbig, Katherine L., and Wiskoff, Martin F., *Espionage against the United States by American Citizens 1947–2001*, Technical Report 02-5, Defense Personnel Security Research Center (PERSEREC), Monterey, CA, July 2002.

13. Wise, David, *Spy, The Inside Story of How the FBI's Robert Hanssen Betrayed America* (New York: Random House, 2002).

14. For example, Webster, William H., "A Review of FBI Security Programs," March 2002, http://www.fas.org/irp/agency/doj/fbi/websterreport.html (accessed August 9, 2010).

Section II

Legal and Policy Context

A good illustration of the issues involved in using the Internet for intelligence is the concern that the search engine companies and other Web service providers collect information from users for their own purposes.[1] The intentions driving search engine providers such as Google, Bing, Ask, etc., are commercial: Advertisers are their first priority, because they pay the bills. Searchers, consumers, browsers—users—are not as high a priority. As discussed below, in the United States, where opt-out policies are applied, the user must ask that personally identifying information not be collected. Even then, Internet service providers (ISPs), search engines, and Web sites collect and utilize information about Internet behaviors for business purposes. In many respects, the great benefits of the Internet as an information provider are supported by advertising and market measurement that depend on data mining of online behaviors. However, there is well-placed concern about whether businesses will regulate themselves when it comes to self-interest over the privacy of the individual. As the U.S. Congress and Americans contemplate the appropriate limits that should be imposed on Internet sites to ensure privacy protection, those contemplating how to exploit Internet information must confront similar issues. Meanwhile, in Europe, strong privacy protections apply to users' data, and users must provide informed consent before a government agency or private company can make use of those data.

Network and Internet service providers and commercial Web sites collect detailed data from users for many valid reasons, including ensuring continuity and quality of service. Sites generally express their policies in privacy policy and authorized use policy statements available on the Web site (by tradition, links are often found at the bottom of the home page). The place of the ISP and some commercial Web sites in the spectrum of network services allows these businesses exceptions to laws forbidding interception of electronic communications and collection and retention of customer-identifiable data—for the limited purposes of service quality assurance and continuity. However, many Internet businesses were initiated for marketing purposes, and rely on their ability to collect data on large groups of customers to carry out their business-to-business activities. Therefore, it behooves customers to understand the privacy and use policies of ISPs, and to make informed decisions about what Web site services to use, based on the customer's comfort level in sharing private data with service providers.[2]

A related concern is the strategy of an Internet information collector: Will she use a proxy or "anonymize" her searching, so that it is not possible to know who is asking about whom? Are privacy options of the search engines used?

NOTES

1. Google, "How Google Works," http://www.google.com/howgoogleworks/ (accessed June 1, 2010).
2. Schlein, Alan M., *Find It Online, The Complete Guide to Online Research*, 2nd edition (Tempe, AZ: Facts on Demand Press, 2001).

5

Liability, Privacy, and Management Issues

LIABILITY FOR SERVICE PROVIDERS

The wide variety of activities on the Internet has been spawned by creative businesses offering many types of social, recreational, hobby, communications, and business functions that work well and scale globally. In the early days of the Internet, it was possible to categorize service providers by the types of online activities offered, but soon "one-stop shopping" firms like America Online (AOL) created services with many types of interactions. Many of those online still use services like AOL, Microsoft's MSN, Yahoo!, and major telecommunications firms' portals for a wide variety of functions, such as Internet access, email, social networking, news, chat, instant messaging, searching, and others. Mobile devices increasingly provide a widening variety of online activities and applications. Today, the role of the commercial Internet portal in connecting users is to provide multiple, bundled services, often with applications allowing more and more integrated and interconnected options. Examples include geolocation, finding nearby sites and people, updating a circle of "friends," interlacing multiple email, IM, and "tweet" contact lists and postings, evaluating local retailers, and updating agendas. As a facilitator of the human interactions enabled by the multifaceted network, the telecommunications company, ISP, interconnected service providers, and hosts must understand the market forces, predominant personal views, laws, and ethical limitations of the activities riding their wavelengths.

Based on historical profiles of crime patterns within communities, it is predictable that a variety of criminals will take advantage of networked services to carry out their acts in a more efficient, anonymous, and pleasurable manner. Already major telecommunications and Internet service providers have been forced to deal with many warrants, subpoenas, and court orders requiring legal intercepts, production of customer records, and service details based on serious criminal activities. No self-respecting drug dealer is without a cellular connection, whether a "throwaway" cell phone or a Blackberry allowing multiple connections and messaging options. A classic case in a northeast state involved a clue at an apparent mob "hit" scene, a calling card from a telephone network that was traced to a man from Florida through his credit card. The man claimed he was in Florida at the time of the murder, but his cell phone records identified precisely where he was and with whom he discussed the murder he committed. He is now serving time for the murder. As important as the records of the cell phone calls were to the investigation, even more important was the capability of identifying the calling card customer.

Telecommunications networks, ISPs, and Web sites generally take the position that they are not responsible for their customers' activities, only providing a virtual venue through which people can carry on legal behaviors. Unfortunately, services like eBay have discovered that the sale of stolen, contraband, and misappropriated items is sufficiently rampant that they have felt compelled to field a first-class team of former law enforcement and prosecutorial personnel to prevent, detect, alert law enforcement to, otherwise respond to, and process data concerning illegal activities. While the illegal activities may be only a small part of the service provided, it is significant to those victimized, such as a purchase for which a customer received no goods. Not all Internet firms take the initiative or incur the expense that eBay has to ensure the integrity of a service that is open to virtually everyone.

Criminal and civil courts have so far agreed with the large majority of ISPs, Web sites, and others online that they are not responsible for the criminal behaviors of their customers. In some instances, courts have recognized the AUP as in effect the governing rule on a Web site, and held the customer who violates the AUP (and therefore the site's terms of service) to be engaged in illicit activities by definition. In various communities, counties, and states, there have been occasional cries to shut down or criminally sanction Web sites that have become a venue where illegal acts take place, but in general, it is understood that Web sites operating properly still may be used in crimes.[1]

Among the special classes of services online are those belonging to universities, colleges, other educational institutions, and some nonprofits. Many educational and nonprofit sites have large storage, a variety of applications, and high bandwidth—just what a cybercriminal may be looking for. Educational sites also operate in a wide-open environment. For example, at the start of each semester, hundreds or thousands of students may "plug in" to the college IT network. The educational system may be required for research, study, communications with teachers, class attendance, test taking, cafeteria access, campus access, bill paying, and a variety of other student, faculty, and staff services. Often, the university email system also accommodates alumni, a special target of solicitations for donations and support for the school. The size and openness of the educational IT infrastructure make it a prime target for cybercriminals, spammers, and marketers. As a consequence, many educational sites have found it necessary to adopt robust and inventive security measures that can guarantee system functions, integrity, and continuity, while keeping out malicious code, inadvertent infections, and deliberate attempts at misuse (e.g., changing grades, cheating on tests and papers, bulk spam).

The above examples are not limited to ISPs, other network service providers, and educational institutions. Unfortunately, many corporations have found that their employees have placed large quantities of contraband and illicit materials in shared storage (e.g., MP3 music files, videos and software in violation of copyrights, porn and child porn). For example, an employee of a high-bandwidth company was arrested for running his own business on the side, selling child pornography from his personal Web site on company servers. Like the service providers, businesses are potentially liable for the content of their IT systems and must face the fact that at least a small percentage of their users will misuse their systems. The larger the systems, the greater the likelihood that illicit content and unauthorized behaviors are taking place on them. System owners must decide who, in effect, will be the sheriff in town.

In all the instances discussed, it is the people who decide to misbehave on computer systems to which they are granted access that cause the risk to service providers of all kinds. Like viruses, illicit acts online should be sought out, discovered, and dealt with by Internet-connected hosts, if only for self-preservation and reputation protection.

LIABILITY FOR EMPLOYERS

Employers in the private sector are governed by a series of constitutional, federal, state, county, and local statutes and legal standards.[2] This is not the appropriate place to itemize them. However, a key question that must be considered in all legal and policy discussions of Internet searching that applies to persons (individuals and legal persons) is the legal standards that must be applied. Therefore, it is necessary to focus on how one can conduct Internet and open-source information collection without incurring legal liability for violating a statute or standard.

Employers must contemplate the laws that apply, whether they are conducting an internal criminal investigation, vetting potential employees, collecting business/competitive intelligence, assessing market competition, doing due diligence, managing brand protection, or assessing security risks and vulnerabilities, to name some of the main reasons for enterprise intelligence functions. This discussion will deliberately omit market studies, because the rules governing Internet social research (a very different animal from intelligence collection) should be applied for market research. However, some of the discussion in later chapters bears directly on such operations.

Two key areas of concern are applicant background investigations and protection of people, assets, and information (i.e., corporate security). While an employer has legal obligations that must be met in assessing candidates for employment, the obligation to provide a safe and secure workplace is also vital. When an employer discriminates in hiring under Title VII of the Civil Rights Act of 1964, liability is created, and lawsuits will probably follow. When an employer fails to anticipate the likelihood of a threat such as an insider victimizing fellow employees, customers, or others, liability may be incurred. It is only a matter of time before the legal theory that an employer should have known and acted on information published and readily available on the Internet finds its way into a courtroom, especially if violence, crime, or serious loss occurs in the workplace. Physical world negligence suits asserting a standard of due care in hiring against employers have succeeded, and it is likely that cyber world torts will as well.[3]

The federal government, counties, states, and municipalities to varying degrees oversee the application of employment laws. The courts apply the laws for criminal and civil judgments. One aspect of the rapid advances in information technology is the lag time between societal changes such as large-scale Internet use and the adaptation of the legal system to new realities.[4] For example, at a time when millions of Internet users illicitly download films, music, and software for personal use in violation of copyright laws, how can an employer judge how much illicit activity of this kind should preclude a person from employment? How many downloads are tolerable? Is it likely that people who misappropriate movies would also commit economic espionage? Can that likelihood be judged by the amount of past illicit downloading done? Business and government are, at this writing, just beginning to contemplate the metrics of adjudications in the Internet era.

Avoiding serious liability will require employers to look carefully at the standards they apply to vetting employees, both for hire and for continued employment, promotion, or clearances. Fortunately, according to court cases reviewed to date, there is no requirement in the United States for an employer to take additional steps to utilize any public information in background investigations, provided that the process includes notice, signed (informed) consent, and a verification process. Should an employer wish to include questions to candidates about their computer use and abuse, and verification of their responses using Internet vetting, it would be prudent to include explicit prior notice about those topics in the process. Suggested methods appear later.

Most application forms and the government's SF-86[5] (among others) ask applicants to list the other names under which they are known. Because a large percentage of Internet users (at least 30%, based on studies by Pew and others) have multiple virtual identities online, it is important in the background investigation process to collect them. Virtual identities include email addresses, nicknames, "handles," and other pseudonyms used for Internet activities. Asking for these aliases does not exceed the current norm for forms used, but four years' study has shown that few employers explicitly ask applicants to include virtual identities on the form. The SF-86, which is used for U.S. government candidates for jobs with clearances, asks for both home and work email addresses and for aliases. Recently added to the SF-86 are questions about prior misbehavior using computers. Yet almost no agencies at this writing explicitly instruct candidates to include their Internet identities, which may have been used in such misbehavior.

The discussion below is designed to help put Internet intelligence gathering in an appropriate legal context. However, few attorneys have focused on this area, and not much case law exists to date, to help in the rapidly developing area of Internet law.

ACCOUNTABILITY FOR EMPLOYEES

Automation of the workplace and widespread changes in social norms for computer use have dramatically changed the landscape in ways that enterprises may not have considered. Habits acquired in personal computer use may invade the business, and business topics are being included in off-hours blogging, social networking, and a variety of other Internet activities both desirable and undesirable from the employer's standpoint. In most workplaces, it is easy to acquire digital goods, including designs, customer lists, marketing plans, information on employees, and other trade secrets. Espionage cases over the past twenty years in both government and industry have highlighted how much more damaging just one insider can be, due to the volume, quality, and scope of the data stolen, particularly when IT systems are exploited.[6]

It must be acknowledged that computers, networks, and data are

- Intrinsically not secure, and perhaps not absolutely securable in the near term
- A gateway to most enterprises' most sensitive and valuable data
- Accessed by employees as trusted users with little oversight
- Protected more strongly against outsiders than insiders
- A higher risk than most employers understand

Recent experience demonstrates that most enterprises have attempted to strengthen their information security and have sought to improve protection through employee security awareness. Laudable though those efforts are, they may be inadequate to the task. Studies of insider crime have demonstrated since biblical times that there is almost always an insider willing to commit serious crimes within any sizable enterprise. After years of frustration with inadequate metrics, questionable survey statistics, and corporate security experience as a practitioner, colleague, and consultant to business and government, my rule of thumb is that six of every thousand employees will commit a felony crime against their employer yearly. I regret having to report this, just as I regret having participated in the arrest of priests, nuns, and FBI agents. One only need look at the high crimes and misdemeanors of the nation's once respected politicians, law enforcement officers, intelligence officials, clergy, business leaders, and nonprofit executives to demonstrate that there is no sacrosanct group of human beings in any workplace. Aspiring to greatness does not prevent crime in the ranks.

So the logical question for every enterprise is how to approach the virtual goods that are at the disposal of every authorized user through information systems. U.S. military and intelligence agencies take the approach that all online activities involving classified data and systems will be logged, monitored, and serious breaches prevented.[7] Alas, even those systems with the strongest protections have been victimized by clever, malicious users. It is clear that it is the person, not the machine, that should be the focus of behavioral assessment, since it is the person who can make a mistake or commit a crime.

Twentieth-century personnel management can be characterized as evolving from the workplace cruelty of the industrial revolution to the civilized protections, led by unions, of the information age. Yet there are those that would contend that the two decades of the 1980s and 1990s saw more layoffs, outsourcing, and ill treatment of workers than ever. It was the generation when the lifelong aspiration to work for just one employer (other than the government) came to a painful end. The trust and emotional attachment between employer and worker ended. You can hear it in the terms used for employees: human resources and human capital. Just another currency.

Perhaps it sounds too strident to observe that an employer, viewed even in the press as likely to downsize or outsource, is apt to be looked upon by employees with a wary eye. The employer, needing to keep key talent, may engage in strategies to use economic leverage to prevent the exodus of its brain trust. Employees, for their part, may collect as much data as they can from the workplace, in anticipation that bringing it with them will enhance their value in the next job. Several surveys suggest that this is actually happening frequently in the twenty-first century.[9]

Employee accountability in this context can be a sensitive topic, given the atmosphere described above. Yet the compact between the employer whose net worth is largely in data and the employee with access to that data must include a strong element of trust if the enterprise is to succeed. In most agencies and firms, a formula for success is holding each individual user accountable for actions taken online. All trusted users should sign a confidentiality agreement. At logon, workers should be reminded that as a condition of access, their use of data and online activities is controlled by programs to prevent misuse, as well as to log events. This accountability should start before the applicant is hired, be stressed during indoctrination and training, and continue with periodic reinvestigations, monitoring, and enforcement of authorized use policies during employment. Internet investigations are a natural part of preemployment screening and reinvestigations. Like the Internet, intranet behavior can be a prime indicator of danger for the enterprise, when users violate the law, policies, and rules. Given the invaluable nature of information assets, today's automated employer owes nothing less to stockholders, customers, and the employees themselves than vigilance and efficiency in protecting its information assets from malicious users.

NOTES

1. Krasne, Alexandra, "What Is Web 2.0, Anyway?" TechSoup, December 2005, http://www.techsoup.org/learningcenter/webbuilding/archives/page9344.cfm (accessed June 1, 2010).
2. Cybercrime information collected in law enforcement briefings of the Computer Crime and Digital Evidence Ad Hoc Committee (which the author chaired).
3. Nixon, W. Barry, and Kerr, Kim M., *Background Screening and Investigations, Managing Risk from HR and Security Perspectives* (Burlington, MA: Elsevier, 2008).
4. Lawson, Thomas C., Expert witness in several negligent hiring cases in California and Arizona, http://www.apscreenemploymentscreening.com/articles/case_samples.pdf (accessed May 25, 2010).
5. Dunne, Caroline, and Sanford, Anna, "The New Age of Social Networking—Issues for Employers," 2007, http://www.paulhastings.com/assets/publications/767.pdf?wt.mc_ID=767.pdf (accessed September 21, 2010).
6. "Questionnaire for National Security Positions," SF-86, http://www.opm.gov/forms/pdf_fill/sf86.pdf (accessed May 26, 2010).
7. Eric Shaw, Kevin G. Ruby, and Jerrold M. Post, "The Insider Threat to Information Systems," Political Psychology Associates, Ltd., 1999, http://www.pol-psych.com/sab.pdf.
8. Moore, Andrew P., Cappelli, Dawn M., Caron, Thomas C., Shaw, Eric, and Trzeciak, Randall F., "Insider Theft of Intellectual Property for Business Advantage: A Preliminary Model," Carnegie Mellon Software Engineering Institute and CERT, appearing in the 1st International Workshop on Managing Insider Security Threats (MIST 2009), Purdue University, West Lafayette, June 15–19, 2009.
9. For example, DOD Directive 5220.22-M, Chapter 8, Information Systems Security, Section 6, Protection Requirements, February 2001.

6

Laws

This chapter contains brief reviews of the statutes that may assist those seeking guidance for the legal limitations on Internet intelligence and investigations. For the most part, federal and state laws contain no restrictions on the use of the Internet to collect information—especially public or published information—for use by investigators. The summaries and views expressed here do not constitute legal opinions or advice, but are conveyed as commonsense interpretations of the meaning of current laws and indications of the intent of Congress and the judiciary, even if the laws themselves do not address Internet investigations directly. Because people have differing views and strong opinions about their privacy rights, some of the interpretations below may be controversial.

CONSTITUTIONAL RIGHTS

The U.S. Constitution's amendments[1] enshrine the following rights relevant to Internet searching:

- First: Freedom of speech
- Fourth: Freedom from unreasonable search and seizure
- Fifth: Freedom from being forced to give witness against oneself or to be denied due process of law
- Sixth: Right of the accused to call witnesses and face an accuser in court

None of these rights preclude Internet searching under the appropriate circumstances. Litigation, to date, concerning constitutional rights has provided no successful challenge to Internet searching. Very few cases have been brought. Litigation will be considered later.

Decisions by the Supreme Court and other federal courts in general have upheld the rights of individuals to protection of their information (e.g., postings) where there is a reasonable expectation of privacy. Under the Fourth Amendment, the location where the reasonable expectation of privacy exists is usually interpreted as in one's home, but has been extended to include other places where privacy can be expected (e.g., in a phone booth or hotel room). On the Internet, the privacy of a venue and users' expectation of privacy may often depend on the authorized use policy of the Web site. Where the terms of use call for recognition of individual privacy rights, presumably a collector of information should abide by the AUP or face the possibility that information found may not be legally usable in any court or administrative procedure. Collection itself may even be deemed illegal, if it is considered to be for an illegitimate purpose.

FEDERAL AND STATE STATUTES

A review of U.S. laws that may impact Internet searching for information on individuals was conducted. These statutes regulate investigations to varying degrees, depending on the purpose, methods used, and resulting actions. Based on this review, the key issues are the methods used to retrieve the data, the uses to which Internet search results are put, and how decisions are made. Following is a summary of those laws deemed most relevant.

> *The Privacy Act of 1971, as amended:*[2] Controls government collection, use, and protection of personally identifying information, and limits the extent to which federal agencies can disclose records: an individual must consent in writing, a court order must be placed, or the disclosure must fall within one of the statute's exceptions. The Privacy Act does not address personal information collected by private parties, such as data brokers, collection agencies, or consumer credit groups. A privacy impact assessment is required when a government agency establishes a new information system used to store data, including personally identifying information.

The Public Information Act (Freedom of Information Act):[3] Governs disclosure of U.S. government information, with exemptions for law enforcement and intelligence investigative files. The Disclosure of Confidential Information Act provides criminal penalties for unauthorized disclosure of specified classes of information by government officers and employees.

Health Insurance Portability and Accountability Act of 1996 (HIPAA), Gramm–Leach–Bliley Act of 1999, and Sarbanes–Oxley Act of 2002:[4] Several statutes, including these three, provide for the protection of sensitive, personally identifying information in the hands of the health industry, financial services, and consumer services enterprises.

The USA Patriot Act, Public Law 107-56, 2001:[5] The Patriot Act does not specifically address investigations of candidates for employment or clearances, except for drivers of hazardous cargo vehicles, who must meet federal standards for licensing based on a background investigation. The Patriot Act authorizes government surveillance and information collection activities, including electronic surveillance, designed to prevent terrorism, under appropriate legal authority (e.g., a warrant, subpoena, or national security request).

The Fair Credit Reporting Act (FCRA), Public Law 91-508 (Title VI § 601):[6] Regulates consumer reports and consumer reporting agencies, establishing standards for the collection and dissemination of credit information and consumer reports, including reports of background investigations establishing eligibility for employment conducted by contract firms. Key provisions include the ability of the subject of a consumer report to review it and correct information deemed inaccurate. The FCRA protects prospective and onboard employees, and must be the basis for policy principles established for Internet vetting by the private sector. The FCRA is examined further below.

Electronic Communications Privacy Act of 1986 (ECPA):[7] Protects wire, oral, and electronic communications while in transit by requiring warrants for interception, and protects communications held in electronic storage, i.e., messages stored on computers. Law enforcement and investigators must obtain warrants or other specified processes to obtain communications and customer account data. Protects private communications from third-party access, such as ISPs. ECPA does not restrict collection of data legitimately posted on the public Internet, or regulate the personal information that may be made available by users who willingly post such information. ECPA also does not protect employees' communications conducted on employers' systems. Some litigation under ECPA has served to clarify its reach.

TITLE X Homeland Security Act of 2002 and TITLE III E Government Act of 2002, amending the Federal Information Security Management Act (FISMA) of 2002:[8] These statutes require that federal programs include information technology training programs and security awareness training for personnel and contractors that include information security risks and responsibilities involved in reducing those risks.

The Computer Fraud and Abuse Act (Title 18, Part I, Chapter 47, § 1030):[9] Forbids, with other federal criminal statutes, criminal activities that occur in the physical world, when they take place in cyberspace, and crimes facilitated by computers. U.S. computer crime is the province of the Computer Crime and Intellectual Property Section of the U.S. Department of Justice, which can be found at http://www.cybercrime.gov/, and which posts much helpful information about computer-related crime and intellectual property protection. Many types of street crimes (e.g., sale of pirated movie DVDs on the streets in Manhattan and Beijing) are also found on the Internet (where millions of users monthly patronize about 1,000 pirate sites offering films, videos, music, and software). Because millions of people engage in criminal activities on the Internet, it is unlikely that most of them, given today's enforcement situation, will ever be charged with crimes.

The Computer Security Act of 1987 (Public Law 100-235):[10] This act, subsequent statutes, and appropriations aim to strengthen the security of government computers, networks, and data, and assign establishment of computer security standards to the National Institute of Standards and Technology (NIST) and other federal agencies, including training of federal systems users and security measures.

The Children's Online Privacy Protection Act (COPPA):[11] Regulates the information that can be collected about preadult Internet users by Web sites and other commercial online services providers. COPPA is an example of the concern that the Congress has expressed in statutes, hearings, and studies about the best ways to protect the privacy of all Internet users from collection of personally identifiable transactional data by ISPs, Web sites, and advertisers.

Copyright (Title 17, U.S. Code) and Uruguay Round Agreements Act (implementing international copyright treaties):[12] Protects authors of original works that are fixed in a tangible form of expression, both published and unpublished, giving the author exclusive rights to do and authorize reproduction, distribution, public performance, or display, with fair use and licensing restrictions. Registration and marking of copyrighted material are not necessary for copyright protections to apply. Infringement of copyright can be a federal civil or criminal matter, enforced by the courts, including damages, injunctions, and impoundment. Providing false contact information to a domain name registry creates a rebuttable presumption that the infringement was willful. Criminal infringement includes fines and incarceration for commercial, for-profit misuse, including illicit distribution by computer network. ISPs are exempt if violations are committed by network users and not the ISP.

Federal background screening laws: Besides the FCRA, federal statutes controlling background screening include the Driver's Privacy Protection Act, the Civil Rights Act of 1964, Title VII of the Civil Rights Act 1996 (commonly referred to as Title VII), the Americans with Disabilities Act, the Federal Bankruptcy Act, the Employee Polygraph Protection Act, and the Family Educational Rights and Privacy Act, as well as guidelines set by the Equal Employment Opportunity Commission. None address Internet vetting.

California statute: Unauthorized Access to Computers, Computer Systems and Computer Data (California Penal Code Section 502-502.08):[13] From the statute: "It is the intent of the Legislature in enacting this section to expand the degree of protection afforded to individuals, businesses, and governmental agencies from tampering, interference, damage, and unauthorized access to lawfully created computer data and computer systems. The Legislature finds and declares that the proliferation of computer technology has resulted in a concomitant proliferation of computer crime and other forms of unauthorized access to computers, computer systems, and computer data. The Legislature further finds and declares that protection of the integrity of all types and forms of lawfully created computers, computer systems, and computer data is vital to the protection of the privacy of individuals as well as to the well-being of financial institutions, business concerns, governmental agencies, and others within this state that lawfully utilize those computers, computer systems, and data."

California Database Protection Act (CDPA), CA Civil Code § 1798.82; Consumer Credit Reporting Agencies Act, CA Civil Code § 1798.16; California Investigative Consumer Reporting Act, CA Civil Code § 1798.83-84; U.S. Comptroller of the Currency Guidance to National Banks, OCC Bulletin 2005-13:[14] The CDPA, which took effect in July 2003, mandates public disclosure of computer security breaches in which confidential information may have been compromised. The law covers state agencies and all private enterprises doing business in California. Any entity that fails to disclose that a breach has occurred could be liable for civil damages or face class-action lawsuits. Personal confidential information includes first and last names in conjunction with the following data: social security number, driver's license or CID, account number, and credit or debit card number with any required security code, access code, or password that would permit access to an individual's financial account. The U.S. comptroller of the currency issued guidance requiring national banks to notify customers of data breaches that include sensitive customer information. California state laws governing background checks include the California Consumer Credit Reporting Agencies Act and the California Investigative Consumer Reporting Act, which expand on the requirements of the federal FCRA.

Examples of other relevant state statutes:[15] California Civil Code § 1798.83-84 and Utah Code §§ 13-37-101, 102, 201, 202, 203, require all nonfinancial businesses to disclose to customers the types of personal information that the businesses sell or share with third parties for marketing purposes or for a fee. Minnesota §§ 325M.01 to .09 prohibit disclosure of an ISP customer's personally identifying information, stored data, and surfing history, except to law enforcement, and provides for civil damages. Nevada § 205.498 requires ISPs to keep confidential all but a customer's email address, and requires keeping email addresses confidential if a customer so requests, subject to fines for violations.

Delaware § 19-7-705 and Connecticut General Statutes § 31-48d prohibit an employer from collecting email contents and Internet surfing data of employees without written notice, imposing civil penalties for violations. Exceptions are made for criminal investigations. At least sixteen states have statutes that require government Web sites to establish privacy policies and procedures.

In federal and state laws, both the U.S. Congress and the states have passed statutes aimed at protecting the privacy of computer and Internet users across the board. Many of the statutes restrict government collection and use of data without placing similar restrictions on the private sector. However, no law found prohibits the collection of publicly posted information on the Internet for a lawful purpose.

FEDERAL RULES OF EVIDENCE
AND COMPUTER RECORDS

The 2009 versions of the Federal Rules of Evidence, Federal Rules of Criminal Procedure, and Federal Rules of Civil Procedure[16] contain almost no references to the Internet, except mention of publication online of government information. The Rules of Evidence do not even contain the words *Internet*, *cyber*, or *digital*. However, they do treat "data stored in a computer or similar device."

In order to address the issues of admissibility and authenticity of evidence as viewed by a court of law, the Federal Rules of Evidence will be considered here, rather than those of each state, selected foreign countries, or some other approach, all of which might fall short of providing consistent and useful guidance. Since the states generally follow the federal approach, and this area of law is evolving with the technologies involved, the federal rules are deemed enlightening and sufficient. They are rooted in the Constitution (e.g., the Sixth Amendment right of an accused to face an accuser).

Federal courts generally consider admitting computer records into evidence under an exception to the hearsay rule, which states (in relevant part): "Hearsay, [which] is a statement, other than one made by the declarant while testifying at the trial or hearing, offered in evidence to prove the truth of the matter asserted . . . is not admissible except as provided by these rules or by other rules prescribed by the Supreme Court pursuant to statutory authority or by Act of Congress." In lay terms, testimony by John that "Mary said Sam did it" usually would not be admitted in federal court. Exceptions to the hearsay rule include a recorded recollection, or a record of regularly conducted activity, such as a business record. Courts have analyzed the content and circumstances of computer records' creation in order to determine if they contain hearsay. If a person created the record (e.g., a document, spreadsheet, etc.), then its admissibility may depend on testimony in order to authenticate the content and assert that it is accurate as recorded (e.g., if it was information that a clerk normally enters in the course of business). If the computer itself created the record by processing data in a programmed fashion, then the record may not contain hearsay, but may require someone to authenticate the information to be admitted. Of course, computer records often contain mixed data, that is, those that are entered by a person, which courts interpret as containing hearsay, and those that result from automated processing. In order to get computer evidence admitted, then, a party must establish the authenticity of the record and that it falls under the hearsay rule exception.[17]

One reason for considering the Federal Rules of Evidence in connection with cyber vetting and Internet intelligence is the reasoning behind the centuries-old court rules, which are based on British Common Law and American practice. The rules point to a central issue: the authenticity and veracity of the data. Essentially, all intelligence functions must face the same questions as the courts: Is this information real or somehow untrustworthy? Is the information likely to be true or false? Courts apply rules like the hearsay one to keep unreliable information out. As the Justice Department's guidance says:

> The hearsay rules exist to prevent unreliable out-of-court statements by human declarants from improperly influencing the outcomes of trials. Because people can misinterpret or misrepresent their experiences, the hearsay rules express a strong preference for testing human assertions in court, where the declarant can be placed on the stand and subjected to cross-examination.[18]

Clearly, computers can be used to create false or misleading records. Internet postings may contain humor, irony, fantasy, exaggeration, deliberate untruth—or factual documents. Since the intelligence analyst often cannot consult the creator of the records, authentication and veracity can be difficult to judge.

INTERNATIONAL TREATIES AND STANDARDS

Among the international bodies addressing legal and privacy issues of the information society are the United Nations, the Organization of Economic Cooperation and Development, and the Council of Europe. The European Commission and European Union, as well as constituent nations, have strong privacy protection laws and directives that can be characterized as enforcement of the "opt in" principle, meaning that in order for personally identifying information to be collected, the individual must agree to that collection. The 1995 EU Data Privacy Protection Act requires unambiguous consent for information to be gathered online, notice as to why the information is collected, the ability to correct erroneous data, and the ability to opt out and to be protected against transfer of one's data to countries with lesser privacy protections. Nevertheless, an individual may elect to post personal information online for all to see.

In the Council of Europe Convention on Cybercrime,[19] ratified by the United States in 2001, and in effect since January 1, 2007, convention signatories pledged to criminalize a wide range of computer-related illegal activities, and to address electronic evidence, facilitate investigation of cybercrime, and obtain electronic evidence to prosecute all types of criminal investigations and proceedings. The convention reaffirms established principles of free expression and privacy, and is the only binding international treaty on the subject to date.

The European Union Data Protection Directive[20] applies to firms operating in the EU and specifies that "personal data" must have "appropriate security," compliant with either ISO/IEC 17799 or BS 7799-2; prohibits an individual's personal information from being accessed and employed for other uses; and requires appropriate measures to protect personal data. The Canadian Personal Information Protection and Electronic Documents Act[21] regulates the use and collection of personal information via the Internet. The act applies not only to Canadian companies but potentially to any entity that collects personal information in Canada or personal information from Canadian citizens. More sensitive information, such as patient records, should be safeguarded by a higher level of protection. Collection or use of personal information without knowledge and consent appear to be allowed by the act for appropriate, official purposes such as verification of the terms of employment.

Existing laws that may relate to Internet searching can be summed up in a few short points:

- U.S. statutes and legal practice do not forbid the lawful use of public Internet postings for intelligence, investigative, and vetting purposes.
- In Europe, Canada, and Asia, legal privacy protections may limit the types of data that can be collected and used from Internet sources.
- Misuse of personally identifying data, including failure to protect it adequately, can result in legal sanctions in the United States and abroad.
- The law tends to favor the agency or business that provides full disclosure and transparency to consumers, employees, and others, allowing them to see the information about them, correct it if necessary, and provide consent when data about them are used in a manner that may impact their well-being.

While the U.S. Constitution and statutes do not directly address issues related to Internet investigations, they shed light on the principles that should be adopted for fairness and ethical cyber vetting. Additional support for the pillars of Internet search policy for government and private enterprises will be found in Chapter 9.

NOTES

1. U.S. Constitution, http://www.archives.gov/exhibits/charters/constitution.html (accessed August 10, 2010).
2. For the Privacy Act, see http://www.usdoj.gov/oip/foia_updates/Vol_XVII_4/page2.htm, which contains amendments (accessed August 10, 2010).
3. Freedom of Information Act, http://www.justice.gov/oip/foia_updates/Vol_XVII_4/page2.htm (accessed August 10, 2010).
4. HIPPA, https://www.cms.gov/HIPAAGenInfo/Downloads/HIPAALaw.pdf (accessed August 10, 2010).
   Gramm–Leach–Bliley Act of 1999, http://banking.senate.gov/conf/ (accessed August 10, 2010).
   Sarbanes–Oxley Act of 2002, http://fl1.findlaw.com/news.findlaw.com/hdocs/docs/gwbush/sarbanesoxley072302.pdf (accessed August 10, 2010).
5. USA Patriot Act, Public Law 107-56, 2001, http://thomas.loc.gov/cgi-bin/bdquery/z?d107:HR03162:%5D (accessed August 10, 2010).
6. Fair Credit Reporting Act (FCRA), Public Law 91-508, Title VI, § 601, http://www.ftc.gov/os/statutes/031224fcra.pdf (accessed August 10, 2010).

7. Electronic Communications Privacy Act of 1986, http://www.it.ojp.gov/default.aspx?area=privacy&page=1285 (accessed August 10, 2010).

8. Federal Information Security Management Act (FISMA) of 2002, http://thomas.loc.gov/cgi-bin/bdquery/z?d107:h.r.03844: (accessed August 10, 2010).

9. Computer Fraud and Abuse Act, Title 18, Part I, Chapter 47, § 1030, http://www.justice.gov/criminal/cybercrime/1030NEW.htm (accessed August 10, 2010).

10. Computer Security Act of 1987, Public Law 100-235, http://www.nist.gov/cfo/legislation/Public%20Law%20100-235.pdf (accessed August 10, 2010).

11. Children's Online Privacy Protection Act (COPPA), http://www.ftc.gov/ogc/coppa1.htm (accessed August 10, 2010).

12. Copyright law, http://www.copyright.gov/title17/, http://www.copyright.gov/circs/circ01.pdf, http://www.copyright.gov/title17/92chap5.pdf (accessed August 10, 2010).

13. California Penal Code, Section 502-502.08, http://www.calpers.ca.gov/eip-docs/utilities/conditions/502-ca-penal-code.pdf (accessed August 10, 2010).

14. California Database Protection Act (CDPA), CA Civil Code § 1798.82, http://www.cybersure.com/documents/seminar/database_protection.pdf and http://www.ffiec.gov/ffiecinfobase/resources/info_sec/2006/occ-bul_2005-13.pdf (accessed August 10, 2010).

    California Consumer Credit Reporting Agencies Act, CA Civil Code § 1798.16, http://law.onecle.com/california/civil/index.html (accessed August 10, 2010).

    California Investigative Consumer Reporting Act, CA Civil Code § 1798.83-84, http://www.privacy.ca.gov/icraa.htm (accessed August 10, 2010).

15. For examples of state statutes, see http://www.ncsl.org/programs/lis/privacy/eprivacylaws.htm (accessed August 10, 2010).

16. Federal Rules of Criminal Procedure, Civil Procedure and Evidence, http://www.uscourts.gov/rules/newrules4.html (accessed August 10, 2010).

17. Kerr, Orin S., "Computer Records and the Federal Rules of Evidence," *U.S. Attorneys' USA Bulletin*, 49(2), 2001, http://www.cybercrime.gov/ (accessed August 10, 2010).

18. Computer Crime and Intellectual Property Section, Criminal Division, U.S. Department of Justice, *Searching and Seizing Computers and Obtaining Electronic Evidence in Criminal Investigations* (Manual), July 2002, Appendix F updated December 2006, http://www.cybercrime.gov/s&smanual2002.html (accessed August 10, 2010).

19. Text of Council of European Convention on Cybercrime, http://www.conventions.coe.int/Treaty/Commun/QueVoulezVous.asp?NT=185&CM=1&CL=ENG.

20. European Union Data Protection Directive and links to individual countries' laws, http://www.authernative.com/MandatoryRequirements.shtml#EUDPD and http://ec.europa.eu/justice_home/fsj/privacy/law/imple-

mentation_en.htm (accessed August 10, 2010). EU Data Privacy Protection Act (Directive), http://www.nextlabs.com/html/?q=european-union-eu-data-protection-act (accessed August 10, 2010).

21. Canadian Personal Information Protection and Electronic Documents Act, http://laws.justice.gc.ca/PDF/Statute/P/P-8.6.pdf.

7

Litigation

The intent of this section is not to provide a review of all relevant court decisions or to litigate the privacy issues of cyberspace. It provides no legal advice or analysis, but rather describes selected litigation and related information deemed to illuminate key issues regarding Internet searching of persons. Few court decisions were found that directly concern Internet searching and few legal reviews of sensitive issues such as privacy. Therefore, topical reviews were conducted of decisions that could be used as precedents in a case where an Internet search led to a lawsuit. Commentary is included in an effort to demonstrate potential relevance to this issue.

INTERNET SEARCH LITIGATION

Few cases involving claims relating to an employer conducting Internet searching on an employee or applicant have been found. In one case, the U.S. Court of Appeals for the Federal Circuit affirmed the firing of a U.S. government employee on a nonprecedential basis.[1] The employee claimed that "his guaranteed right to fundamental fairness was seriously violated" when his supervisor used Google to search his name and learned and improperly considered that he previously had been removed from a position by the Air Force. However, the court found that the employee himself told his supervisor that he had been subject to employment proceedings before, ruling his due process rights were not infringed in over one hundred supported charges of misconduct.

A legal comment on the above case noted that if an employer "hunts down information on the Internet as a pretext for firing an employee for a truly improper motive, such [as] unlawful discrimination based on race, gender or age, such conduct would not be embraced by the law," while "on the other hand, if an employer learned on the Internet that an employee was engaging in conduct harmful to the employer, such as disclosing company trade secrets or defaming the company, that may be grounds for termination."[2]

Numerous other cases have been filed, but none so far have resulted in decisions against employers where the public Internet is concerned. In a 2006 New Jersey case, a bartender and a waitress fired for MySpace postings deemed unprofessional sued their restaurant ex-employer, claiming that the privacy-protected postings were not meant for public viewing, and a hostess who showed the postings to a supervisor "for laughs" was later coerced into giving her logon credentials, resulting in superiors viewing the site and firing the pair.[3] It is safe to say that there will be plenty of litigation exploring the limits of privacy protections on the Internet. However, it is also obvious that public postings have no current, legal privacy protections, and courts have consistently held so.

ANONYMITY

In 1958, the Supreme Court held Alabama's demand for the identities of all NAACP's members and agents unconstitutional, declaring that anonymity was essential to free speech and association, exercise of which would be impaired by disclosure. The court held that forcing the NAACP to disclose its membership lists was "likely to affect adversely the ability of [the NAACP] to pursue their collective effort to foster beliefs which they admittedly have the right to advocate."[4]

Comment: Anonymity enables a wide range of public activities on the Internet, in which those posting information publicly are responsible for deciding whether or not, and in what manner, attribution is included. A number of federal and state courts have held that an enterprise cannot cause a court to require disclosure of the posting individual merely because the material is insulting to the enterprise.

In *Griffin v. State of Maryland*, the Maryland Special Court of Appeals upheld the murder conviction of Griffin, approving a Cecil County Court judge's ruling allowing introduction of Griffin's girlfriend's MySpace page to corroborate a key eyewitness' testimony that he had declined to testify in a first trial with a hung jury due to threats on the witness' life. The judge allowed the MySpace page into evidence due to compelling circumstantial evidence, including the use of the girlfriend's photo with Griffin, her date of birth, number of children, and Griffin's nickname, among other things. Defense counsel objected that the MySpace profile owner "Sistasouljah" had not been conclusively verified as the girlfriend prior to introduction into evidence. The trial and three-judge appeals panel unanimously agreed that despite the use of a pseudonym, she had identified herself by photo and personal background information.[5]

Comment: This ruling may suggest that judges will accept good circumstantial grounds for identification of a person with Internet postings, provided that the details are sufficient and clear. In this case, the murderer was included in a photo on the MySpace posting with his girlfriend, whose blatant threat against the eyewitness, her date of birth, boyfriend's nickname, number of children and other details provided convincing corroboration to support the prosecution's introduction of the MySpace page. A Maryland state policeman testified about the profile outside the jury's hearing, prior to the judge's allowing its introduction into evidence. The lesson from this case for Internet investigators is that every detail that corroborates or may shed doubt on the identification of online content is important, and should be assembled to verify the relevance, attribution and authentication of the facts reported.

EXPECTATION OF PRIVACY

In 1967, the Supreme Court established the principle that individual privacy protection (rather than property protection) extends the Fourth Amendment shield to include what a person "seeks to preserve as private"—in this case, a telephone call in a public area. The court used a two-part test to determine when an individual has a "reasonable expectation of privacy": whether government action violated an individual's subjective expectation of privacy, and whether that expectation of privacy was reasonable (an objective test).[6] One year later, in 1968, Title III of the Omnibus Crime Control and Safe Streets Act was passed, requiring law enforcement to seek a warrant for electronic surveillance.[7] Subsequent, lower federal court decisions have found, under more recent laws, including those recounted above, that a reasonable expectation of privacy has a variety of nuances, depending on the type of communication and the situation.

Comment: Courts have ruled unanimously that publicly posted information on the Internet carries no reasonable expectation of privacy. More on this topic appears below.

The Supreme Court ruled on a constitutional privacy suit brought by patients and doctors against a New York State statute requiring physicians to report prescriptions for "potentially harmful" drugs to the state. Because the statute included security requirements, use, and retention limits for the computer files maintained, the court found the statute constitutional, stating that the privacy arguments were not sufficient to invalidate the law, which was a reasonable exercise of the state's police powers in view of the privacy and security safeguards employed.[8]

Comment: Security protection for personally identifying information on employees, applicants, and other persons ensures that information collected through background investigations, including Internet searching, poses no unreasonable security threat to candidates and employees. Requiring disclosure of Internet activities that could relate to employment as a condition of a successful background screening is a proper exercise of employer discretion, provided that the information collected is handled and utilized in a lawful, fair, secure manner.

The Supreme Court ruled that a police pen register did not constitute a violation of the Fourth Amendment, because the user of a telephone had no reasonable expectation of privacy in the numbers dialed from a home phone.[9] (A pen register is a device that records numbers dialed to and from a telephone, without providing call content.)

Comment: Posting of information by an individual on the public Internet makes that information available to everyone. When Web sites post data about all users who agree to be profiled, those users have no Fourth Amendment right to protection of those data, because consent to Web site access includes such postings. Most Web sites have privacy and use policies that spell out what happens to data provided by users.

The U.S. Court of Appeals for the Armed Forces upheld the conviction of an officer on child pornography and obscenity-related charges, finding that seizure of email and other computer data under a federal warrant was proper, and that after an email was received by the recipient, the sender's privacy interest in its stored content was low, and collection by law enforcement was not subject to the controls relating to interception of an email in transit.[10]

Comment: Much data posted to the Internet, such as blogs, chats, profiles, comments, photos, videos, and message board content, may be regrettable, and individuals involved may wish it was not online. However, an individual's control and privacy interest may be limited after posting.

In *U.S. v. Charbonneau*, the federal court ruled that a participant's email and postings in an Internet chat room used to distribute child pornography hold no reasonable expectation of privacy, and the defendant's motion to suppress the evidence was denied. Once the email is sent, the sender loses privacy protections when the email (like a letter) is in the hands of the recipient. A posting in a chat room, where an undercover agent is observing postings, has even less privacy protection, and anything said on the chat is admissible in court.[11]

Comment: This decision appears consistent with findings in all court jurisdictions where open-source, public information, such as that posted on the Internet, is concerned. Chat rooms and their logs are worthy of further discussion, which appears below.

In *Davis v. Gracey*, the U.S. Court of Appeals for the 10th Circuit dismissed the claimants' assertion that evidence seized on a warrant should be suppressed under the First and Fourth Amendments, the Privacy Protection Act (PPA), 42 U.S.C. 2000aa-2000aa-12, and the Electronic Communications Privacy Act (ECPA), 18 U.S.C. 2510-2711, ruling that a good faith reliance on a court order or warrant is a complete defense to any action brought under the ECPA. To be in good faith, reliance on the warrant or court order must be objectively reasonable. The court ruling enabled a federal district court trial and conviction of the claimants based on the evidence.[12]

Comment: This is an example of defendants' claims of privacy rights that would supersede a warrant (i.e., a finding by a judge that a crime has been committed and evidence of the crime should be seized in the manner specified). It is possible that persons denied employment or a clearance as a result of information found on the public Internet will claim a violation of their privacy rights. Nevertheless, privacy rights clearly do not apply to public data.

The 9th Circuit Court of Appeals held in 2007 in *United States v. Ziegler* that while an employee of a commercial firm had a reasonable expectation of privacy in his locked (nonshared) office space, the employer had the right to monitor his computer use, retrieve copies of his hard drive using a company key, and turn the copies over to the FBI, resulting in his conviction on Internet access to child pornography charges. The court said that computers are "the type of workplace property that remains within the control of the employer even if the employee has placed personal items in it."[13]

Comment: Like the employer's own systems, public information is not a province to which an employer is denied access in considering candidates for employment or clearance. The only potential issue is the manner in which the employer collects, analyzes, and utilizes the open-source information found.

In *Konop v. Hawaiian Airlines*, the Ninth U.S. Circuit Court of Appeals overturned a federal district court, ruling that a personal, restricted Web site on which Konop, a pilot, posted critical comments about his airline employer and labor concessions sought by the airline were considered protected activity and unauthorized access could constitute violations of the federal Wiretap Act, 18 USC §§ 2510-2520, and the Stored Communications Act, 18 USC §§ 2701-2710. Airline executives accessed Konop's Web site using other employees' login information and clicked to affirm that they would abide by the site's confidentiality policy—violating that policy against unauthorized access. Hawaiian later placed the pilot on medical suspension, which Konop claimed was in retaliation for his union activity. In court, the airline argued that the pilot's postings were false, defamatory and outrageous, but the appeals court held that they were within the bounds of labor laws, and returned the case to a lower court, reinstating Konop's lawsuit.[14]

In *Pietrylo et al. v. Hillstone Restaurant Group*, Brian Bietrylo and Doreen Marino sued after their termination by Houston's Restaurant (Hillstone) for posting derogatory and obscene comments on a password-protected MySpace profile. A third employee was allegedly coerced into providing her login to a manager, who shared the site's contents with other managers, who fired Pietrylo and Marino. A New Jersey Court held, and the New Jersey Federal District Court affirmed, that the restaurant's managers violated the Stored Communications Act and New Jersey Wiretapping and Electronic Surveillance Act by accessing the MySpace page without authorization. However, the court ruled on an invasion of privacy claim that the plaintiffs had no reasonable expectation of privacy on MySpace.[15]

Comments: It is clear that courts will have little sympathy for employers who gain illicit or illegal access to postings and then take adverse action against employee-posters. However, the extent to which a posting is protected has limitations. Coercing someone to provide unauthorized access appears to be a step less acceptable than being given access voluntarily. However, if the site policy clearly restricts access to and use of content, it is unlikely that the employer will have free rein to act solely on what is found in postings. As yet untested are situations in which large numbers of persons have authorized access to defamatory postings, and the courts in the New Jersey case indicated that the employees did not have a valid invasion of privacy claim, since they had no reasonable expectation of privacy on MySpace.

In June 2009, the City of Bozeman, Montana, was widely criticized when it was published by AP and others that applicants for city positions were being asked to provide passwords to access social networking and other Web sites to which candidates belonged. The city quickly rescinded its policy, but its application form online still requests a listing of all Web sites that applicants use.[16]

Comment: Bozeman officials conceded that they went too far in requiring applicants to provide passwords, which might provide access not only to social networking sites but also to such protected activities as banking, medical services, and insurance. Nevertheless, Bozeman is at the forefront in asking applicants for their history of Internet use and being in a position to review postings that are public to confirm that applicants meet all the requirements of the position.

DUE PROCESS

The U.S. District Court for the District of Columbia enjoined the U.S. Navy against discharging a U.S. Naval officer whose postings on AOL, a major ISP, appeared to embrace a gay lifestyle, and against using information obtained without process by a navy paralegal concerning the officer. The court held the government to a strict interpretation of the ECPA's requirement for obtaining process (warrant or subpoena) to obtain the officer's identity from AOL, and opined that the officer's public Internet postings did not constitute proper grounds for the investigation as conducted, in view of the Internet's invitation to fantasy and anonymity.[17]

Comment: A central issue in this case was the navy paralegal's identification of the naval officer without due process from AOL. The court considered and commented on the public Internet postings that were the basis for the investigation. This decision may be an indication that it is not Internet postings alone that should constitute the basis for adjudications. In addition, the degree of misbehavior in such postings is pivotal in deciding whether they are leads for investigation, grounds for action, or the basis for adjudications that could be adverse to the subject. This is one of the few cases involving the adverse use of Internet postings to be litigated.

In *Raytheon Company v. John Does 1–21*,[18] Raytheon succeeded in identifying twenty-one employees who violated company policy and their employment contracts:

Summary

On February 1, 1999, Raytheon filed suit against 21 employees it alleges posted or discussed confidential corporate information on a Yahoo! message board, in violation of their employment contracts and Raytheon's published employment policy, and claiming, in addition, that this conduct constituted a misappropriation of Raytheon's trade secrets. To identify the "John Does" Raytheon obtained a court order allowing its counsel to take out-of-state discovery from Yahoo! global, AOL, EarthLink, and various other ISPs, seeking documents and information identifying the 21.

Analysis

By framing its lawsuit primarily as a breach of contract action, Raytheon limited the defendants' ability to rely on a "free speech" defense because typically in situations where an employee has signed a contract which specifically precludes disclosure of trade secrets or other confidential corporate information, the availability of that defense is limited to "whistle blower" cases. In addition, it is also possible that any jurisdictional defenses normally available to defendants outside of Massachusetts may have been limited or eliminated by the terms of the employment agreements.

The privacy issue raised by the out-of-state discovery from Yahoo!, AOL, and the ISPs—the right of the authors to remain anonymous, if you will—is very limited. In order to access Yahoo's message board and post, the authors each agreed to the terms and conditions set forth in Yahoo's "term and conditions" agreement concerning the use of the message board, including providing Yahoo! with a valid email address and to the terms and conditions of their ISP.

Yahoo's message board disclaimer [changed from the quote provided, and now posted at http://info.yahoo.com/legal/us/yahoo/utos/utos-173.html] states that while Yahoo! will take reasonable measures to respect the privacy of users, Yahoo! reserves the right to turn over user identification information if Yahoo! in good faith believes that disclosure is necessary in certain circumstances, including to comply with legal process or the law. After being served with Raytheon's subpoena, Yahoo! apparently provided Raytheon with the author's email addresses or other information.

In May, 1999, Raytheon dismissed the lawsuit after several of the identified employees had apparently resigned.

Comment: The contracts used by Raytheon are analogous to the notice and consent that are appropriate for notice to and consent of applicants for jobs and clearances. Such procedures are appropriate not only to add Internet searching to existing background investigative checking, but also to send a clear message to candidates that proper use of information systems is a vital requirement of the job. An individual with a history of improper computer use is more likely to misuse an employer's systems, or post items damaging to the employer. In this case, the Raytheon employees made the offending anonymous postings in violation of their confidentiality agreements and employment contracts. Should a prospective candidate have a similar history of postings harmful to his or her employer, the candidate's judgment and integrity (and therefore eligibility for a clearance) would be called into question. Better to deter an applicant before incurring the expense of hiring than to risk suffering a loss because the applicant misuses information systems.

A New Jersey court dismissed an initial and amended claim of violation of privacy by state employees subject to financial disclosure whose disclosure forms were posted on the Internet. The court twice ruled that there was no "difference of constitutional magnitude" between prior publication in hardcopy form and publication on the public Internet, even with employees' names and addresses posted for anyone to see.[19]

Comment: This ruling may have relevance in that Internet postings by other parties about an applicant may be usable in investigation and adjudication processes, even if the applicant claimed that the data were posted without his or her consent.

LIBEL/DEFAMATION

Federal and state courts have had numerous libel (defamation) suits brought against both named and anonymous posters of allegedly libelous materials online. Key findings have included the federal court's decision in *John Doe v. 2TheMart.com* in 2001, which held that the First Amendment protects the anonymity of Internet speech, and that use of a civil subpoena to ascertain the identity of those posting allegedly offensive remarks could have a significant chilling effect on Internet speech, and thus the exercise of First Amendment rights. The court set out a list of criteria to be met so that a party could not intimidate critics into silence by using civil subpoenas to learn the identity of anonymous posters.[20] Such decisions also track Section 230 of the Communications Decency Act of 1996,[21] which immunizes "providers and users of interactive computer services" from liability for defamatory material posted by third parties.

While the decisions on libel and disputes over offensive Internet postings do not relate directly to Internet vetting of persons, they indicate that a court is unlikely to empower a party to use the civil court process to discover someone's identity and confront him or her for online behavior, unless there is a serious offense and no other method is available. Note that when a person's identity can be deduced from public postings (e.g., when two email addresses or user identities appear in the same posting, attributed to the same individual), the expectation of privacy is not present, because the Internet page is publicly accessible.

Comment: Anonymous identities were used to mask the true identities of persons in the libel suits reviewed, enabling speech unfettered by the discretion expected from a speaker using a true name. Attribution for offensive postings may not be discoverable unless the poster makes a mistake, and allows an "anonymous" identity to be deduced. Availability of legal process (a warrant) may be called into question by the circumstances, for example, the alleged damage done and the nature of the relationship between the Internet service provider and the user in question. The courts appear to make a distinction between evidence of offensive speech and that of felonious behavior. Even when a valid warrant enables discovery of the user's registration information, investigators sometimes find that the identifying information is incomplete, false, or insufficient to identify the user. If an applicant has a prior history of anonymous postings of defamatory materials, serious questions of judgment, discretion, maturity, and adherence to enterprise standards, these could indicate ineligibility for employment.

In *Endicott Interconnect Technologies Inc. v. National Labor Relations Board*, the U.S. Court of Appeals for the District of Columbia overruled the NLRB, concluding that an employee's dismissal for disparaging comments he made to a newspaper reporter and a message the employee posted to the newspaper's Web site public forum, criticizing the owner's managerial abilities, were so disloyal as to overcome collective bargaining rights enumerated in the National Labor Relations Act.[22]

Comment: The Appeals Court's ruling took into consideration that First Amendment and labor law protections apply to public communications by employees, but said, "We conclude that White's communications were so disloyal to EIT as to remove them from section 7's protection and that the Board erred in holding otherwise." The employee had a right to say publicly what he wished, but the employer had a right to take appropriate action to protect its reputation and ability to function (in my opinion).

This is consistent with the Supreme Court's decision in *Garcetti v. Ceballos* (2006) that official communications made by public employees are not protected by the First Amendment and that public employers may discipline employees if official communications are deemed improper.

INVASION OF PRIVACY TORTS

Common law (tort law) invasion of privacy appears not to apply well on the Internet, based on established law and practice, according to Harvard's Karl Belgum's comparison of three conflicting views of Internet privacy,[23] and Robert Sprague, writing in the *Hofstra Labor and Employment Law Journal*.[24] Four commonly recognized types of invasion of privacy are misappropriation of the name or likeness for another's commercial benefit, public disclosure of private facts, intrusion into seclusion, and "false light," or untrue public attribution of views or circumstances. These "four common law torts are generally considered to be irrelevant when it comes to online privacy issues," according to the review. The essential reason is that such claims have limited applicability, since voluntary public posting of information about oneself is the norm, "and no consensus has emerged that time spent on the Internet constitutes time in 'seclusion.'" Further, "on a more general level, the common law privacy torts fail to protect online privacy because they do not protect actions taken in public, and the Internet is arguably a public environment."

Comment: There is clearly room for invasion of privacy torts where false information is posted to damage another's reputation, or where a person's name or likeness is misappropriated for commercial use. Otherwise, there may be no legal or logical basis for civil privacy claims where data about someone are posted on the public Internet.

In *Oja v. U.S. Army Corps of Engineers*, a complaint that the Corps had wrongfully posted personal information about Oja on a government Web site was dismissed and upheld by the U.S. Ninth Circuit Court of Appeals because it was filed over two years after the first posting. Oja had asserted that every day constituted a renewed posting. The court applied the first publication rule, dating the posting when first placed online, relying on state laws on defamation for analogy, saying the ruling would uphold the provisions of the federal Privacy Act to "economiz[e] judicial resources while preserving the plaintiff's ability to bring the claims."[25]

Comment: The Ninth Circuit's application of the two-year statute of limitations to Oja's claim may raise questions while answering others.

Some claim that Internet postings can "live forever," as cached copies can come back to haunt someone years after original postings, and continued posting increases the likelihood that the Web page image will be preserved somewhere. The damage done by the content of an Internet posting can depend in part on the duration of its exposure, and the number of people who view, copy, download, and share that content. Since the court dismissed the claim on technical grounds (i.e., that it was filed too late), the court did not address the underlying claim.

SANCTIONS FOR PUBLIC POSTINGS

Increasingly, individuals are being sanctioned by employers, the courts or others based on their public postings—which are correctly viewed as publications laid out in plain view of the public. Following are a few examples:

In *Stacy Snyder v. Millersville University*, the U.S. District Court for the Eastern District of Pennsylvania upheld denial of an education degree and dismissed her suit demanding monetary damages. A photograph of Snyder with a pirate hat holding a beverage with the caption "drunken pirate" appeared on her MySpace page, on which she also inappropriately included material regarding her student-teaching assignment. The court found that Millersville University appropriately found her eligible for an English degree rather than a teaching certification, dismissing her claims of First Amendment and other violations and demand for monetary damages.[26]

In 2009, Vaughan Ettienne, a New York police officer with many online postings including his own body-building profile, testified against Gary Waters, a parolee whom Ettienne arrested after chasing him through Brooklyn, NY, on a stolen motorcycle for felony possession of a handgun and ammunition. Officer Ettienne had undergone a workplace suspension for testing positive for steroids. At trial, the defense attorney confronted Officer Ettienne with excerpts from his MySpace profile, which contained provocative statements such as "Vaughan is watching 'Training Day' to brush up on proper police procedure" (a reference to a 2001 movie portraying a corrupt Los Angeles police detective) and comments about how an officer could rough up a cuffed suspect. The defense alleged that Officer's Ettienne had gone into a steroid-induced rage, which could have caused him to assault Mr. Waters and in an effort to justify excessive force, Officer Ettienne planted a 9 millimeter Beretta on him. The jury acquitted

Waters of the felony possession charge but found him guilty of the misdemeanor of resisting arrest. Officer Ettienne was quoted as saying about the acquittal, "I feel it's partially my fault," and about the online profile, "It paints a picture of a person who could be overly aggressive."[27]

In *Cromer v. Lexington-Fayette Urban County Government*, Case No. 20088-CA-000698, 2009 KY App., a Lexington, KY, police officer's dismissal for unacceptable MySpace postings was upheld on appeal. The officer had arrested a well-known singer for DUI, which caused an increase in visitors to the officer's MySpace page. The dismissal noted that Cromer had identified himself on his profile as a Lexington police officer in word and image, and posted materials that brought discredit and disrepute to the police, including profane language, disparagement of homosexuals and the mentally disabled, as well as the people and city of Lexington, inappropriate comments on the use of force, a photo of the officer with the singer after the arrest for DUI, an instance in which he did not arrest a friend for DUI and other derogatory items.[28]

INTERNET PRIVACY FOR THE TWENTY-FIRST CENTURY

Robert Sprague, an assistant professor at the University of Wyoming's College of Business, contributed an excellent review of the law and the evolution of privacy protection in America in the *Hofstra Labor and Employment Law Journal*.[29] Among the relevant issues treated were

- "Essentially no protection" of applicants' privacy when prospective U.S. employers use the Internet to investigate them, especially when someone self-publishes on the Internet in a blog or social networking profile.
- However, publicity given to private facts could be tortious (e.g., intimate details of one's private relationships revealed publicly).
- "Certainly no one can complain when publicity is given to information about him which he himself leaves open to the public eye...." "Current privacy law suggests that a job applicant who posts embarrassing or personal information on a blog or within a social networking site which can be accessed by anyone with an Internet connection should have no expectation of privacy, and therefore, no recourse, when that publicly-available information is viewed, and potentially used, in an employment decision." Professor Sprague cites cases that, while not specifically about preemployment Internet

vetting, nevertheless upheld the principle that postings that are public cannot be held to have privacy protections (citations included in endnotes).

- Several states protect as private "lawful conduct" that is off-duty and does not involve the employer. Litigation generally supports the employer when the employee conduct impacts the employer adversely, and supports the employee when the employer uses non-job-related off-duty conduct to sanction.

Professor Sprague addresses the conflict between those using the Internet with the intent to share intimate or potentially objectionable materials only with a small group, and the millions who can see such materials on the public Internet (i.e., a desire for relative confidentiality vs. wide access). He says, "Even though information published on the Internet is potentially accessible by millions of people, from a practical standpoint, only a few people may actually view the information. And that is often the intent of the publisher of the information." He suggests that protecting confidentiality, if not privacy, is a goal that might be achieved as follows:

> Since current privacy laws will not protect Internet information, perhaps the "lawful conduct" statutes provide a good start to protect that information. Many of these statutes are incorporated into states' antidiscrimination prohibitions. The Internet provides employers the opportunity to learn a substantial amount of information they would otherwise be prohibited from asking (such as religion, disability, marital status) in a typical employment interview. Even if an employee were to volunteer such information during an interview, the employer is still prohibited from using it in the hiring decision. But there is no way to know if an employer has used the same information gleaned from an Internet search in deciding whether to even interview an applicant.
>
> One way to protect job applicants from the content of their Internet information would be to amend "lawful conduct" statutes to prohibit employers from using publicly-available personal information that could be obtained through an Internet search in their hiring decisions. As an alternative, or in addition, personal information obtained by employers through an Internet search could be treated as credit reports. Under this model, employers could be prohibited from acquiring personal information that could be obtained through an Internet search without first informing the applicant in writing, and would be required to inform the applicant if this information was used as part of an adverse decision, as well as to provide the applicant with a copy of the information found and used. This latter requirement would at least inform the applicant

there was possibly damaging information on the Internet so steps could be taken to remove, alter, or correct the information.

Comment: While it is disputable whether publicly posted information deserves some level of privacy based on the intent of the poster, it is a cogent suggestion to address fair treatment of Internet-collected information along with all other information used in hiring and employment decisions. The Fair Credit Reporting Act (FCRA) and nondiscrimination rights exist, even if an employer elects to risk circumventing them. Putting the investigative results of cyber vetting into the same category as checking private data repositories seems the right thing to do and probably would not require changes to current law. Explicitly notifying applicants and employees when checks of the Internet will be done, and when adverse decisions are based on Internet search findings, fits neatly within extant, objective criteria. Creating a right in law that public information must be ignored—even job-related derogatory information—does not seem well founded or likely to gain general support.

In a recent federal criminal prosecution, the legal theory was advanced that the accused adult violated the Computer Fraud and Abuse Act—unauthorized use of a computer system—because she violated the MySpace user agreement by assuming a fictitious teenage identity to harass a teenager, who subsequently committed suicide.[30] The accused woman was convicted for misdemeanors under what was called the first U.S. cyber bullying case.[31] While the legal theory remains controversial, and this area of Internet law could be described as somewhat fluid, the general practice of users on MySpace and similar social networking sites is to use a "false" pseudonym, and the sites encourage the practice.

Comment: It is common for user agreements to forbid access to a Web site for an illegal or unauthorized purpose (e.g., misappropriation of other users' identifying data, other site content, or spamming).[32] However, it is doubtful that a claim based on a user agreement between the investigator and the Web site would prevent an employer from using data posted on a Web site in an adverse finding about the subject for bad conduct. Where a claim could arise is if an investigator elicited information from or about a subject by fraud (e.g., pretended to be the subject or a friend to see privacy-protected social network postings). However, mere misrepresentation would not be equally actionable (e.g., if the investigator gained access to the subject's privacy-protected postings by misrepresentation as a "new friend" voluntarily admitted by the subject). If a subject could claim a violation of the subject's privacy by the investigator, it could render the adverse use of the information found by the investigator improper. It appears that the investigator can use information that the subject posts openly. However, the investigator must collect posted information by legal means (which could include deception that is not illegal or unethical). A subject might use the argument that a user agreement prevents any investigative use of a social site posting, but since the posting is visible to hundreds of millions of people, the basis for such a claim would be questionable.

While this chapter addressed several legal issues tangentially related to Internet vetting, its main intent is to help establish a framework for principles that can be applied to the policies and practices needed to incorporate life online into the security schema of life as we previously knew it.

NOTES

1. *Mullins v. Department of Commerce*, U.S. Court of Appeals for the Federal Circuit, 06-3284, appealed from U.S. Merit Systems Protection Board, http://www.ll.georgetown.edu/federal/judicial/fed/opinions/06opinions/06-3284.pdf (accessed August 10, 2010).
2. Sinrod, Eric, Office of Duane Morris LLP, San Francisco, http://technology.findlaw.com/articles/00006/010851.html (accessed August 10, 2010); Sinrod, Eric J., "From Googling to Firing?" CNETNews.com, May 30, 2007, http://www.duanemorris.com/articles/article2527.html (accessed August 10, 2010).
3. Searcey, Dionne, "Employers Watching Employees Online Stirs Policy Debate," *Wall Street Journal*, April 23, 2009, http://online.wsj.com/article/SB124045009224646091.html (accessed June 1, 2010); "Former Bartender and Waitress Sue One-Time Employer over Their MySpace Post," http://3lepiphany.typepad.com/ (accessed August 10, 2010).
4. *NAACP v. Alabama ex rel. Patterson*, 357 U.S. 449 (1958), http://caselaw.lp.findlaw.com/scripts/getcase.pl?court=US&vol=357&invol=449 (accessed August 10, 2010).
5. *Griffin v. State of Maryland*, Case No. 1132, Lash, Steve, *Baltimore Daily Record*, May 31, 2010, http://findarticles.com/p/articles/mi_qn4183/is_20100531/ai_n53902808/, http://mdcourts.gov/opinions/cosa/2010/1132s08.pdf (accessed September 2, 2010).
6. *Katz v. United States*, 389 U.S. 347 (1967), http://caselaw.lp.findlaw.com/scripts/getcase.pl?court=US&vol=389&invol=347 (accessed August 10, 2010).
7. Omnibus Crime Control and Safe Streets Act of 1968, http://www.justice.gov/crt/split/42usc3789d.php (accessed August 10, 2010).
8. *Whalen v. Roe*, 429 U.S. 589 (1977), http://caselaw.lp.findlaw.com/scripts/getcase.pl?navby=search&court=US&case=/us/429/589.html (accessed August 10, 2010).

9. *Smith v. Maryland*, 442 U.S. 735 (1979), http://caselaw.lp.findlaw.com/scripts/getcase.pl?navby=search&court=US&case=/us/442/735.html (accessed August 10, 2010).

10. *U.S. v. Maxwell*, 45 M.J. 406 (1996), http://webcache.googleusercontent.com/search?q=cache:http://www.armfor.uscourts.gov/opinions/1996Term/95_0751.htm (accessed cached copy August 10, 2010).

11. *U.S. v. Charbonneau*, 979 F.Supp. 1177 (S.D. Ohio 1997), http://www.swlearning.com/blaw/cases/child_porn.html (accessed August 10, 2010).

12. *Davis v. Gracey*, http://scholar.google.com/scholar_case?case=16037774558711975401&q=Davis+v.+Gracey,+111+F.3d+1472&hl=en&as_sdt=10002&as_vis=1 (accessed August 10, 2010).

13. *United States v. Ziegler*, 474 F.3d 1184 (9th Cir., 2007); see the following paper for reviews of similar actions: http://www.howardrice.com/uploads/content/Civil%20Actions%20For%20Privacy%20Violations%202007%20-%20Where%20Are%20We.pdf (accessed August 10, 2010).

14. *Konop v. Hawaiian Airlines*, No. 99-55106, D.C. No. CV-96-04898-SJL (JGx), 2002, http://www.internetlibrary.com/pdf/Konop-Hawaiian-Airlines-9th-Cir-Jan-8-01.pdf (accessed September 4, 2010).

15. *Pietrylo et al. v. Hillstone Restaurant Group*, Docket No. 2:06-cv-05754 (D.N.J. 2008), U.S. District Court for New Jersey, Civil Case No. 06-5754 (FSH), July 24, 2008, http://www.employerlawreport.com/uploads/file/PIETRYLO%20v%20%20HILLSIDE%20RESTAURANT.pdf (accessed September 4, 2010).

16. Frommer, Dan, "Montana Town Demands Job Applicants' Facebook Passwords," June 19, 2009, Business Insider SAI, http://www.businessinsider.com/montana-town-demands-job-applicants-facebook-passwords-2009-6 (accessed September 4, 2010); Weinstein, Natalie, "Bozeman to job seekers: We won't seek passwords," Cnet, June 20, 2010, http://news.cnet.com/8301-13578_3-10269770-38.html (accessed September 4, 2010); the current City of Bozeman, Montana application for employment asks for "any and all, current personal or business websites, web pages or memberships on any Internet-based chat rooms, social clubs or forums, to include, but not limited to: Facebook, Google, Yahoo!, YouTube.com, MySpace, etc."—but not for passwords. http://privacy.org/Background_Check_Form_Interview_MASTER.pdf (accessed September 4, 2010).

17. *McVeigh v. Cohen*, 983 F.Supp. 215 (D.D.C. 1998), http://www.netlitigation.com/netlitigation/cases/mcveigh.htm (accessed August 10, 2010).

18. *Raytheon Company v. John Does 1–21*, Commonwealth of Massachusetts, Middlesex Superior Court, Civil Action 99-816, http://www.netlitigation.com/netlitigation/cases/raytheon.html (accessed August 10, 2010).

19. *Price v. Corzine*, 2006 WL 2252208 (D.N.J. 2006) and 2007 WL 708879 (D.N.J.), http://www.howardrice.com/uploads/content/Civil%20Actions%20For%20Privacy%20Violations%202007%20-%20Where%20Are%20We.pdf.

20. *John Doe v. 2TheMart.com*, USDC C01-453Z, April 26, 2001, http://cyber.law.harvard.edu/stjohns/2themart.html (accessed June 1, 2010).

21. Section 230 of 47 U.S. Code, http://codes.lp.findlaw.com/uscode/47/5/ II/I/230 (accessed August 10, 2010); Communications Decency Act of 1996, http://www.fcc.gov/Reports/tcom1996.txt (accessed August 10, 2010).
22. *Endicott Interconnect Technologies v. NLRB*, U.S. District Court of Appeals, No. 05-1371 & 1381, decided July 14, 2006, http://openjurist.org/453/f3d/532/ endicott-interconnect-technologies-inc-v-national-labor-relations-board (accessed September 4, 2010).
23. Belgum, Karl G., *Who Leads at Half-time? Three Conflicting Visions of Internet Privacy Policy*, 6 RICH. J.L. & TECH. 1 (Symposium 1999), http://www.rich-mond.edu/jolt/v6i1/belgum.html, found at http://cyber.law.harvard.edu/ privacy/WhoLeadsatHalftime(Belgum).htm (accessed August 10, 2010).
24. Sprague, Robert, "Rethinking Information Privacy in an Age of Online Transparency," *Hofstra Labor and Employment Law Journal*, 25, no. 2 (2009): 395, http://law.hofstra.edu/pdf/Academics/Journals/LaborAndEmployment LawJournal/labor_vol25no2_Sprague.pdf (last visited March 29, 2010). Excerpts: "Certainly no one can complain when publicity is given to informa-tion about him which he himself leaves open to the public eye. . . ." "Current privacy law suggests that a job applicant who posts embarrassing or per-sonal information on a blog or within a social networking site which can be accessed by anyone with an Internet connection should have no expectation of privacy, and therefore, no recourse, when that publicly-available informa-tion is viewed, and potentially used, in an employment decision." Footnotes: See, e.g., *Dexter v. Dexter*, No. 2006-P-0051, 2007 WL 1532084, at *6 & n.4 (Ohio Ct. App. May 25, 2007) (upholding custody for father where mother had posted on her MySpace page, among other online statements consid-ered by the court, that "she was on a hiatus from using illicit drugs [during the trial] but that she planned on using drugs in the future. . . . [T]hese writ-ings were open to the public view. Thus, she can hardly claim an expecta-tion of privacy regarding these writings."); Sanchez Abril, Patricia, *A (My) Space of One's Own: On Privacy and Online Social Networks*, 6 NW. J. TECH. & INTELL. PROP. 73, 78 (2007) ("Categorically, everyone would agree that those who carelessly post shameful pictures of themselves or incriminating information on profiles that are accessible to everyone on the Internet can-not reasonably claim privacy in their posting."); Crawford, Krysten, *Have a Blog, Lose Your Job?* CNN Money.com, February 15, 2005, http://money.cnn. com/2005/02/14/news/economy/blogging (citing four cases of employees being fired for what they had posted online, observing that most noncon-tract employees are at will, meaning they can be fired at any point for any or no reason at all without any recourse, and are therefore extremely vulner-able to such employment actions); Simonetti, Ellen, *I Was Fired for Blogging*, CNET News.com, December 16, 2004, http://www.news.com/2102-1030_3-5490836.html?tag=st.util.print ("The official reason for my suspension [and eventual termination]: 'inappropriate' pictures. The unofficial reason (implied through an intimidating interrogation): blogging.").

25. *Oja v. United States Army Corps of Engineers*, 440 F.3d 1122 (9th Cir. 2006), Privacy Act of 1974 two-year statute of limitations
26. *Stacy Snyder v. Millersville University et al.*, U.S. District Court for the Eastern District of Pennsylvania, Case No. 07-1660, decided December 3, 2008.
27. Dwyer, Jim, "The Officer Who Posted Too Much on MySpace," *New York Times*, March 11, 2009, http://www.nytimes.com/2009/03/11/nyregion/11about. html?_r=1&pagewanted=print (accessed September 4, 2010).
28. *Cromer v. Lexington-Fayette Urban Co. Gov't*, #20088-CA-000698, 2009 Ky. App. Unpub. Lexis 71, http://www.aele.org/law/Digests/empl71.html (accessed September 4, 2010).
29. Sprague, above.
30. Jesdanun, Anick, "Using a Fake Name on the Internet Could Be Illegal," AP, May 2008, http://www.newsfactor.com/story.xhtml?story_id=11100A799 HN3&page=1 (accessed November 2009).
31. Steinhauer, Jennifer, "Verdict in MySpace Suicide Case," *New York Times*, November 26, 2008, http://www.nytimes.com/2008/11/27/us/27myspace. html (accessed April 20, 2010).
32. Based on review of MySpace, Classmates, Facebook, YouTube, Yahoo!, Monster.com, Match.com, and Google privacy policy and user agreements.

8

International and Domestic Principles

U.S. AND INTERNATIONAL PRIVACY PRINCIPLES

A large number of discussions, held in academic, government, and private venues over the past two decades, have resulted in generally recognized privacy principles originally recognized in U.S. statutes in the 1970s. For purposes of this text, the core principles first published by the U.S. Department of Commerce in 1998,[1] as amended with input from several sources, including the State of California and the Center for Democracy and Technology, deserve mention.[2] Based on considerable legal analysis and debate by privacy advocates, these principles are withstanding the test of time and litigation. It should be noted that U.S. law lacks the privacy rights set out in Canadian, European, and Asian laws. Therefore, the principles represent useful guidelines for the proper collection and use of Internet information about individuals. The principles are

1. Notice to individuals when personally identifiable information is collected (awareness)
2. Limits on use and disclosure of data for purposes other than those for which the data were collected (choice)
3. Limitations on the retention of data
4. Requirements to ensure the accuracy, completeness, and timeliness of information

5. The right of individuals to access information about themselves
6. The opportunity to correct information or challenge decisions made, based on incorrect data (recourse)
7. Appropriate security measures to protect the information against abuse or unauthorized disclosure (data security)
8. Redress mechanisms for individuals wrongly and adversely affected by the use of personally identifiable information (enforcement, verification, and consequences)

ADJUDICATIVE GUIDELINES

The U.S. government has established presidentially approved adjudicative guidelines for eligibility for access to classified information.[3] Currently, federal practices include notice, consent, verification, appeal, correction, and confidentiality, which directly conform to the privacy principles cited. In over forty-two years of involvement at various levels, from background investigators to overseers in the federal agencies and National Security Council, I have observed a passionate dedication, in professionals involved in security, investigative, intelligence, and adjudicative work, to the rule of law, fair play, and the privacy principles listed. Since the adjudicative guidelines contain both behaviors of concern and mitigating factors to be considered in a determination of eligibility for access to classified information, they represent well-established benchmarks for any employer with a need to protect valuable intellectual property in the workplace.

The following brief summary of the federal adjudicative guidelines for eligibility for access to classified information (strictly my own interpretation) lists types of behavior that might be found by Internet searching and substantive concerns that could, if verified, lead to denial of a clearance:

1. Allegiance to the United States: treason, sabotage, anti-U.S. acts, extremism
2. Foreign influence: foreign relatives, close relationships, sympathies or coercion
3. Foreign preference: dual citizenship, loyalty to another nation or anti-U.S. group
4. Sexual behavior: illegal or unbalanced behavior, coercible (*not* sexual preference)
5. Personal conduct: dishonesty, bad judgment, unreliability, rule violations

6. Financial considerations: financially overextended, dishonesty, unexplained affluence
7. Alcohol consumption: DUI, drunk and disorderly, abuse of alcohol, binge drinking
8. Drug involvement: illegal drug use/dealing, dependency, drug abuse
9. Psychological conditions: emotional disorders, mentally ill, unreliable or unstable
10. Criminal conduct: a serious or multiple minor crimes, whether or not charged/convicted
11. Handling protected information: disclosure of or failure to protect classified or sensitive information
12. Outside activities: conflicts in employment (foreign), in loyalty or protecting classified information
13. Use of information technology systems: illegal, unauthorized, noncompliant acts

A recent or recurring pattern of questionable judgment, irresponsibility, or emotionally unstable behavior can itself be disqualifying.

The federal adjudicative guidelines focus on the reliability factor: an individual exhibiting prior misbehavior described in the guidelines may be a poor choice for a government position that requires loyalty, discretion, and good judgment. The guidelines' preamble includes: "The adjudicative process is the careful weighing of a number of variables known as the whole person concept. Available, reliable information about the person, past and present, favorable and unfavorable, should be considered in reaching a determination." The adjudicative guidelines provide a series of factors to be considered in assessing whether the acts in question should or should not disqualify an individual in a specific case from eligibility for a clearance, including the behaviors':

- Seriousness
- Timing, including start, completion, and recency (elapsed time)
- Number of repetitions (frequency)
- Likelihood of recurrence
- Voluntary reporting of the information about the behavior
- Promptness in efforts toward correction
- Truthfulness and completeness in responding to questions
- Willingness to seek assistance and follow professional guidance, where appropriate
- Resolved or appears likely to favorably resolve the security concern

- Has demonstrated positive changes in behavior and employment
- Demonstrates proper motivation by complying promptly
- Unusual circumstances
- Conflict of interest
- Occurred prior to or during adolescence with no evidence of subsequent conduct of a similar nature
- Potential to serve as a basis for coercion, exploitation, or duress
- Resolution plan with a signed statement of consent
- Treatment successfully completed

Often, assessments addressing the possibility of mitigating factors can help adjudicators understand past mistakes that are unlikely to recur, such as common juvenile misbehavior. In an era where a candidate is as likely to act out online as in the physical world, it is important to consider such behavior in assessing the candidate, both for questionable conduct and for mitigation. Further, many enterprises should consider the orientation and training needed if a hiring or clearance decision is made, in the context of established authorized use policies, data sensitivity and value, vulnerability of information systems, and culture of the enterprise.

While not a part of the government clearance criteria, a principle that appears to be emerging in employment standards nationwide is the question of relevance to the duties of the position that past misbehavior may represent. In the case of Internet searching, any kind of prior misdeed could be found, from prior arrests to drug or alcohol abuse to unethical behavior.[4] If an Internet search revealed that the subject had engaged in cybercrime or computer-related illicit acts (e.g., piracy, counterfeiting, malware, spam, harassment), then a candidate whose job would include authorized access to a workstation on the employer's network could be considered ineligible based on computer-related misbehavior. One of the prime reasons to consider Internet vetting as part of background investigations is that it is one of the few ways to ascertain whether the applicant can be trusted to use the employer's information systems properly, and if special training is needed prior to entrusting access to the candidate.

One observation about why more agencies and businesses have not implemented enhanced attempts to address information systems behavior issues in the application, interview, background investigation, Internet vetting, orientation, and training processes is that the complexities of employment law, recruitment, and related issues act as deterrents. One aim of this book is to enable any enterprise to address the serious issue of prior computer systems misbehavior legally. The U.S. government has recently started asking candidates for clearances whether or not they have engaged in forbidden uses of computer systems.[5] Based on legislation, privacy policy, and established personnel practices, it is possible to add appropriate, legal measures that are explained further in this book.

NOTICE AND CONSENT

A review of the relevant statutes and litigation revealed an exception to the privacy safeguards that could potentially limit employers' use of data found on their own systems or elsewhere on the Internet. That exception is proper notice to the employees, contractors, and other users of the employers' information systems, and consent from the same group, to access what legally belongs to the employers: systems, networks, and data owned by the employer. Because of the rapid development of technology and its ever-changing uses, the laws and customs that apply could be described as in a state of flux. However, prior agreement by employees and applicants, as well as others contracting with an enterprise, enables mutual understanding about how the owner intends to protect information and the systems on which it is kept.

The proliferation of mobile devices used for both work and personal activities has complicated employees' views about what is private vs. open to an employer. For example, an employee may keep online bank, brokerage, and email accounts on a personal computer, and even on a cell phone, issued by the employer for work. Most employers tolerate a limited amount of time online to conduct personal business during the workday, but the sensitive personal information of the employee is now hosted on the employer's computer. Likewise, many employers issue mobile phones with which they can contact the employee using "push to talk," instant messaging, email, or paging. Again, the device may host "private" employee data. When employees use their own cell phones to receive email and conduct other personal communications in the workplace, the data of the employer and employee may again be mixed. Having clear understandings between the employer and employees about the limits of privacy for any information, communications, or Internet uses involving the enterprise's computers, network, or data storage platforms can help set all parties' expectations and may head off conflicts.

The principle of notice and consent is also often applied to contractual agreements not to compete against an employer (often for a fixed period of time after leaving) and not to breach the confidentiality of proprietary information without the employer's prior consent.

An effective way to inform enterprise users and document terms of access to information systems is the notice or reminder posted on computer logon screens, including the U.S. Department of Defense's banners, such as

> You are accessing a U.S. Government (USG) information system (IS) that is provided for USG-authorized use only.
> By using this IS, you consent to the following conditions:
>
> - The USG routinely monitors communications occurring on this IS, and any device attached to this IS, for purposes including, but not limited to, penetration testing, COMSEC [communications security] monitoring, network defense, quality control, and employee misconduct, law enforcement, and counterintelligence investigations.
> - At any time, the USG may inspect and/or seize data stored on this IS and any device attached to this IS.
> - Communications occurring on or data stored on this IS, or any device attached to this IS, are not private. They are subject to routine monitoring and search.
> - Any communications occurring on or data stored on this IS, or any device attached to this IS, may be disclosed or used for any USG-authorized purpose.
> - Security protections may be utilized on this IS to protect certain interests that are important to the USG. For example, passwords, access cards, encryption or biometric access controls provide security for the benefit of the USG. These protections are not provided for your benefit or privacy and may be modified or eliminated at the USG's discretion.[6]

Litigation concerning digital forensic evidence taken from computer systems by employers and law enforcement has produced a steady stream of case law that upholds the employer's ownership of the systems, networks, and data, and rights of monitoring and collection for any lawful purpose. Courts have almost universally upheld actions based on evidence found on computer systems provided for employees' use. Claims centered on the employees' privacy rights, reasonable expectation of privacy in the workplace, and on personal use of employers' systems have favored the employer and the government over the employee. Rulings to date reportedly have all been in favor of employers who have established policies regulating how employees are to use work systems and who have notified employees that their use of employers' systems constitutes consent to monitoring for security and compliance purposes. In some cases, this has included employees' Internet use. A possible exception might be an employee's use of a personal (nonwork) email system for communications with an attorney.[7]

GOVERNMENT STANDARDS

The U.S. government has long-established standards for personnel security, based on presidential executive orders, cabinet directives, and departmental/agency policies. The nucleus of U.S. standards on classified information includes such documents as executive orders on access to classified information, adjudicative guidelines for eligibility for access to classified information, personnel and information systems' security policies and procedures, and related directives. In addition, classified information is protected by the espionage statutes. Since September 11, 2001, the Homeland Security Presidential Directive and Patriot Act, among others, have focused on protecting U.S. critical infrastructures. In the private sector, the Economic Espionage Statute of 1996 prescribes stiff penalties (e.g., fifteen to thirty years' imprisonment) for theft of intellectual property. Trade secrets statutes in many states mirror federal prohibitions against misappropriation of employers' data.

While in-depth review of U.S. government clearance standards is not necessary here, it is worthwhile to note that when protecting highly valuable and sensitive information, additional security measures, including more careful vetting of candidates, are required. Similarly high standards apply for law enforcement and private security personnel. Today's enterprises, in both government and business, including critical infrastructures, often place invaluable information at the disposal of all authorized users of enterprise information systems. Since the early 1990s, security breaches in government and industry have increasingly involved computers, both at work and at home. In truth, the full extent of the security problems that have arisen due to the greater amounts of time spent online at work and at home is as yet unknown. However, anecdotal evidence suggests that in recent years, agencies and companies have been grappling with computer-related security issues that are more numerous and involve online behaviors previously not seen. As yet, government clearance procedures do not explicitly include Internet vetting, or require preemployment disclosure of details of the candidate's life online. Many federal agencies, and some state and local law enforcement agencies, are finding evidence of Internet misbehavior in interviews and polygraph examinations, and sometimes when background investigators Google candidates. It stands to reason that the established standards for clearances will require enhancements when Internet behavior is added as a focus in government background investigations.

Executive Orders 12958, 12968, and 13231 contain the standards by which classified information and critical infrastructures will be protected, and by which individuals will be granted access to classified information. These orders do not directly address Internet vetting. EO 13231, Critical Infrastructure Protection in the Information Age (October 16, 2001), includes the following, in part:

(a) The information technology revolution has changed the way business is transacted, government operates, and national defense is conducted. Those three functions now depend on an interdependent network of critical information infrastructures. The protection program authorized by this order shall consist of continuous efforts to secure information systems for critical infrastructure, including emergency preparedness communications, and the physical assets that support such systems. Protection of these systems is essential to the telecommunications, energy, financial services, manufacturing, water, transportation, health care, and emergency services sectors...

(d) Recruitment, Retention, and Training Executive Branch Security Professionals. In consultation with executive branch departments and agencies, coordinate programs to ensure that government employees with responsibilities for protecting information systems for critical infrastructure, including emergency preparedness communications, and the physical assets that support such systems, are adequately trained and evaluated. In this function, the Office of Personnel Management shall work in coordination with the Board, as appropriate.

To date, federal agencies have not included Internet vetting in standards established to evaluate the background of those who will be given access to classified, law-enforcement-sensitive, or critical infrastructure information systems. Efforts to strengthen the critical infrastructures of the United States only rarely have placed special emphasis on personnel security, and on the evolution needed in information systems security based on changing vulnerabilities, social behavior, and societal norms. While observers are concerned about ethics online and the implications of increasing misuse of information systems, as yet there is no consensus that personnel security measures must move more quickly to adapt to evolving computer security vulnerabilities. Increased protection mea-sures for the most essential of our critical infrastructures, the staff, have not been included in enhancements to security, even though they were deemed critical by the Joint Security Commission in its report *Redefining Security* to the secretary of defense and director of central intelligence on February 28, 1994, which called for "new strategies for achieving security within our information systems." Unfortunately, most of the new strate-gies have focused on self-protection of computer systems and not on the human element, including digital footprints of human actions online.

The news media reported in the 2008 postelection, preinauguration period that then President-elect Barack Obama asked potential candi-dates for high-level appointments to disclose their Internet identities (email addresses, profiles, and nicknames) for their background vetting.[8] This requirement demonstrates the recognition that those selected for responsible positions should not have a history of Internet activities or posted data that indicate they were involved in illegal, illicit, or socially unacceptable behaviors. Public Internet postings were considered too obvious to overlook for cabinet and subcabinet-level posts. Since the elec-tion, equal recognition of the same principle for other federal employees (even intelligence community and law enforcement members) has not emerged.

A search for explicit authority for the government to use open-source intelligence (including Internet vetting) when investigating candidates for access to classified information turned up very little of value. Executive Order 12333, United States Intelligence Activities (December 4, 1981, as amended August 27, 2004), does authorize collection of "information that is publicly available or collected with the consent of the person concerned." This is an exemption from prohibitions against the U.S. intelligence com-munity targeting of U.S. persons (citizens and permanent resident aliens). The FBI, other law enforcement agencies, and other state and federal agencies would also be authorized to collect information concerning any person suspected of a crime or who applies for employment or access to classified information. The reason why this standard has relevance is that modern standards of intelligence collection and background investiga-tion include legally permissible Internet searching. Even the American Bar Association recommends Internet searching, noting that it can reduce the cost and improve the speed and results of legal research.[9]

PARALLEL GUIDANCE: INTERNET RESEARCH ETHICS

When considering guidance for new types of activities, it is important to consider how ethics are applied in different but parallel endeavors. During the past twenty years, the behaviors of individuals and groups online have become subjects of study by sociologists, linguists, anthropologists, psychologists, and a host of other researchers. Fascination with virtual worlds, new types of communication, and networks of people distributed across the globe, but connected by the power of the Internet, has attracted the attention of both serious and casual students of human behavior. Communities online have developed modes of existence and interaction all their own, and created values that have moved researchers to recognize a variety of ethical approaches to their work. Based on published materials, these ethical approaches shed light on the issues, strong beliefs, and alternative approaches that should be considered by intelligence practitioners on the Internet. Those are covered in Chapter 9.

NOTES

1. U.S. Department of Commerce, *Elements of Effective Self Regulation for Protection of Privacy*, National Telecommunications and Information Administration Discussion Draft, U.S. Department of Commerce, 1998, http://www.ntia. doc.gov/reports/privacydraft/198dftprin.htm (accessed August 10, 2010).
2. Dempsey, James X., Executive Director, Center for Democracy and Technology, testimony to U.S. Senate Committee on the Judiciary, April 13, 2005, and California state privacy principles, http://www.cdt.org/privacy/guide/basic/generic.html and http://www.privacyrights.org/ar/princip.htm (accessed March 13, 2010).
3. Adjudicative Guidelines for Eligibility for Access to Classified Information summary, http://www.state.gov/m/ds/clearances/60321.htm (accessed August 10, 2010).
4. Based on thousands of Internet searches conducted by the author's firm.
5. *Questionnnaire for National Security Positions*, Standard Form-86, Section 27 questions, "Use of Information Technology Systems," http://www.opm. gov/forms/pdf_fill/sf86.pdf (accessed August 10, 2010).
6. Copied in April 2008 from a Defense Personnel Security Research Center computer system banner logon screen.
7. Westmoreland, Jill, "Minimizing Employer Liability for Employee Internet Use," *Los Angeles Business Journal*, July 31, 2000, http://www.thefreelibrary.com/Minimizing+Employer+Liability+for+Employee+Internet+Use-a063986324 (accessed August 10, 2010). This article contains good advice about an employer's need to notify and obtain consent from employees regarding

monitoring of their online behaviors. *Marina Stengart v. Loving Care Agency, Inc.*, New Jersey Court, A-16-09, ruled that Stengart has a reasonable expectation that personal emails to and from her attorney would remain private, although copies were on her workplace computer, http://lawlibrary.rutgers.edu/courts/supreme/a-16-09.opn.html (accessed May 5, 2010).

8. Hurwicz, Macy, "Barack Obama Staff to Have Email and Facebook Vetted," *Telegraph*, November 13, 2008, see http://www.telegraph.co.uk/news/3453916/Barack-Obama-staff-to-have-email-and-Facebook-vetted.html (accessed August 10, 2010).

9. Bliss, Lisa R., "Using the Internet to Save on Legal Research Costs," *American Bar Association Litigation News*, July 10, 2009, recommends using Internet searching to reduce legal research costs to ascertain data about cases, background information, media coverage, and blog entries about cases and parties, but verifying findings. See http://www.abanet.org/litigation/litigationnews/top_stories/legal-research-costs-internet.html (accessed August 10, 2010).

9

Professional Standards and the Internet

Laws are designed to deliver public safety, privacy, and ensure human rights. Ethical and behavioral standards are created to carry out laws and ensure that fairness, openness, and choice (among other values) are employed in professional endeavors. One problem with using relatively new criteria to judge eligibility, capability, and past behavior is that the law is slow to catch up, and the ethical standards and guidelines that normally follow the law are even slower to develop. Internet vetting, when addressed in the few standards and guidelines where it is mentioned, has been discouraged, because of the issues that inexpert collection, assessment, reporting, and adjudication of Internet search results can engender. A review of the most important guidance available is revealing, instructive, and shows that this emerging area of standards is at an early stage of development.

Blogs, chats, discussion forums, networking sites, game sites, mutual interest groups, and massively multiplayer online role-playing games (MMORPGs) present a rich panorama of different types of human interaction, varied "ground rules" in access, privacy, and use, and a challenge for those seeking to impose a definitive set of ethical tenets for those involved. As difficult as it seems for lawyers and ethicists to address guidance (not really surprising, since their focus is steeped in traditional authority, from times before the Internet), it is strange that those studying the Internet in depth have yet to be consulted for the guidance necessary. If we wait for the lawyers, how much risk will be absorbed by enterprises unable to react in "Internet time"? Authorized use and privacy policies of the Web sites themselves provide a starting point and are only now being used to enforce requirements for users, over seventeen years after the explosion of the use of the Internet. At this time, it is especially important to understand the medium and adopt a practical policy for addressing the legal and ethical issues without waiting for uninitiated legalists to reach final conclusions. We should start with the standards that exist.

ASIS STANDARDS

ASIS International, an organization of over thirty thousand security management professionals worldwide, provides internationally recognized standards on various security topics. In February 2008, ASIS published its Preemployment Background Screening Guideline, which was reviewed in 2009.[1] Following is a summary (in my words, not the copyrighted ASIS guidelines) of the guideline's contents on Internet vetting:

A new trend is the use by employers of online searches on applicants. Employers should approach online searches with caution because

- Postings may include information not intended for an employer to see, access to which may be controlled by passwords, terms of use, and privacy laws and policies. While anything on the Internet may be considered public, posted materials may be intended for private use only.
- Employers or recruiters doing background checking on the Internet are not required to abide by FCRA, as are contracted investigators, so an applicant may not be notified when Internet data are used in an adverse decision (and will not find out that it was based on what was found online).
- Unlawful discrimination in hiring could occur if an employer used protected status under equal employment laws (e.g., race, religion, age) as the basis for an adverse decision.
- Job requirements should guide an employer's consideration of online content.
- Internet postings may be difficult to attribute to an individual, due to shared virtual identities, false postings, unverified name match, or malicious posting of deceptive material.

The ASIS guideline deserves a detailed analysis, because it is accepted as a standard by a large number of businesses and some government agencies. While the volunteers who oversaw the composition of the guidelines (like other ASIS standards and guidelines) worked conscientiously and

110

diligently to create consensus on baseline principles, their conclusions about the Internet, legal questions, and relevant privacy issues did not include mention of dissenting but authoritative views. While the ASIS guide adopts a legal approach designed to protect employers against potential lawsuits for using Internet vetting, it eschews adoption of an Internet search methodology adequate to protect employers against online misbehavior by candidates and designed to protect an employer against negligent hiring (which could occur if easily found Internet postings are ignored). The ASIS guideline fails to address the proper, legal manner in which Internet vetting could be accomplished, while discouraging such vetting.

Meanwhile, it appears that an increasing minority of employers conduct Internet searches on applicants for employment. According to a June 2009 CareerBuilder.com survey of over 2,600 hiring managers,[2] 45% (up from 22% in 2008) checked social networking sites to find out information regarding potential candidates, and 35% reported finding data on social networking sites that caused them not to hire candidates. While the ASIS guidance appropriately says "approach with caution," it does not address appropriate ways to deal with what employers are finding online, that is, clearly inappropriate behaviors disqualifying to candidates, and the unanswered question of how best to employ cyber vetting.

The ASIS guideline expresses concern about the possible risk to someone's privacy if an employer accesses material that "a person did not intend for an employer to view." It is not clear where ASIS found the legal principle that says a person's intent about access to and use of publicly available information supersedes an employer's right to view it and take it into consideration. Public Internet postings are not protected in law, nor is a right to privacy ascribed to someone's publicly visible, illegal, illicit, or offensive behavior. An employer might find it difficult to defend the hiring of someone whose Internet profile notoriously featured illegal, illicit, or offensive behavior. The guideline fails to weigh the possibility that an arrogant or ignorant person boldly can post evidence of his or her ineligibility—and the employer should consider it. Employers include government, law enforcement, and private sector entities whose staffs must be able to meet the highest levels of scrutiny. Unfortunately, I have seen numerous instances in the past four years of illegal, illicit, and antisocial behaviors posted on the public Internet for anyone to see. Fortunately, we found many of them in time to help protect employers against clearly unqualified persons.

It is true, as the ASIS guideline says, that an employer need not abide by the FCRA when the employer (and not a consumer reporting agency) checks the Internet, declines to hire the person, and does not notify the applicant of the reason. Under the FCRA, it is within the employer's legal rights not to notify the person, when any investigation is conducted in-house. While in an ideal world, applicants would be able to find out why they are not hired, there are many legitimate reasons why an employer may choose not to hire someone. Most employers will disclose the reasons, if the applicant merely asks. Provisions of the FCRA do not directly address Internet vetting. An employer or contract background investigator can abide by FCRA and still conduct Internet vetting legally and properly, using the correct approach.

The ASIS guideline raises the possibility of discrimination under Title VII of the Equal Rights Act of 1964 if Internet vetting is done. Title VII describes the grounds that would be illegal reasons to deny employment, such as racial, sex, or religious discrimination. A decision not to hire based on an Internet search has no relationship with Title VII, which does not address Internet vetting. Only if the employer discriminates as defined in the law would the employer be in violation of Title VII, whether or not an Internet search occurred. Internet vetting itself is not a discriminatory act, but decisions made to search or not to search, or based on prohibited discrimination that originates from items found in a search, could be discriminatory. Protected classes should not be identified as such in reports of Internet investigations (i.e., exactly as required for traditional background investigations). Employers should use policies and procedures that ensure candidates fair, nondiscriminatory treatment, regardless of the methods used to collect information about the applicants.

The ASIS guideline raises a valid question about the relevance of Internet search results to job requirements. A candidate's prior misbehavior online can certainly be an indicator of future information systems misuse during employment, as can illegal or illicit behavior that an employer wishes to avoid in selecting applicants for employment. In a recent case, we found that a person had been hired to a senior research position after an extensive and expensive effort by the employer to find the most qualified candidate. The person hired had hidden the fact that he had been sanctioned by the government for scientific misconduct in research, to which he had admitted. Government records, when first checked, contained no reference to the punishment or misconduct. An Internet check revealed government publications saying that the individual had been prohibited from government research contracting for three years. In this case, the employer had incurred tens of thousands of dollars in recruitment, hiring, and other expenses, when a simple Internet check prior to finalizing the hire could have revealed the misconduct and the lack of candor by the candidate.

The ASIS guideline raises the issues of identification and attribution, but omits the issue of seriousness (because often juvenile postings are humorous and exaggerated). These are key concepts for employers considering Internet searching as part of background investigations. Identifying which references may refer to the subject, may be posted by someone "spoofing" or masquerading as the subject, or may represent a fantasy or an untruth requires careful analysis. A recent contestant on a national TV talent show admitted that photos of her in underwear on the Internet were genuine, but she was slandered by other, pornographic photos that were doctored to include her image and were unscrupulously posted. Producers recognized the difference.

It is important that investigators and adjudicators exercise great care in using the findings of Internet searching. Like analyses of all investigative results, online data may or may not be factual or relevant. Investigators and employers must make proper use of data collected from the Internet for it to play an appropriate role in an application or clearance process. Critical information may be missed without Internet searching. With Internet searching, the employer must employ proper procedures, but will reap the reward of identifying prior behavior that needs to be addressed, whether the candidate is hired, cleared, retained, or not. It should be noted that based on the author's experience, only a small percentage of references to subjects of Internet vetting will create issues to be adjudicated, while most references will be positive or neutral to a candidacy.

NATIONAL ASSOCIATION OF PROFESSIONAL BACKGROUND SCREENERS (NAPBS)

The NAPBS, founded in 2003 as a nonprofit trade association, represents the interest of companies offering tenant, employment, and background screening. NAPBS promotes ethical business practices, compliance with the Fair Credit Reporting Act, and fosters awareness of issues related to consumer protection and privacy rights within the background screening industry. Members must abide by the standards and code of conduct, and go through an accreditation process. Following are standards from the NAPBS Member Code of Conduct:[3]

Individuals shall

2.1. Disclose all relevant information to those having the right to know.
2.2. Define "right to know" as a legally enforceable claim or demand by a person for disclosure of information. Such a right does not depend upon prior knowledge by the person of the existence of the information to be disclosed.
2.3. Not knowingly release misleading information nor encourage or otherwise participate in the release of such information ...

... All Accredited Agencies and their Employees shall avoid injuring the professional reputation or practice of colleagues, clients or employers. However, nothing in this code limits an Agency from engaging in fair, competitive business practices.

The NAPBS approach depends on the FCRA standards,[4] which are worth a second look:

The FCRA says that a consumer has the right to be told if information in a consumer report results in an action against him/her (e.g. denial of an application for employment, credit or insurance); to see the contents of a consumer reporting agency's file concerning the consumer; the right to dispute and correct inaccurate or incomplete information (which must be corrected, if a mistake is verified); and to consent prior to a consumer report being provided to an employer.

NAPBS advocates a highly ethical approach to conducting background investigations, and by virtue of its relatively high dues and charges (e.g., for accreditation) is primarily focused on large agencies and their practices.

ASSOCIATION OF INTERNET RESEARCHERS (AOIR)

The AoIR thinks of Internet research in terms of observing human behaviors online, for many purposes, most often sociological, psychological, or behavioral studies of human interactions online or of works of art. In this arena, a host of ethical questions arise as researchers interact with individuals in "virtual worlds," social networking sites, blogs, Internet Relay Chat sites, and encounter new types of content (e.g., videos, graphics, photographs) and the like. Questions of disclosure, informed consent, identifying and quoting without permission, etc., have been addressed in rich AoIR discussions from the varied perspectives of the social sciences, the humanities, ethical and legal scholars, and Internet users over the past few years. In confronting national and international laws, ethics and definitions of privacy, autonomy, and netizens' expectations, AoIR has captured and inspired spirited discussions of many related issues. The AoIR has developed standards titled "Ethical Decision-Making and Internet Research" to help researchers make ethical decisions in areas that are admittedly fluid and hard to define, particularly in an international context.[5] Among the salient guidelines are

- An "ethical pluralism" approach (recognition of different ethical frameworks).
- An Aristotle-like attempt "to discern what [doing] the right thing at the right time for the right reason and in the right way may be," through a combination of judgment and the rules that apply in an individual situation.
- Questions to ask, including Internet venue (e.g., home pages, blogs, chat rooms, etc.), with the relevant ethical expectations (e.g., posted site policy) to judge the degree of privacy expected, and who are the subjects (e.g., adults or minors) of research.
- Considerations of timing, communications, and how materials will be used, to protect human subjects' rights to privacy, confidentiality, autonomy, and informed consent.
- Relevant legal requirements and ethical guidelines not only in the country of the researcher, but in those of the subjects as well (recognizing the international nature of the Internet, e.g., the contrast between EU and U.S. data protection standards).
- Assumptions (and the validity thereof) of participants/subjects of a study, such as the difference between people observed in private exchanges vs. those who view themselves as authors.
- The ethically significant risks that the research might pose for a subject, such as intimate content, that could result, if disclosed, in harm to a subject. The principles of "above all, do no harm," and assessing how the benefits to be gained from the research may in some way offset/balance the risks posed, are important benchmarks for ethical decision making. However, a utilitarian approach (as in the United States, where research gains may be viewed as outweighing risk to personal privacy) differs markedly from a deontological approach (as in Europe, where personal privacy almost always outweighs possible research benefits).

115

- The AoIR guide provides case studies that are highly useful in assessing ethical questions online. For example, it examines the question of whether chat rooms are public spaces, and how notifications about a researcher's presence may impact those using the chat room.
- AoIR also provides a list of references and outlines of different leaders' processes for ethical decision making and sample consent forms.
- Valuable concepts: AoIR's thoughtful review provides concepts of ethics worth considering in any humanistic endeavor, including:
  - Obligations of researchers to inform subjects, respect individuals' private lives and families, and keep confidential the information subjects provide.
  - The potential impact of research on a group using a Web site for its own purposes, that is, when the group must confront the unexpected intrusion of outsiders (possibly even insiders whose role as researchers is suddenly revealed) and the realization that users' customs are not honored. This may come down to recognizing the "human rights" of an avatar or online community of avatars.
- The changing nature of Internet activities that themselves attract researchers, but which can be considered in some senses the province of the users, and out of bounds for others.

The concept of online research itself has become as nuanced as the Internet's wide variety of activities. Virtual lives, MMORPGs, chat, blogs, and list serves (among others) present people in new dimensions. The researchers for science, sociology, and the humanities have considerably different motivations from the researchers for intelligence, criminal investigations, background vetting, and enterprise protection. As a confessed American (and utilitarian, in the terms of AoIR), the author would suggest that where intelligence and investigations are concerned, materials posted for millions to see on the Internet are "fair game." The naïve view that publicly posted content is somehow protected from investigators defies common sense. However, the AoIR's guide and similar thinking must inform the policies applied to unannounced presence in online venues by investigators, and the uses to which collected content can be put, which should ideally be influenced by the basic human rights and mutual respect to which we are all entitled. In the end, bad behavior is unworthy of protection in public postings.

Besides the AoIR standards, a book and journal articles by Heidi A. McKee and James E. Porter provide priceless views from the minds of Internet researchers and their subjects, ethicists, and those overseeing Internet research.[6] For example, the gamers generally feel that their avatars in virtual worlds deserve privacy. Researchers are advised to be intimately familiar with the online community they examine (i.e., they should spend many hours online), because naïve or clumsy intervention can wreck the cyber venue's mode of existence. Even public forum participants have perceived expectations of privacy and are uncomfortable with outsiders capturing content about them. McKee and Porter amply illustrate the fact that for many millions of people, the Internet is a different dimension of life, where participants' expectations and beliefs about their rights may differ from long-established understandings of behavior in the physical world. Further, the authors' findings help define sensitive situations for both researchers and their subjects, where added care is required because exposure could cause ridicule, embarrassment, or negative publicity, pertaining to illegal activity, personal health, sexual activity, religious beliefs, sexual preferences, family background, traumatic or emotionally distressing life experiences (death, injury, abuse), bodily functions, or idiosyncratic behaviors, as well as information that the online community wants kept confidential.

The stock that Internet behavioral researchers place in the feelings and beliefs of the subjects is not as appropriate for investigators and intelligence personnel, because it is the feelings and beliefs themselves that are among the facts being collected. The more potentially problematic for the subject that the information may be, the more valuable it is likely to be in understanding the subject's motivations and behaviors. However, the worry that any subject may have about exposure of his or her online activities to investigators should be mitigated by the protections afforded by such laws as FCRA and Title VII, which prohibit misuse and discrimination. Illegal activity is an appropriate target for investigators, and netizens who engage in it should not be able to shield themselves by their feelings that it should remain ignored. Because of the misprision of a felony laws (requiring reporting of apparent crimes to a judge or civil authority such as law enforcement), it could be a problem for Internet researchers to conceal, and not report, felonious behavior they encounter.[7] Researchers focused on computer network protection face similar but different ethical issues in addressing the welfare of the Internet ecosystem.[8] In any case, the ethics of researchers and those of investigators have different purposes and foundations, and properly should proceed in their separate ways. Proposed guidelines for Internet investigations appear in Section III, Chapters 11 to 13.

LIBRARIANS

The intelligence officer, sociologist, scholarly researcher, and student come together as customers of the librarian, whose services have changed dramatically with the growth of electronic books, publications, and materials, and Internet availability of so much data. Indexing and search automation have revolutionized the finding of facts about people, businesses, government, topics, and any academic subject.[9] Not only do librarians provide essential assistance for all types of researchers, but significant resources are available for free in libraries from subscription services and publications that would otherwise cost an Internet researcher. The approach of the librarian is to enable each patron, while maintaining his or her confidentiality and privacy. Like the investigator, a librarian looks to the Internet as an additional tool to find all the available, authentic, reliable information on a topic. The Internet is viewed as a pathway to publications. This view too should inform the intelligence collector, since any informed user should understand that by placing information online, he or she makes it available to the largest collection of readers on the planet.

INSIDE AND OUTSIDE THE WORKPLACE

Government and business attorneys initially considering Internet vetting often focus on the law's concern to make any background checking relevant to the specific position being applied for. In doing so, they often limit the universe of concern to the workplace tasks and systems to which a person will be assigned. This is a fundamental mistake in today's society, because people use their personal computers for work, work-related communications, to talk with both insiders and outsiders about work, look for new work, and network with many other people in and out of work. In addition, people commit violations of law, ethics, rules, employment standards, and good behavior while on the Internet from home, on their personal and their employers' systems. In many cases, misbehavior is associated with an employer or with a person whose employment is publicly known. For example, many individuals use their work ISP for

Internet connections from home, and use their work email address for all kinds of personal communications, whether from work or home.[10]

In some cases, employees use their personal computers to leak or disclose information that is detrimental to their employer, such as complaining about their employer online. Other examples abound. Even those whose workplace systems have stringent controls are not sufficiently scrutinized, if the employer ignores what the employee may be doing using a home computer. In the course of four years' investigations, the author found many users in online activities tied to their employer, without an authorized purpose. A favorite example is the fact that nearly one thousand members of one of the armed services used their DOD-issued email addresses as their identifier in establishing their MySpace profiles, posting voluminous facts about their service for anyone to see. Did they not think that adversaries in every nation on earth could surf the Net? Their service likes to use social networking sites to publicize and recruit, but issues users instructions not to reveal military activities improperly.

Monitoring proprietary systems is no longer enough for an employer to conduct due diligence in the pursuit of protecting intellectual property or verifying that employees have not engaged in dangerous breaches of security. While it may not seem rational, many employees mix their roles in and out of work in their Internet activities. By doing so, they involve their employer by necessity in their off-hours, online world. Whether in emails, postings, instant messaging, "tweets," or other online communications, at least 30% of today's workers have a prolific presence online.[11] Millennial employers ignore such millennial employees at their peril.

REPUTATIONAL RISK, PUBLIC AFFAIRS

As both business and government have recognized, the instant news and information dissemination taking place online pose an interesting dilemma for today's enterprise. On the one hand, it is possible to get a message across immediately, cheaply, and to a targeted audience. On the other hand, because reports spread virally and are not fact checked, it is possible for misinformation and damaging information to get broad exposure. Retraction, correction, and remediation of false reports can take much longer, and be much more difficult, than the originals. Reputational risk has risen for all enterprises.[12]

Blogs, message boards, and other postings are more than a minor annoyance to nearly every major corporation. Not only must the public affairs and stockholder services offices work diligently to discover and refute false reports, but it is normal for large enterprises to have a handful of true but damaging reports online at any one time. Irresponsible employees often post items using "anonymous" identities, usually including a free email account from a major provider such as Yahoo!, Google, Microsoft, or AOL. While it is sometimes possible to trace these anonymous posters, it is nearly impossible to undo the damage. Reputational risk is a major challenge to every enterprise, because everything from stock value to regulators' views of the company ride on what is said about it. Insider revelations can be major violations of SEC regulations and other rules. When an individual becomes disgruntled in the information age, it is possible for the Internet to magnify the damage done by only a few choice postings, true or not. While the HR department may still struggle with proper uses of the Internet in vetting, the other departments, including legal, marketing, public relations, security, and investor support, are busy daily with scanning the Web for posts about the company. Trade media, now all online, are only one of the types of Internet publications of which they must remain aware.

When an employee, contractor, supplier, or partner posts damaging materials about an enterprise, it is in the enterprise's best interests to discover and take appropriate action on the event. In considering any prospective candidate, the enterprise should consider if the applicant has a history of posting damaging material. This is but one of many examples of illicit behaviors that can be trivial or immensely important in the life of a corporation or government agency.

BOTTOM LINE

It is more important to have defensible standards about Internet searching for information collection and intelligence purposes than to count on the specific standards themselves, especially since the legal underpinnings are fluid. The lack of definitive legal rules has resulted in perhaps less Internet vetting than should be done. Uncertainty can be the enemy of sound ethical approaches. Anecdotal evidence suggests that individuals in many companies and government agencies are using the Internet in vetting candidates, looking up fellow employees, superiors, and business associates, and otherwise using Web information as a key part of their decision making. Among the issues raised by this behavior is the potential liability of an enterprise without any rules or policies, the possible use of Internet search results in illicit or inappropriate ways, and the mistaken use of incomplete, inaccurate, unreliable, and false data.

The proposed standards in Section III include many of the elements that are informed by the extant legal and ethical approaches provided for guidance to disciplines both inside and outside intelligence and investigations.

NOTES

1. ASIS International, "Preemployment Background Screening Guideline," 2009, http://www.asisonline.org/guidelines/guidelinespreemploy.pdf (accessed August 10, 2010).
2. Haefner, Rosemary, "More Employees Screening Candidates via Social Networking Sites," http://www.careerbuilder.com/Article/CB-1337-Getting-Hired-More-Employers-Screening-Candidates-via-Social-Networking-Sites/?ArticleID=1337&cbRecursionCnt=1&cbsid=ed3b3595c5334cb0b74dab5465 7de7a4-334768959-RS-4&ns_siteid=ns_us_g_careerbuilder_survey (accessed August 10, 2010).
3. NAPBS, http://www.napbs.com/i4a/pages/index.cfm?pageid=3279 (accessed August 10, 2010).
4. Fair Credit Reporting Act summary, http://www.yale.edu/hronline/careers/screening/documents/FairCreditReportingAct.pdf (accessed August 10, 2010).
5. Ess, Charles, and the AoIR ethics working committee, "Ethical Decision-Making and Internet Research: Recommendations from the AoIR Ethics Working Committee," approved November 27, 2002, by Association of Internet Researchers (AoIR), an international association of students and scholars in the field of Internet studies, http://aoir.org/, available online at www.aoir.org/reports/ethics.pdf (accessed August 10, 2010).
6. McKee, Heidi A., and Porter, James E., "Playing a Good Game: Ethical Issues in Researching MMOGs and Virtual Worlds," *International Journal of Internet Research Ethics*, 2, 2009, www.ijire.net/issue_2.1/mckee.pdf (accessed September 21, 2010); McKee, Heidi, and Porter, James E., "The Ethics of Digital Writing Research: A Rhetorical Approach," *CCC*, 59.4, 2008; McKee, Heidi A., and Porter, James E., *The Ethics of Internet Research, A Rhetorical Case-Based Process* (New York: Peter Lang Pub., 2009).
7. Title 18, U.S. Code, Part I, Chapter 1, Section 4, "Misprision of a Felony," http://www.law.cornell.edu/uscode/uscode18/usc_sec_18_00000004----000-.html (accessed August 10, 2010) and similar state statutes.
8. Kenneally, Erin, Bailey, Michael, and Maughan, Douglas, "A Framework for Understanding and Applying Ethical Principles in Network and Security Research," U.S. Department of Homeland Security working

group on ethics, 2010, http://www.caida.org/publications/papers/2010/framework_ethical_research/framework_ethical_research.pdf (accessed August 10, 2010).

9. Cassell, Kay Ann, and Hiremath, Uma, *Reference and Information Services in the 21st Century, An Introduction*, 2nd ed. (New York: Neal-Schuman Publishers, 2009), which contains excellent pointers for Internet researchers and librarians.

10. Based on over five years' collection and analysis of Internet data by the author.

11. The 30% estimate for those with a prolific presence online is derived from statistics published by the Pew Internet and American Life Project, http://www.pewinternet.org/.

12. Rochette, Michel, "Reputation Risk" (presentation), Towers Perrin, May 9, 2007, http://www.soa.org/files/pdf/lsprng07-001-rochette.pdf (accessed June 1, 2010).

10

The Insider Threat

A primary reason for considering Internet vetting is the fundamental changes that have occurred since the 1970s in the workplace, and since the early 1990s on networked computers. The insider threat deserves in-depth analysis, because it has such a large impact on all types of organizations, but that will be left for another day. Studies on industrial crimes, shrinkage, losses ascribed to embezzlement, and espionage have shown increases in insider crime for the past twenty to thirty years. However, the relevance of survey statistics in a field with so little tangible, public evidence is minimal. Are we seeing better reporting, better detection, or a higher incidence of insider crime? We certainly are seeing a higher level of attention paid to the insider threat in government and industry.

The insider threat is not well understood outside the confines of the individual enterprise because statistical record keeping and reporting are inconsistent at best. Like economic espionage, the problem has been addressed over time much more rarely by law enforcement than by internal investigations and administrative resolutions. Most of the time, in my experience, the perpetrator is laid off, fired, or otherwise moved out. I am aware of some instances where felony crimes were addressed internally, and the employee retained, because of the wishes of high-ranking executives. In any case, insider threat mitigation varies greatly.

As mentioned in earlier chapters, an insider with access to information systems, networks, and data is in a position to do great damage to the enterprise with substantially less prospect of detection than in the physical world. After all, the data remain in the possession of the employer, even if the insider copies those data and sells them to the highest bidder.

From the standpoint of vetting applicants and insiders, employers need to include online behavior, from both intranet and Internet sessions, in evaluations of eligibility. The consequence of omitting online behavior is that insiders will not be evaluated in the one dimension where they can probably do the most damage, and cause the greatest losses. As we have learned from studies of espionage and financial services embezzlement, people initially cleared have gone on to commit the crime even though their initial background investigations and even updates and periodic polygraphs favored continued clearances.[1] This suggests that without periodic reinvestigations and reviews, insiders can commit serious crimes against their employers undetected.

Security, intelligence, and law enforcement practitioners sometimes think too narrowly of venue and territoriality in connection with securing the enterprise. Work computing has moved "off campus," and into hotel rooms, airports, coffee shops, and homes. Symantec and IDC estimate that 73% of the workforce will be mobile by the end of 2011. "Whether inside the employer's space or cyberspace or outside, the vulnerabilities of work-related data are increasing," Symantec's white paper said. "According to industry analysts, 70 percent of security incidents resulting in data loss are perpetrated by insiders. Risk assessment studies by Symantec reveal that an organization with 20,000 employees is likely to suffer up to 400 potential data loss incidents per day."[2] To be perfectly clear, the vulnerability includes vital employer data processed on both work-issued and personal devices, at rest and in transit, at work and outside.

Recent conversations with intelligence, defense, and law enforcement leaders indicate that some cyber vetting is under way. Several agencies (which will go unnamed) ask candidates to sit down with a background investigator, log on to Internet services they often use, and take a tour of the content together. Agency leaders believe that this is the best way to review postings (which may be accessible to anyone, or many people) and verify that they are appropriate for an employee of whom the highest behavioral standards will be expected. Asking the candidate to log on also avoids the potentially problematic option of asking for passwords. Not all agencies then follow up with independent searches, designed to ascertain whether the candidate has revealed all the relevant online activities. Concealment is one of the most common potential problems found among applicants.[3] While it is good to know that the agencies with the highest stakes (i.e., those whose employees hold the highest clearances, carry weapons on duty, and must keep secrets) are beginning to address Internet vetting, it is clear that the process is not uniform or well developed.

As employers contemplate what types of monitoring, if any, to deploy in securing internal information systems, they should also consider whether and how to ascertain what candidates do online, and to verify what candidates provide by searching the public Internet for signs that insiders may pose a high risk of crimes and misbehavior, leaks and inadvertent disclosures. It is not unusual for people to post items that are not consistent with their employer's code of conduct or business standards, although this involves only a small minority of employees.[4] However, serious crimes or security breaches revealed by Internet searching prior to or during employment would be strong indicators of high risk for insider crime or security lapses. As pointed out before, it only takes one malicious or negligent insider to do grave damage using an employer's information systems to which he or she is granted full access.

BENEVOLENT BIG BROTHER

In order to address the insider issue, employers with high-value data, including defense and intelligence contractors, law enforcement, electronics firms, aerospace, biotechnology, nanotechnology, software, leading-edge manufacturers, and market leaders of all kinds, have had to step up monitoring and control over proprietary computer systems, networks, and data.[5] This has been complicated by the need to communicate globally, from workplaces and outside locations, and to access sensitive data from anywhere, anytime. The standard formula up to now has been a combination of technical security controls, information assurance activities, user security awareness training, nondisclosure agreements/contracts, and enforcement mechanisms. Included have been new digital data rights management systems, multifactor authentication, and advanced logging solutions. Some of these protections allow an employer to prevent online misbehavior, remind users of rules when they exceed their authority, require supervisory approval for some uses of data, collect real-time forensic evidence of abuse, and enforce standards quickly. Nevertheless, such solutions can only be a part of the insider threat solution, because determined insiders can circumvent controls.

Every employer also must face the question of how employees view the information systems security controls and enforcement, and the potential chilling effects (as well as impediments to efficiency) that security measures can cause. In an era of wild financial swings, layoffs, and restructurings, the written and unwritten compacts between employers and workers are at greater risk today than ever before. Employers exert efforts to treat employees and contractors humanely and structure compensation and benefits, workplace ambience and atmosphere to make the strongest possible positive impression on insiders. The natural balance and conflict between personnel and security departments figure into the workplace ethos and are both vital to making the automated enterprise successful in making information a strategic differentiator for success.

Among workers who are most familiar with the information systems they use, such as IT personnel, electronics engineers, programmers, and designers, there is a high recognition of the necessity for good behavior online, and the need to monitor and enforce IT discipline. One good reason is the general realization among more sophisticated users that infiltration often occurs when user credentials are acquired by outsiders bent on penetration. Social engineering is a key "cracker" method for intrusions, but password cracking programs, stolen laptops, inadvertent disclosures, and shared logon credentials are also frequent causes. There is a double-edged sword for employers who are successful in online security training and awareness for insiders: They are better prepared to help protect enterprise systems, but they are also more likely to understand the value of the data to which they have access and the potential reward of theft. At the end of the day, the more savvy the user, the greater potential threat posed. Since history tells us that the actual number of malicious users is only a very small percentage of the overall population, the risk does not appear unacceptably high. However, the insider is one case where the potential impact of a security incident is so high that additional preventive methods are needed.

So the benevolent dictatorship of the enterprise must confront the inevitable balance between big brother and big buddy. A great advantage of knowing each insider through close association with supervisors, mentors, and teammates is that the temptation for abuse and crime are greatly reduced, and the probability of early intervention or detection is greatly enhanced. When information assurance, technical and human methods are combined, the insider threat is reduced to an acceptable minimum. However, both the employer and insiders should remember that their future success depends on protecting the intangible property represented by enterprise data.

NOTES

1. Herbig, Katherine L., and Wiskoff, Martin F., *Espionage against the United States by American Citizens 1947–2001*, Technical Report 02-5, Defense Personnel Security Research Center (PERSEREC), July 2002; Mitre Report (numerous authors), "Analysis and Detection of Malicious Insiders," submitted to 2005 International Conference on Intelligence Analysis, McLean, VA; Shaw, Eric, Ruby, Keven G., and Post, Jerrold M., "The Insider Threat to Information Systems, The Psychology of the Dangerous Insider," *Security Awareness Bulletin*, 2-98, June 1998; Randazzo, Cappelli, et al., "Insider Threat Study: Illicit Cyber Activity in the Banking and Finance Sector," National Threat Assessment Center, U.S. Secret Service and CERT Coordination Center, Carnegie Mellon University Software Engineering Institute, August 2004.
2. Symantec and IDC, "Worldwide Mobile Worker Population 2007–2011 Forecast," Symantec White Paper, March 2008.
3. InfoLink Screening Services (Kroll), Applicant hit ratio analysis, 2005 (no longer available online). Title 18, Section 1001, U.S. Code, makes it a crime to deliberately falsify or conceal information, including applications for employment, provided to the U.S. government, with a term of up to five years' confinement and fine of up to $10,000 or both.
4. Numerous instances of malicious, untrue, unauthorized disclosures or similarly damaging online postings have been observed by the author over the past ten-plus years.
5. GAO, "Employee Privacy, Computer-Use Monitoring Practices of Selected Companies," report to the ranking minority member, Subcommittee on 21st Century Competitiveness, Committee on Education and the Workforce, House of Representatives, September 2002, http://www.gao.gov/new.items/d02717.pdf (accessed August 21, 2010); Needleman, Sarah E., "Monitoring the Monitors: Small Firms Increasingly Are Keeping Tabs on Their Workers, Keystroke by Keystroke," *Wall Street Journal* online, August 16, 2010, http://online.wsj.com/article/NA_WSJ_PUB:SB100014240527487 037489045754119837902722268.html (accessed August 21, 2010).

Section III

Framework for Internet Searching

The philosophy of open-source intelligence in a world of information dominated by the Internet depends on a foundation and framework designed to address the strategic and ethical issues that confront all organizations. While an enterprise may expect that every insider using the Internet will abide by the law, regulations, and enterprise policies, it is unwise to expect that there will be no major problems or misuse. This and subsequent chapters provide a structure by which an organization can exploit Internet information according to generally accepted understandings of risks, benefits, and the needs of individuals and their employers.

11

Internet Vetting and Open-Source Intelligence Policy

If you are doing research, investigations, or intelligence collection on the Internet, there is not much to worry about in terms of legal restrictions. By its nature, the Internet is a network of networks, designed to facilitate the sharing of information. Certain criminal laws prohibit computer fraud and abuse, including unauthorized access to or use of information that is accessible through the Internet but protected, interception of electronic communications in transit, and misuse of computer systems and data in ways specified in the law. Because of the designs of computers, networks, and databases, it is simply not possible beyond a point to secure them. Those who believe that any information that can be accessed is theirs to use as they see fit are sadly mistaken (but this feeling has a rather large following). Abuse is not tolerable—illegal or illicit behaviors are wrong. When we went online, we moved to a virtual neighborhood where most residents only use unlocked screen doors. That does not mean that burglary is no longer illegal.

Before an enterprise embarks on a process to exploit the Internet for open-source information, it is a very good idea—in fact, a necessity, according to the best attorneys I know—to have a policy for how to do so.[1] Like other intelligence collection methods, including human intelligence, signals intelligence, etc., open-source intelligence requires a set of standards that both enable success and avoid the pitfalls inherent in the practice. For a business, government agency, nonprofit, or other organization, it is important to recognize that Internet research, which has become indispensible for society, is at a relatively early stage of development, including the legal framework, policy, and procedural foundation that are needed.

LEGAL AND ETHICAL LIMITATIONS

Before using the Internet for open-source intelligence research, it is important to know some of the legal restrictions imposed by law, regardless of the purpose of the search. Normally, it would not be necessary to address this issue, since open-source research exploits published materials (free or for a fee) to collect and analyze information, and produce reports on topics of interest. However, the Internet differs in several important respects from the county library (although even the county library these days provides computers for information retrieval).[2] Information accessible on the Internet can be categorized into different types, depending on who has it, what is in it, where it is kept, and how it is accessed. Further, retrieving data electronically in a legal manner requires abiding by federal and state laws that, while straightforward, are not necessarily common knowledge. Using data from Internet searches also can differ from data sourced from established authority.

A wide variety of hosts on the Internet provide information,[3] such as

1. News media, including newspapers, broadcast news, blogs, news wholesalers, associations, interest groups, educational institutions, etc., publish online. These providers are often free, but some charge for access to their stories. The content is generally copyrighted, and permission is needed to reuse reports. Essentially, these sources are considered published information (i.e., data designed to be available to the public). Fair use includes quoting and using facts reported as leads.

   Businesses, government agencies, and other organizations have Web sites to provide information to the public, stockholders, citizens, customers, partners, and stakeholders of all kinds. The content may be copyrighted, but often the intent of postings is to share the information as widely as possible for public relations, awareness, safety, marketing, sales, and networking, or to provide public access to periodic updates, such as quarterly and annual reports.

2. Most businesses and agencies today have internal applications and databases designed for conducting enterprise functions, and those private systems are connected to the Internet to allow access to authorized individuals (e.g., employees, contractors, partners, and sometimes customers). The degree of security varies for those allowed access, but internal systems are not intended for public access.
3. Entertainment and social networking sites are optimized for public use and allow for somewhat private group use as well. These Web sites create networks of individuals where content can be shared, sometimes with access restrictions, connections can be made, and a variety of materials, such as blogs, photos, audio and video files, and other content, can be posted. Some content may be copyrighted, but much is intended for wide dissemination, and some items are intended for a restricted audience of friends and colleagues. Merely requiring membership to see content may not make data posted on these sites private, since millions of users have access to postings without privacy protection.
4. Businesses such as Internet retailers, financial firms, service providers, etc., have Web sites with functions designed to attract and inform customers (completely open to the public), provide data to registered users (restricted use, but relatively open, nontransactional information content), present account information exclusively to account holders (private access), and conduct transactions for registered and authenticated users (closed, limited-access systems designed to prevent fraud and to facilitate online payments). The degree of security afforded to these three or four levels of access (envisioned by the Federal Reserve years ago, in its guidance to the nation's online banks) is greatest at the transactional level.

The first level of control for those setting Internet search standards is to ensure that practitioners understand the difference between public Web sites and those where restrictions on authorized use of content may impact the decision to collect and utilize posted information. By the time the data collected are reported, it may not be clear to a report reader where the items originated and what limitations, if any, need to be considered for their use. Therefore, the actions (if any) taken on an Internet intelligence report can violate a law, policy, or standard if the method of the search or its product is illicit or improper. One way to address this concern is to require explicit sourcing for each item reported from the Internet, with a notation if the item was retrieved in a manner not authorized by the Web site hosting the data, or not published on the public Internet. Clients of investigative and intelligence reports (e.g., HR, legal and security departments, policy makers) should establish clear expectations for collectors and analysts, so that the enterprise does not inadvertently use reported data in an inappropriate manner, inconsistent with its policy.

The anonymity of users on the Internet can benefit an intelligence officer, who might access many Web sites to find instances of illegal or threatening behavior without revealing his or her role in intelligence. However, the possible uses of the information obtained might be limited by the manner of collection. It is useful to think of stored (not in-transit) information collected by investigators, intelligence, and security personnel in categories:

- Published data intended for use by everyone
- Published data intended for a limited group of people
- Data stored in a limited-access place for authorized users only
- Data stored in a secure place for the personal use of their owner only

Because of the nature of the Internet, openness of users' postings, and availability of effective search and collection methods, a good investigator will soon find that it is possible to gain access to information that the investigator was never intended to see. Contents of the information may very well show the type of behavior or document facts that are most useful for judging the trustworthiness, character, or proclivities of the subject, and hence most useful in assessing the subject. But because of the method of collection, an item retrieved in this manner may not be admissible as a piece of evidence, usable as a derogatory element in a report, or usable as a question for interviewing the subject directly. The suitability of an item for use in due diligence investigations (e.g., cyber vetting) therefore may depend on its method of collection and whether the source can be cited openly. This is not to say that the item cannot be used at all in the evaluation or due diligence process. When a piece of information is found that cannot be used openly in an adverse action, it may still be useful in formulating interview questions, as a lead for further investigation (e.g., interviews of friends, coworkers, or acquaintances of the subject), and as a pointer to other potential sources online or offline, where public variations may be found (e.g., by using the handle or user name found in the private posting to find similar public postings). In addition, it is worth noting that having intelligence about a subject of importance, even if that intelligence cannot be used in a proceeding or report, can be very helpful in protecting the security of an enterprise's people, assets, and information. For example, the orientation and training (including indoctrination) of an employee with a history of Internet misbehavior can include material addressing the high standards that apply for workplace computing. Monitoring and mentoring are other possibilities.

Since investigative personnel often operate alone and rarely get supervisory scrutiny over each step they take, investigators must adhere to the proper ethical standards on their own. At this writing, there are almost no guidelines for Internet searching. Therefore, there is virtually no scrutiny being given to the questions of whether the Internet is used, how cyber vetting may be carried out, and the use of results in follow-up investigation. When ethical standards are established for the use of the Internet in investigations, there is a high likelihood that most investigators will follow those standards most of the time. Today, it's up to the individual investigator.

POLICY

In any enterprise, government or private, there are four stakeholders with a critical need to address the policy applied to Internet searching for investigative and intelligence purposes: the chief legal officer, the chief security officer, the chief personnel officer, and the chief information officer. Each of these executives has his own operational reasons for needing to address Internet searching, but enterprise strategy and risk management require that the four agree on the following simple principles:

1. Internet searching is a form of open-source intelligence that may, if used properly, contribute important insights in an investigation.
2. Internet searching should be comprehensive, that is, find a high percentage of available information relevant to the subject.
3. Internet searching results should be screened for accuracy and reliability, that is, verified for credibility and pertinence to the subject of interest.
4. Internet searching, analysis, and reporting should be conducted by experienced, capable analysts using technical tools in an efficient, productive manner.
5. Internet searching should be conducted in a safe manner, to avoid causing harm to or increasing the vulnerability of those vetting or vetted.

6. Due diligence decisions should be made on the basis of the quality, quantity, timeliness, and credibility of the intelligence presented; that is, Internet intelligence can add to, but does not fundamentally change, the legacy decision-making process.

In a large enterprise, it would be interesting to see how many hours daily are spent online in pursuit of strictly business goals.[4] Based on the trends evident in user statistics, it appears that every department in every organization with Internet access on employees' workstations now depends on Internet information for productivity. There is no doubt that Internet searching is already a critical factor in timely information retrieval, assessment of options, and rapid communications, benefitting the enterprise greatly. If the Internet were not a relatively reliable source of information, the productivity gains from its use would not be so evident. However, when the best available intelligence assessments are critical, it is imperative to require added scrutiny of the Internet information used, so that decisions have the best available basis and misjudgment is less likely.

Legal departments of enterprises have been forced to oversee a growing practice of electronic disclosure, based on the contents of corporate data that may relate to a particular matter under litigation or investigation.[5] Email files are especially difficult, because their volume, archiving, searching, and applicability to almost any issue are likely to be burdensome on the enterprise and also likely to produce evidence against the interests of the enterprise. Several general counsels of major businesses with which I have consulted, and some government agencies, in the past have advocated systematic destruction of emails, to avoid the "false positives" that are caused when employees include inaccurate, untrue, scurrilous, and defamatory information in their emails. Because emails occupy that nether world between the formal business letter and the informal personal note, it is generally up to the user to keep the content true, proper, and civil. However, so much email contains content inconsistent with enterprise policy that it has become a legal issue for almost every organization. Civil litigation nearly always includes a motion for disclosure from enterprise documents and data (e-discovery), including email, imposing procedural and technical issues with ever-growing volumes of documents stored electronically. Recent laws help regulate electronic disclosures in civil cases (e.g., changes to Rule 16, U.S. Federal Rules of Civil Procedure, addressing the timing, scope, and cost of motions for e-discovery), but the law does not do much to mitigate the need to preserve data. Unfortunately, data on the public Internet may well point to those within corporate walls, and the likelihood that Web references will help investigators to make successful electronic disclosure demands has grown with the volume of data escaping the enterprise and residing on the Internet.

In a world of secrets, classified information, and vital intellectual property, the virtue of discretion has suffered a nearly fatal blow. The Internet has become the antisecret. Self-exposure has increased with the changing social norms propelled by the Web. Those trained in the protection of classified information (and perhaps coming from an earlier generation) have a natural tendency to be more discreet, say less, and disclose less. Among other things, discretion involves choosing not to tell others something, just because one knows it, and being careful not to embarrass oneself by exposing something potentially harmful to oneself or one's family, community, one's employer. The Internet generation appears to be less discreet and more apt to disclose data that should be protected. As indicated earlier, even one or a few indiscreet individuals can jeopardize the security of an enterprise. Therefore, a key requirement for protecting classified data and IP is the collective and individual discretion of those with access to it, and the ability of the enterprise to detect instances of disclosure and exert discipline to discourage it.

INFORMATION ASSETS PROTECTION

The following chapters will specifically outline procedures to be used for Internet searching for intelligence, but it is important to have an ethical strategy based on core tenets. Among core tenets for a business or government enterprise are

- Enterprise information is a key asset to be protected.
- The enterprise will take all reasonable, legal measures to protect its systems, networks, and data, in order to protect its information assets.
- All authorized users will be required to adhere to enterprise IT policies, and should expect that their systems use will be scrutinized for compliance, data protection, and effectiveness as needed at any time (as expressed in authorized use policies).
- Authorized users of any systems, business or personal, can create Internet records that could adversely impact the enterprise, because outsiders, unauthorized users, and adversaries of the enterprise may see Internet postings. Therefore, users should be

very careful what they post on the Internet. The enterprise may take measures to detect Internet postings that could be of concern, and will discipline any authorized user found posting material deemed to be harmful to the enterprise.

- The enterprise respects the individual privacy of its authorized IT systems users, and will take steps to ensure the protection of their personally identifying information. While enterprise IT systems are proprietary and exist for business use only, it is understood that users' data will at times share enterprise IT resources. The enterprise reserves the right to review all information residing on its systems at any time, for any purpose, and will take appropriate action if any information found is deemed to be improper, illicit, or pose a potential risk for the enterprise.
- The enterprise expects all authorized users to be of assistance in protecting systems, networks, and data, and failure to help protect the enterprise will be subject to discipline.

Full disclosure of the above principles will help users to understand the value of IT systems and the need and intent that their employer has to protect itself in the interconnected world of computers. Awareness establishes a legal basis for security measures and admissibility of information found about misuse. Awareness is also a first step in enlisting users as part of the security solution, which depends on all users' cooperation.[6] Lastly, it is a necessary legal step in establishing the intent to protect proprietary information as a valuable asset.

In an ideal world, the Internet would allow all users to experience the freedom to express whatever they wanted to, and to enhance the creativity and productivity of all the businesses and agencies online. In the real world, the Internet has become not only a crucial asset for U.S. users, but also a source of significant risks. Prior to the rise of the Internet as a risk, the enterprise could guard its physical files, libraries, and other physical assets. Since computing, networking, and data have become essential to success and efficiency, it is critical to exploit their benefits, while guarding against the added risks posed by the virtual world to which we are all connected.

NOTES

1. Discussions by the author with chief privacy officers and chief legal officers at several government agencies and corporations over the past five years.

2. Cassell, Kay Ann, and Hiremath, Uma, *Reference and Information Services in the 21st Century, An Introduction*, 2nd ed. (New York: Neal-Schuman Publishers, 2009), with a description at http://www.neal-schuman.com/reference21st2nd (accessed August 21, 2010).
3. Schlein, Alan M., *Find It Online, The Complete Guide to Online Research*, 2nd ed. (Tempe, AZ: Facts on Demand Press, 2001); Sherman, Chris, and Price, Gary, *The Invisible Web, Uncovering Information Sources Search Engines Can't See* (Information Today, 2001).
4. Hannula, Mikva, and Lönnqvist, Antti, "How the Internet Affects Productivity," Tampere University of Technology, Finland, http://www.tut.fi/units/tuta/teta/mittaritiimi/julkaisut/internet.pdf (accessed June 1, 2010).
5. eDiscovery, see http://www.uscourts.gov/SearchResults.aspx?IndexCatalogue=AllIndexedContent&SearchQuery=e%20discovery (accessed August 21, 2010).
6. Wilson, Mark, and Hash, Joan, *Building an Information Technology Security Awareness and Training Program*, Special Publication 800-50, National Institute of Standards and Technology, October 2003, http://csrc.nist.gov/publications/nistpubs/800-50/NIST-SP800-50.pdf (accessed June 1, 2010).

12

Tools, Techniques, and Training

If your enterprise or unit needs a process for Internet searching, analysis, and reporting, it is important to ensure that those tasked with carrying out the process have adequate training and preparation to do so. Yes, everybody Googles. That does not mean that everybody knows what they are doing, or can properly assess the results. If investigative and intelligence conclusions are to be reached, strategies evaluated, and decisions made based on Internet data, there are basic attributes that are required for the execution of searches, which could be characterized as "user requirements," in the sense of software systems requirements.[1] The search and analysis processes should deliver results that are, to the greatest extent possible:

- Reasonably complete and comprehensive
- Accurate, with identifiable references properly attributed to the subject
- Useful for the purpose the search was conducted
- From sources believed to be reliable
- Verified or verifiable through multiple sources and analysis
- Current and properly dated
- Efficient, that is, accomplished within allocated budget
- Timely, that is, accomplished within established deadlines
- Designed and conducted in a manner that does no harm to searchers or subjects

When my private intelligence practice began, we found that for search terms (people, firms, topics) with many references, it is possible to engage in endless collection and review of links, with the hope that the next click will bring you to the holy grail of the search. After a point, it's like the slots player at the airport in Las Vegas: How often will you win, and how many more times must you drop in a coin and wish? The house has the game stacked against you, and more play simply means more loss. Therefore, it is important to establish at the beginning how much searching, review, and capture of results is enough for a given purpose, or at what point the prospect of winning any more diminishes to near zero. When important decisions are to be made based on results, it becomes all the more important that the completeness of the search is sufficient that no major reference is overlooked; the search engines and sites most likely to be productive have all been queried; and the additional leads found in initial search results have been incorporated into follow-up searches. For fairness in using cyber vetting, a similar process must be applied for all candidates (or all candidates in certain categories, such as those seeking high-level clearances), so that there will be no discrimination in who is searched or the reach of the search. Since most of the references will be positive or neutral, the goal of the search is not to find what is derogatory (since that may not exist), but rather to meet the requirements set for a "full search." The full search is to be defined by policy, which should define the scope of the search as its most important attribute.

When I searched FBI indices for references to a person of interest, in twenty-eight years, I have never found only one person with the same name. On the Internet, the prospect that you will find only one of a kind, whether it is a person, business, or another search term, is very low. Some people's names are also common words (e.g., Baker, Price), so many references found will have nothing to do with the subject. Accuracy is essential because there are not always secondary identifying factors to use in evaluating whether to attribute a reference to the subject of interest. It is possible to report items that may or may not be identifiable with the subject, but doing so may detract from the value of the report and raise questions that need resolution. Factors that can help determine whether a reference is identifiable with a subject (besides having the same name) include geographical location, identifying numbers (e.g., social security number), physical description, age/date of birth, education, employment, city or community, activities, hobbies, sports, photos, advocacy (i.e., espousing the same position on topics), family, friends, and associations. The name of the subject can also be important, because name variations, nicknames, misspellings, and the like are common. The decision to report a questionable reference should depend on the potential seriousness of the behavior, if it proves true and attributable to the subject.

In vetting people and firms, it is often possible to find many references attributable to the subject with a relatively high degree of accuracy. However, often the purpose of the search is to determine whether there are any derogatory references (e.g., arrests, civil suits, bankruptcies), and mountains of data that merely confirm what the requester already knows (e.g., address, employment, education) provide no added value. Required report contents should therefore be determined before the search begins, based on the purpose of the search. A report can contain a complete profile of the subject, including all known, verified attributes; only specified biographical items; or only derogatory or previously unknown data. Establishing the manner in which results will be reported makes the report ideally suited to the purpose for which it was requested, and perhaps a much shorter task to accomplish (e.g., report only bad behaviors).

Reliable sources exist on the Internet, but not all sources are equally reliable. Some sources (e.g., media reports) are generally reliable, but we all know of examples where the news media got the story wrong, and there's a reason that nearly every newspaper runs a corrections column. The analyst must assess the nature of the source: Is this a publisher whose purpose is to convey information (e.g., an obituary, list of graduates), to present well-documented events (e.g., a court case), or to argue for a viewpoint (e.g., a blog advocating a side on an issue)? An address directory is likely to be correct in most instances, but a social site posting may be a cruel joke. An Internet intelligence analyst must apply classical library standards to the evaluation of the reliability of the sources used, and the confidence placed in the particular items reported. Where appropriate, it will be necessary to find other sources to help verify the item or at least shed light on the authoritativeness of the source.

Verifying information found on the Internet can be tricky. For example, finding a biographical profile of a subject can be very helpful, but the first questions are: Who posted it? Was it fact-checked? Is there independent confirmation of its contents? Many Internet searchers accept the contents of a LinkedIn profile as factual, but forget that the subject himself or herself posted it. Likewise, other business and social networking and job placement sites contain autobiographical curricula vitae. Since a considerable percentage of resumes, job applications, and self-descriptions contain exaggeration and outright untruths, it helps to compare fact-checked biographies with those of the subject. Even then, profiles should not be presumed accurate, since a business will ask an executive to provide the bio posted, and there are few sources online that post CVs that are authored by someone independent of the subject. This illustrates the difficulty of verifying what you find online. Among many examples of "facts" found online in the past four years by the author are

- An erroneous police department posting of a "most wanted" person who had already been arrested, tried, convicted, and served time for the offense
- A government database accessible on the Internet that contained no reference to a severe punishment issued to a person who was found on the Internet listed in the same government agency's newsletter as having been punished
- A young entertainer whose face appeared in obscene poses as well as "wet t-shirt" photos online, but the obscene pictures were phony, "Photoshopped" frauds
- Four individuals with the same first name, middle initial, and last name, of similar ages, living in a six-mile radius in a top-ten city suburb, two of whom had similar backgrounds
- Several individuals whose criminal records appeared in online references, but not in court records retrieved by a paid data broker, and several others who had more criminal and civil court records than were found by data brokers

Just because it can be difficult to verify facts found online does not mean that it is a bad idea to collect and analyze online intelligence. Some policy makers currently forbid their staffs any use of the Internet in vetting, to avoid the possibility of error. Unfortunately, every database, whether government or privately owned, is apt to contain errors.[2] The key analytical issues to be confronted are whether the purported fact in question is material to decision making; whether the fact has more than one authoritative source, reporting substantially the same thing (and not all coming from the same place); and whether it is necessary to take additional steps, prior to using the fact in a judgment. Once the analyst, reporting supervisor, and client settle on a mode of operation for critical fact verification, it is relatively easy to handle issues that arise. For instance, prior to using a finding in an adjudication, an interview with a third party or the subject of the inquiry may be necessary, and often, this step can provide the most fair resolution when the derogatory information should not stay "on the record" if it is not true. The issue of verification illustrates why sound policies are necessary for Internet intelligence, just as they have been for centuries in taking testimony from witnesses or references.

Before a judge, the currency of information can make the difference between a law enforcement officer obtaining or being denied a warrant.[3]

The reason is simple: If the information is out of date, it may not justify the warrant. This principle is analogous to the U.S. adjudicative guidelines for access to classified information, which ask whether the misbehavior found is very old, and may represent a lapse that occurred before the individual corrected himself or herself.[4] On the Internet, finding the "time/date stamp" for references is not always simple. Some postings are undated, some carry an automatically updated current day, some only have a copyright at the bottom of the page, and some relate when the item was originally written and when it was last updated. In looking at a person's or entity's history, it can be important to determine when certain events occurred, so it is important for analysts to record dates where available. Standard references include the reported date of publication and the date that the item was retrieved from the Internet. Because the content of the Internet changes frequently, items found are apt to disappear. Merely reporting the text of a posting with its Universal Resource Locator (URL; Web page address) may not provide a client a view of the Web page as posted, because the client cannot return to the same source Web page if it is removed from the Web site or altered. A copy of the page should therefore be retained. When historical information is found (e.g., date of graduation, period of employment), it is helpful to include the date posted in order to judge the accuracy of the content. Like all investigative activities, Internet collection requires attention to dates and times whenever they are available.

Efficiency and timeliness in investigations can become key issues, especially when a deadline is set to complete reporting. In Internet inquiries, it is possible to find a large number of potential references using search engines and databases, but reviewing, analyzing, and reporting the results can be very time-consuming. When my practice started, our method was to use various search engines and favorite Web sites from a long list we compiled, to find the references to a subject. The list of URLs used grew and grew, as more and more potentially productive Web sites appeared on the Internet, all offering a portal for finding information. We found that "serial searching" can take days, and it would not be unusual to spend several workdays on one subject. Manually going from link to link is slow. Soon, we found ways using metasearch engines, automated searching, and a refined list of URLs better suited to the subject, to reduce the search time required for a subject with many references from up to forty hours down to about two hours. Nevertheless, it is necessary for the analyst to "grind out" the review of each potential reference, because available computer software applications have not yet reached the stage where a program can replace the human analyst.[5]

In order to ensure that Internet searching input into an investigative report is completed in a timely fashion, using the least possible analyst resources, an enterprise should determine a reasonable scope for each project, allocating the time available to complete the tasks within the deadline. When the analyst finds it impossible to complete all assigned tasks, or finds additional leads that appear to offer more or better information, the report may still be completed on time, with a notation that some references could not be reviewed, and indicating what type of information may still be available. When Internet vetting becomes the norm, it will be necessary for employers to define what constitutes a complete search, because there may be unfound data in any inquiry. Since every collection project will vary, it is reasonable to define a standard in terms of the time spent, tools used, references reviewed, skills of the analyst and reviewer, and similar attributes of the effort. By defining the expectations for each type of search, or each individual search conducted, the enterprise can ensure that a sound, fair method is applied. Additional experience inevitably makes the process more efficient, and new tools often help make searching more efficient and effective. Since it is not prudent to avoid Internet searching entirely, or conduct incomplete and inept spot searching, a best effort approach within the available resources and time constraints is productive, cost-effective, and ethically sound.

TRAINING ANALYSTS

The level of training of an analyst conducting Internet intelligence operations has a direct correlation with the level of success achieved. Therefore, in such activities as Internet vetting, trained analysts should be used to the maximum extent possible. It is common for business and government employees today to be self-taught in such computing functions as common desktop applications (e.g., browsers) and Internet search. There are several courses available to law enforcement, private security, and investigators in the private intelligence realm,[6] but they can be costly and should be updated as the ever-changing Internet offers new tools and techniques. Once an analyst has received introductory-level training, the single best way to learn is to conduct research in the sites, search engines, and databases online, and topics relating to Internet resources that can improve the analyst's productivity. Providing the tools for the analyst to use is crucial, as is tutoring in the use of those tools. Chapter 17 specifically addresses automated search tools. An analyst who will be expected to conduct

Internet vetting routinely should be given at least a basic set of automated tools, because these help ensure that a large number of potential sources are queried in every search. Not only do more advanced methods and tools assist the analyst in providing more efficient services, but also they help confirm that the process is fair, complete, and effective.

One way to help ensure that proper policies and procedures are applied to Internet searching is to require that analysts log their activities and preserve the results of searches. When search engines and automated searching are used, the analyst can capture and store the list of references found. When Web pages are located containing substantial information that will be included in the report, the analyst should print the pages in PDF form and store the pages or include copies with the investigative report. When newer analysts are in training, tutors can help them to review the links found, references reviewed, items chosen for reporting, and the recording of URLs and pages chosen. Should a report be disputed or facts called into question, it is then possible to return to the original search material and review it for any normal reporting attribute—completeness, accuracy, verification, etc.

Since each enterprise may be held responsible for the integrity and methodology used by investigators in producing Internet intelligence, the policies and procedures established to guide the investigators are important. Allowing individuals to determine when and how to search, and how to use results and make decisions based on self-determined criteria, could potentially result in collection and reporting that conflict with enterprise principles or create liability. An organization properly may place no restrictions on individual employees' use of Internet search tools for their own, work-related enlightenment. However, all enterprises should recognize the potential power of adding competent Internet searching to the collection and analysis of the information used in business decision mak ing. In my practice, I have found that when two or more analysts focus on the same topics, the results are often better than when only one person does the task, and a reviewer can strengthen the results that an individual analyst obtains. Everyone has access to the library, but it takes a librarian-analyst with practice and training to get the best results from the great global library of the Internet.

OPEN-SOURCE INTELLIGENCE PROCESS

For those contemplating becoming a professional in open-source intelligence, complete training is recommended. Since organizations are apt to task employees with Internet searching as one of their "other duties as assigned," what follows is a brief summary of how a relative Internet novice can work to high intelligence standards when carrying out Internet intelligence duties. As with all work activities, great improvement comes from better training and more experience.

The purpose of intelligence and investigation is to find facts that allow decision makers to reach conclusions. To do so, open-mindedness, objectivity, a broad scope of general knowledge, curiosity, and determination are very helpful to the researcher. Whether the subject is a person, company, organization, or topic, all of the subject's attributes are potentially important, and so should be found and considered by the collector and analyst in formulating which attributes are most helpful for decisions. However, the focus of the inquiry may be defined more narrowly by the client. The client's requirements and the collector's standards control the scope, value, timing, and format of reports. Often, delinquent behavior plays a powerful role in decisions, and thus finding evidence of delinquency is an object of inquiry. Verification of the truthfulness, trustworthiness, qualifications, and eligibility of individuals, organizations, and groups is also a frequent goal. In vetting, some think that the goal is to find instances of misbehavior, but in reality, the purpose is to prove whether the subject is in fact worthy. Sometimes, investigators cut their process short when they find significant indicators of unworthiness, but it is just as important to find mitigating circumstances and verify the occurrence, seriousness, frequency, and impact of alleged wrongdoing, within the time available and guidelines for collection. All inquiries seek certainty, but all collectors must admit that a certain degree of doubt is healthy, even for cases where convincing evidence has been found. In the end, the people entrusted to investigate must seek the truth, but the process should always include verification wherever it is available. It is then up to the client to make judgments based on the findings.

The intelligence collection process begins when the collector chooses sources and methods designed to find the facts needed to meet the goals of the case, within the resources and time available, to the client's specifications.[7] Sourcing is critical to success. Where the Internet is concerned, the analyst must begin with the assumption that the Internet may have changed, even in the recent past, and it may be necessary to add, delete, or otherwise change the mix of online sources to be used. Continual monitoring of activities using Internet sources is increasingly important to decision makers in such areas as investments, risk management, brand protection, employee vetting, operational security, and competitive intelligence. Specific Internet sources are listed in later chapters.

Responsible open-source intelligence depends on application of the well-established principles of all research, with added emphasis on assessment. When an authoritative or unique source provides ostensibly factual information, and especially when online sources with no history of reliability are used, due diligence requires asking and answering a set of appropriate questions. A short list of those questions includes

1. How factual is the information? Determining the accuracy of online information may not be easy. The Internet's wide range of sources and purposes includes fantasy, games, social interaction, comedy, deliberately altered content, controversial opinions, argumentation, religious zealotry, scientific controversy, and artistic expression, to name just a few. Media online and various organizations report results of surveys, opinion polls, and statistical trends that seem to change and vary and that have differing credibility. Even data reporting measurements and geospatial data can be skewed, falsified, or superseded by corrections not present in a posting. For example, some satellite map photographs might not provide recent, accurate, up-close, or clear views of the sites depicted. Some Wiki postings are deliberately slanted to manipulate the reader.

   Reports of events online are a good case in point. Web postings describing events involving civil disorders taking place in China, Iran, Burma, Venezuela, North Korea, and other media-controlled countries may lack the scope, accuracy, and verification expected from countries with a free press. The usual intelligence and news media sourcing are unavailable, so analysts may have to rely on unverified eyewitness reports from Twitter, blogs, emails, posted videos, etc. The inherently risky reporting of events abroad becomes even more problematic when sources cannot be authenticated, facts verified, and potentially explosive content (e.g., bloody police-protester confrontations) put in context in a timely manner. While the opportunity for almost anyone to post on the World Wide Web from anywhere has brought the world closer to us all, the need to derive consistent meanings from millions of voices is challenging.

   To determine the facts from Internet sources, analysts must consider the sources:

   - Identity
   - Bias

- History
- Sponsorship
- Closeness to the facts/events
- Expertise
- Potential to err
- Accuracy
- Timeliness

The authoritativeness of the source is no guarantee of the factuality of events, observations, and items reported, but it can help address the accuracy, completeness, honesty, and intent of reports. The next logical test is whether other sources report the same things. Traps in multiple-source verifications include repeated reporting of the same individual source's data, which occurs when source specificity is absent. The media are especially inclined to pick up reporting from other publications and repeat an original report as their own, without verification. Sometimes, mere repetition leads to acceptance of a report as fact. Also, summaries of multiple reports, estimates, surveys, and projections can provide differing impressions, depending on timing and circumstances. Data completeness can clash with deadlines, and conclusions may differ as time goes on.[8] So, while the ideal of multisource verification should be sought, each item should be judged on its own merits.

2. What is the attribution of the posting? Did the subject really make the online "confession," complete with video, for the world to see? Collectors should approach an online posting skeptically, as an artifact that can be analyzed for the likelihood that it is what it appears to be, or may not be what it seems. If the posting contains facts, it may be necessary to verify them offline. A classic case was a photo of a wild-looking young man at a New Year's Eve party with a caption something like "Joe on Meth." Perhaps Joe was drunk or even on drugs, but the photo, which was tagged with Joe's true name, apparently was posted by an anonymous "friend." Fortunately, it was possible to identify the friend from his user name, and clearly, interviews would be in order before attributing the use of drugs to Joe. Some clients would prefer not to pursue this kind of posting, but if Joe is addicted to drugs, he may not be a prime candidate for hiring or granting a clearance.

150

3. How can the online data be verified? This is the classic intelligence dilemma, because there may be only one source for an item that could cause an adverse judgment. In processing this type of information, the intelligence collector must look for separate reports and sources confirming the report, and try to find other ways that the item can be verified. Sometimes, the Internet can provide evidence hiding in plain sight, as in the case of a subject with several reported instances of foreign travel to countries hostile to the United States, who had posted numerous photos of herself in various scenes at tourist sites in those countries.

In a way, too much has been made about the parts of the Internet that cannot be trusted. Intelligence analysts do not seem to have great difficulties assessing supermarket tabloids as intrinsically different from the mainstream press, and experienced Internet analysts will also be able to weigh the credibility of online sources. As with all intelligence reporting, when an item may not be supported by independent evidence, there is a way to portray that information to the client while cautioning the client that it lacks verification.

Reporting of Internet investigative results should be done to the same standards required of reports from other sources. Topical headings can be used to organize the data into related groups. Each item should have a source citation—the URL from which the item was taken. Where the item may be material to a decision, a copy of the Web page should be captured (PDF format preferred) and appended to the report. Examples of reports are included in Chapter 18.

QUALITY CONTROL

In order to provide professional results, Internet intelligence collectors should draft reports that are reviewed prior to submission to the client. The reviewer and collector must develop and apply methods to ensure that the report of an Internet search is

- Accurate, that is, the search terms used are correct and the results are captured in a forensically valid manner. In most cases, this means that spelling must be double-checked, and Web pages containing content of search results are captured. Digitally signing findings also ensures that the analyst can verify that the image remains the same when reviewed later. Some utilities (e.g., programs that download Web pages) normally date/time stamp the action for later verification. To be accurate, the contents of findings, for example, names, places, dates, descriptions, must be verified, or at least consistent with known facts. Items should be labeled or flagged if their content is actionable, comes from a unique source and remains unverified, or if there is doubt about accuracy, particularly if the item is derogatory in nature. *The single greatest danger in using Internet intelligence is in accepting findings as fact without verification, which impugns the integrity of the report.*

- Thorough, that is, as many logical search engines, sites, and potential sources of data on the topic as possible are queried for references. It is a common mistake for Internet searches to be conducted quickly and sloppily, omitting logical sources out of ignorance or laziness. Further searching on new terms, based on findings, can result in more and better results. If the search is part of an open-source intelligence collection process, the results will not be professional if it is not comprehensive. Because Internet collection and analysis can be time-consuming, there is an optimal balance in each situation between the time/labor available, research goals, and judging when "enough is enough."

- Timely, that is, contains up-to-date information, delivered within any required deadlines. Good analysts search, analyze, and report more rapidly than others, but it is hard to say that any research is complete and final, since there are so many different sources, and often, so many references to include or discount. *A key danger in Internet intelligence searching and analysis is the compulsion to continue searching, and the analyst's sense of when the process is as complete and accurate as possible is the art of the process.*

- Fair, that is, includes references and details that have a high probability of being accurate and complete, without false references, major missing pieces, or subjective input from the analyst (including the analyst's prejudice), and adherence to the standards set for the conduct of the process. People are rightly concerned about their personal privacy in the Internet age. However, individuals (and others) publicly post a great deal of data of potential relevance to an Internet search for background vetting, due diligence, or the like. To be fair, a search report must not violate the Title VII discrimination standards (e.g., race, religion, national origin) and must respect the rights, including privacy rights, of subjects of inquiry. *At this writing, fear of violating privacy rights or feelings of*

individuals is the single biggest reason why necessary Internet searching
is officially avoided by some government and business employers.

In the intelligence community in the information age, the Internet provides just another type of open-source information—another INT, if you will (like HUMINT and SIGINT[9]), perhaps WEBINT. Incorporating online findings into all types of intelligence and investigative reporting should not pose very difficult challenges, and is already being done to a large extent. To the degree that specialization and further automation are required to derive the best possible information from WEBINT, there is progress being made. For background vetting and some types of investigations, additional policies and procedures are required, to meet the same level of reliability as that found from other sources. The tools, techniques, and training, along with quality controls used, will determine success in adopting Internet searching as an added resource for collection.

NOTES

1. User requirements for Internet searches were developed by the author and his team doing business as iNameCheck, 2005–present.
2. Holstege, Sean, "Legal-Worker Database Flawed, National Hiring System Shows 4% Error Rate," *The Arizona Republic*, June 30, 2007, http://www.azcentral. com/arizonarepublic/news/articles/0630pilot0630.html?&wired (accessed June 2, 2010). This story actually shows a rather good rate of error compared to such notorious records as the three major credit bureaus or the Immigration and Naturalization Service, based on decades of news media reports.
3. Federal Rules of Criminal Procedure, see http://www.law.cornell.edu/ rules/frcrmp/ (accessed August 21, 2010).
4. Adjudicative Guidelines for Eligibility for Access to Classified Information summary, http://www.state.gov/m/ds/clearances/60321.htm (accessed August 21, 2010).
5. Five years of reviewing available software for individual Internet search analysts has produced only a few viable systems.
6. The author's firm and at least two other businesses offer Internet search methodology training, which can range from ninety minutes to sixteen hours, and can be customized for the class.
7. Intelligence cycle as described simply by the CIA, https://www.cia.gov/ kids-page/6-12th-grade/who-we-are-what-we-do/the-intelligence-cycle. html (accessed June 2, 2010).

8. Salcito, Kendyl, "Gatekeeping," Center for Journalism Ethics, School of Journalism and Mass Communication, University of Wisconsin–Madison, http://www.journalismethics.ca/online_journalism_ethics/gatekeeping. htm (accessed August 21, 2010).
9. HUMINT is the intelligence community's acronym for human intelligence, and SIGINT for signals intelligence.

13

Proper Procedures for Internet Searching

Proper procedures are needed for Internet searching when an organization establishes a policy for the use of intelligence gleaned from the Internet, such as for background vetting, due diligence, competitive intelligence, and clearances. Practical methodology will be covered in Section IV. This chapter is concerned with the strategy adopted by an agency or private entity for formal controls on the collection, analysis, and reporting of information from the Internet in compliance with management policy. Such controls became necessary because of the proliferation of sources of information accessible from the Internet, and the wildly varying nature (quality, accuracy) of the data. If the Internet is used for certain types of data, such as government records, scientific research citations, press accounts, or product descriptions, there is only limited concern about the attributes of that data (as set out in Chapter 12, such as verification). However, social networking, blogs, chat, and even posted videos and photographs have decidedly less reliability. One way of looking at the nature of data available over the Internet is to examine the disclaimers ever present on Web sites that essentially exempt the host from the necessity of vouching for the accuracy, completeness, and usability of the data presented. Such disclaimers speak to the expectation that the percentage of data with errors could be relatively high (or perhaps the Web site hosts do not trust computers).

CRITERIA

As outlined in previous chapters, application of criteria for assessing the credibility and value of information found on the Internet rests with the collector and reviewer. When information is collected to support a decision-making process of consequence, the value, accuracy, and reliability of any source used must be considered. This is all the more important with Internet data. Each organization must decide for itself whether to have a policy and set procedural standards for using Internet sources, but among the areas where it is prudent to have such criteria are

- Vetting individuals for hiring, employment decisions, clearances, and due diligence
- Vetting firms as suppliers, partners, and for mergers and acquisitions
- Product and brand protection
- Competitive intelligence
- Enterprise security
- Criminal and administrative investigations

A philosophical baseline analogous to the hearsay rule[1] applies to records based on Internet intelligence: If the source is a record created in the normal course of business, with a "business grade" expectation of accuracy and reliability, then the information would normally be deemed credible. If the source is based on rumor, word of mouth, recollection, or a record created long after the fact, then additional verification will be needed before affording the information credibility. The analogy is useful to an enterprise, because when information rises to the level of intelligence or evidence, it must meet higher standards. Statistics are a good example of the dilemma facing the analyst, because the old joke about lies, damn lies, and statistics often applies. The Internet can be a particularly useful tool to find different sources for statistical information on the same topic, so it stands to reason that a report can include numbers from various sources found on the Internet. The key to ensuring that such reports are reliable is that the data presented are up to the same standard, whether from the Internet or other sources.

Based on the principles presented to this point, the procedures that should be considered for implementation by organizations for the types of Internet intelligence listed above include

- Establishing a cadre of trained, skilled Internet investigative analysts as part of the organization's security, research, legal, or personnel departments, or as an independent entity, such as a library, serving the whole enterprise.

- Providing tools, training, policies, and procedures for the Internet analysts, and ensuring that they are utilized when the Internet is exploited for decision support.
- Subjecting reporting that includes Internet data to periodic ethical and analytical review, to ensure that the quality and reliability meet organizational norms and comply with laws, regulations, and ethical guidelines.
- If the organization decides to outsource Internet investigations (alone or as part of its strategy of background vetting, corporate intelligence collection, etc.), the same approach and standards as outlined above should be required of the service provider chosen.

At the highest level of performance, it is also possible to set out the key requirements that Internet analysts are expected to meet in their day-to-day functions, which include developing primary and alternative Internet sources, along with criteria for credibility thereof; keeping up with Internet changes, to add new sources when possible and replace those no longer useful; following the development of tools to make searching more efficient; monitoring guidelines for the use of Internet data in specified areas (e.g., vetting); reviewing specific Web site authorized use and privacy policies; maintaining high ethical work standards; and keeping up with the laws and litigation applied to Internet searching. If an organization treats Internet investigative analysts as a specialized group of professionals, their work product will support enterprise decision making. Without this kind of approach, it is possible that costly errors can arise from incomplete or flawed information found by inept Googling in the normal course of business, and it is probable that such important decisions as hiring will be subject to charges of discrimination, because random and unskilled searching by HR individuals will seep into the hiring process and threaten its integrity.

Organizations often avoid taking necessary steps toward progress until they are forced to take the time and resources by events outside their control, including regulation and competition. In the case of Internet intelligence, a tipping point was reached at least seven to ten years ago when the quantity, quality, and price of data on almost any subject became too great to ignore. The risk of inaccuracy and the skills needed to exploit the Internet efficiently have held back many firms, which often allow staff to use the Internet as they see fit. Professional researchers, including librarians, understand that the Internet is now an essential part of information collection and analysis on any topic. Law enforcement, intelligence analysts, corporate investigators, librarians, and researchers have similarly high standards for the reliability of sources. Provided that they have institutional support, such professionals can be trusted to exploit the Internet for all of their normal tasks. However, without such institutional support, they are left to their own devices and personal discretion in the handling of Internet information. Because of their experience and training, this type of professional analyst should have a role in establishing the procedures, if not also the policies, to be applied by enterprises in utilizing Internet data.

A metaphor used above for the Internet is a neighborhood where all the doors are screen doors. Because skilled investigators are able to look into the homes, past the screen doors, it is important to include ethics training with the legal training provided for them. Investigators who are active in social and professional networking and in tracking people online will become aware of a great deal of privileged information, including subjects' personally identifying information, provocative and interesting anecdotes, startling and disturbing human behaviors, and facts that may include misbehavior by high-ranking or well-known members of their own enterprise. Because many of today's investigators are part of the very open, highly networked world of Internet information sharing, it is especially important that they understand the discretion and confidentiality with which they are routinely entrusted. Periodically updated reminders of their ethical responsibilities are necessary to ensure that these investigators do not divulge information to which they have become privy in the course of their work, especially online. Further, the ease of collection and reporting of sensitive personal information about subjects and others found online must not lead investigators to be casual in their handling of the data, discriminate against people who live alternate lifestyles, or otherwise act irresponsibly with confidential data. Because many subjects investigated online are likely to be highly sensitive to the impact on their personal privacy (regardless of the fact that they have posted their information for anyone to see on the Internet), investigators need to take special care to protect the data found.

Based on the legal and policy standards reviewed, it appears that litigation is inevitable if individuals are sanctioned by employers for Internet behavior on or off the job. That probability makes it imperative to have a firm basis for Internet searching for background investigations (just as employers do for prior employments).

SECURITY

Conducting Internet searching exposes the investigator to a multitude of security issues that are of concern to anyone on the Internet, but also to additional risks that arise from the nature of searching.[2] It is essential that analysts understand the nature of the dangers they face online, but these dangers are endemic to Internet users in general.[3]

Significant risks for Internet searchers include

- Malicious code found on Web sites, in downloads (e.g., in documents, spreadsheets, images, browser add-ons, and HTML) and other content
- False references, including misidentification (e.g., same and similar names), deceptive postings, "humorous" but untrue texts and images, and nonidentifiable information
- Social site postings that reveal too much about the person (e.g., contact information, family and friends, confidential business data, with too few privacy protections)
- Failing to isolate the computer used for searching from that used for business, banking, online purchases, and storage of sensitive personal information (due to the risk of infection)
- Assuming that downloaded data are low in risk
- Searching in such a way as to create a security risk for the subject of the search (e.g., by leaving a communication online retrievable by others)

Numerous government, business, and media reports have documented that there are organized criminal groups, "crackers," and malicious individuals that use the Internet to commit fraud and a variety of crimes, including identity theft and remote takeovers of others' computer systems through implanted programs ("bots") controlled through networks of directed systems ("nets"), comprising "botnets." Controllers of botnets use them to harvest banking, commercial account, and credit card information and commercial secrets, launch spam email campaigns, conduct distributed denial of service attacks, and for takeover attempts aimed at additional computer systems. Among the botnet masters have been Russian organized crime, American crackers, Chinese programmers, and occasionally, intelligence operators for nations testing Internet warfare methodology. Botnets allow controllers to hide their identities, conduct mass attacks, spread malicious code to more potential victims, and "park" data on unwitting parties' systems without detection. The key factors allowing botnets to control literally millions of computers is that users simply fail to keep security up to date, and cannot detect implanted malware (in summary, poor computer hygiene).[4]

The prevalence of viruses, worms, and other malware is not the only issue Internet intelligence analysts must anticipate. Porn is everywhere online. So are illicit and illegal offers of prescription drugs, software, and gambling, to name a few of the most popular off-color distractions. Porn is a special issue, because child pornography is considered intrinsically illegal in the United States: Production, possession, trading in, or sharing child porn is a felony. Many porn sites emphasize youthful images and actions, whether the individuals involved are underage or not. If a search encounters porn, analysts must be very careful not to capture images that are child pornography. Because of this, many researchers avoid capturing images and systematically purge content that could remotely contain offensive images.

Those who intend to spend considerable time conducting Internet intelligence collection and analysis should consider the following approaches:

- Use a separate computer system for Internet searching. This might be a remote system (a "virtual workstation"). The analyst and system administrator should be prepared to rebuild the collection machine, if necessary, if it becomes debilitated by code or content downloaded from searches. If damage occurs to the machine, at least the analyst's and employer's primary systems are not impacted. A corollary is that since email is often used for transmitting malicious code, users should consider separating the system used for email from that used for the most sensitive personal and business data.
- Consider the right choices for browser, data capture, storage, and antivirus scanning. Since Internet Explorer from Microsoft is a prime target of malicious code writers, an alternative browser may reduce the vulnerability of infection. Other options include Firefox, Opera, Chrome, and Safari.
- Consider how to capture content. Because Web pages are apt to change and there is no guarantee that a page will be cached or remain available, it is often important to save an image of the page. Options include copy and save into a document or spreadsheet, save an HTML copy, or print into a PDF document. Some documents or spreadsheets do not actually save "embedded" Web content, but rather save a link, so that a document might not be exactly what was composed, if the Internet page changes. Using a PDF

printed copy of the page does not guarantee an exact duplicate of the page's appearance (due to the different ways that Web pages are composed), but most often the text is captured accurately and the analyst can be sure that the saved PDF will retain its content indefinitely. In addition, the PDF copy can be digitally signed, providing verification that it is identical to the image originally captured.

- Consider how and where to store content. Files containing the results of Internet searches may contain sensitive and valuable data. Evidence, intelligence, and information of use in decision making should be stored in a secure, reliable manner. Personally identifying information should be protected against unauthorized access and misuse. Stored data should be indexed to facilitate retrieval, secured to limit access and deny use to unauthorized parties (usually through encryption), auditable, and support chain of custody (should court use become necessary). Besides the potential need for retrieval for further processing, files may contain data of value in subsequent investigations (e.g., a background investigation on an associate of an employee).

STANDARD METHODOLOGY

An organization is well advised to incorporate Internet sources into standard operating procedures, including methodology applied to investigations and intelligence collection. Based on the specific attributes of Internet searching as a source of information, especially as facts found online are used in decision making, it is important to have standard procedures in place. These should be consistent with policy and constitute a first line of defense for any allegation of unfairness or lack of professionalism in conducting investigations. A large number of agency heads with whom I have spoken about cyber vetting have expressed the belief that their liability for *not* including the Internet in background investigations far outweighs potential liability from what is found. All have expressed confidence in judging facts from fiction in postings. Yet few have a standard for how to handle the Internet, as opposed to other sources with which their investigators are far more familiar.

As with any relatively new venture, Internet investigations benefit from establishment of norms that all can understand, and the standards adopted will help any enterprise in taking advantage of the wealth of data available online.

NOTES

1. The hearsay rule in federal and state courts is generally defined as a statement made out of court that is offered as proof in court; see http://legal-dictionary.thefreedictionary.com/Heresay+rule (accessed August 21, 2010).
2. Stone, Paul, "Internet Presents Web of Security Issues," American Forces Information Services, U.S. Defense Department, http://www.defense.gov/specials/websecurity/ (accessed June 2, 2010). Among the concerns found was "too much information" online about DOD command-level persons.
3. U.S. CERT's computer security tips, including browsing dangers, can be found at http://www.us-cert.gov/cas/tips/ (accessed June 1, 2010).
4. Williams, Paul, "Organized Crime and Cybercrime: Implications for Business," CERT Coordination Center, Carnegie Mellon University, 2002; Botnet definition, http://searchsecurity.techtarget.com/sDefinition/0,,sid14_gci1030284, 00.html (accessed June 2, 2010), also with descriptions of other online security issues.

Section IV

Internet Search Methodology

This section focuses on how to conduct effective Internet searches for investigative and intelligence purposes on subjects such as people, entities, and topics. Some search projects may be limited by restrictions imposed by the client's policies or procedures, or those of the investigative unit. The aim of the guidance presented here is to provide the best possible search methodology, limited only by the law and ethical practices.

Each subject is different, so each collection task should be approached with a combination of routine steps and customized steps to fit the specific subject. The routine steps should consist of established subtasks (usually the bulk of the work), and may include automated functions that retrieve data from an array of identified search targets. In addition, subtask variations appropriate to the geographical area, government jurisdictions, and biographical details should be added as appropriate. Customized subtasks should include queries of professional and personal reference sources and connections peculiar to the individual subject. It is useful for analysts conducting subtasks to maintain lists of search engines' and Web sites' Universal Resource Locator (URL) addresses for ready reference.[1] The search should be designed to survey the Internet, consult key Web sites, and find references that are responsive to the purpose of the task, and if possible, avoid unnecessary collection. For example, a search on a person or business might normally include looking at white and yellow pages directories to verify or discover addresses, telephones, faxes, email addresses, etc., but if contact information is not needed, that subtask can be disregarded.

NOTE

1. Berners-Lee, T., Masinter, L., and McCahill, M., "Uniform Resource Locators (URL)," Network Working Group, December 1994, http://www.ietf.org/rfc/rfc1738.txt (accessed June 2, 2010).

14

Preparation and Planning

Planning is essential to success in all intelligence and investigative collection. Exploitation of the vast quantities of data on the Internet potentially relevant to any topic can be greatly enhanced by preparation, some of which may consist of a group of queries from a list of URLs normally used for the type of subject being searched (e.g., people, businesses), and some preparation that will be done just before and during searching.[1] First, frame the question: What is known about the person, entity, or topic? Next, the search should be based on the following:

- Nature of the data needed
- Purpose of the search (including potential uses of results)
- Best sources, including standard search engines and Web sites
- Geographical location
- Government jurisdiction(s)
- Resources available
- Time available (deadline)

After deciding on an initial search strategy, keyword choices should be made. Keywords should include all logical and likely variations of the name, nicknames, email addresses, and other identifiers that potentially could appear in Internet postings. Reverse directories can be consulted for coinhabitants, significant others, and relatives. Sometimes, postings by people or entities close to a subject can include items containing important information about the person or entity of interest. It may be desirable to combine keywords and use Boolean operators (and, not, or) to home in on the data specifically sought, and perhaps find leads to further information. More about search strategy appears below, but it is important not to underestimate the value of preplanning.

Databases available via the Internet include paid and free sites. An initial consideration includes whether to use a subscription service (e.g., LexisNexis) to find a profile of the subject based on such input as utilities, government and court records, real estate records, employment listings, licenses, and permits. One reason to consider this type of record check first is the rapidity with which it is possible to find a relatively reliable profile of a person or entity and confirm facts that will facilitate Internet searching, largely by allowing the analyst to eliminate references not identifiable with the subject. One aspect of subscription services that should be borne in mind is that records used for their reports contain errors, and so facts provided should be verified. If a subscription service is not available, it is possible to use a pay-as-you-go service like Intelius[2] or U.S. Search,[3] both of which provide reports on a graduated price scale, so that a "complete background" could be $100, but determination or verification of address and telephone number might be $4.50. Depending on the purpose and deadline of the search and the resources allocated to it, a decision should be made about whether to use a fee-based service. Such a decision could also be deferred until the end of an Internet collection project, if most of the information needed is on hand, or if it is expected that the data will be available from free online sources. As with all investigations, identifiers are needed for accurate fee-based searches, such as address, date of birth, or social security/tax number.

Internet vetting of people in support of employment background investigations can be the singular tasking of an analyst, and if so, the analyst should assemble a routine list of planned searches. However, when other types of investigations are conducted, the starting point may not be a detailed application or resume, but rather a few initial facts that may only include a telephone number, email address, name, or nickname. In these types of cases, the search plan is fundamentally different from repeated production of background facts. The analyst-investigator must use a series of searches to build the person's profile from whatever facts are available, and preparation must include a wide list of potential Web sites and sources that can help establish the identity of the subject and verify identifying information.

Many people think that by using a major search engine (e.g., Google, Bing, or Ask) and querying a handful of popular Web sites (e.g., MySpace, Facebook, Blogspot), they will find all the relevant information needed. However, that approach will not provide a thorough search. Most competent Internet investigators have a list of favorite search engines, Web sites, and databases that they routinely include in collection, and they will recognize leads from references found and frequently find productive sources outside their normal URL list, based on experience and initiative. Because so many social and business networking sites create communities of relatives, friends, fellow employees, association members, and "birds of a feather," it is often possible to find references to and even writings by a subject in postings under the profile of those close to him or her. Therefore, not only before the search begins, but also as it is progressing, experienced analysts will find and incorporate new search terms designed to unearth hidden references. Productive searches may be done on a combination of the subject's name and that of an associate. It is worth mentioning that true integration of Internet searching into the investigative and intelligence processes means that when close associates of a subject are identified, solid leads for whom to interview as developed references will be found.

Another important element in planning searches is to list Web sites where data may reside that have not been indexed by the major search engines, and therefore may be part of the "invisible Web."[4] More will be presented on that topic below. Essentially, there are numerous databases accessible through Internet links that are not indexed by search engines. In order to find out if there are references to the subject in unindexed data, one needs to use the search interface provided on the host Web site to find stored information. Government, university, library, private business, and media Web sites (to name just a few) provide access to databases that may contain substantial information about a search topic. For example, the current and archived stories of many news media sites can be searched online. Sometimes, there is a charge for accessing the full story behind a "hit" on the term searched (which may be presented in a brief excerpt). Often, an analyst must take care to conduct keyword searches in accordance with the database search protocol, which may differ from standard Google Boolean protocols. Dangers of this type of search include spending money to review and eliminate false positives and failure to find a record identifiable with the term searched. In any case, planning to include unindexed Internet content in searches is a necessary part of professional collection.

Whatever the experience of the analyst, it is possible to start the search plan with a list of Web sites (URLs) where it is most likely that relevant references will be found. In manual searching, as well as in mapping out potential automated searches, having a list of URLs categorized by content is necessary to carry out comprehensive search plans. A great benefit of major search engines is that they can provide excellent lists of sites on which various types of data should be located. Planning a search should include a quick review of the types of sites where the subject's references will most likely be found. Among the sources and tools available (lists provided later) that may be cataloged for use in a search are the following:

- Directories
- Search engines (including metasearch engines)
- Specialized tools (archives, media, including news, video, audio, photos, music)
- Unindexed sites (e.g., invisible or dark Internet data)
- Private or proprietary sites

Additionally, sites containing blogs, social networking, government records, local news, associations, educational institutions, and similar content should be considered. Some of these may host substantial quantities of relevant but unindexed data.

While there is no substitute for training and experience, many people have taught themselves to be relatively competent Internet analysts by conducting many searches. Students often learn approaches to finding data on the Web that elude others because of the academic disciplines available on campus, including librarians, instructors, and fellow students who freely share their secrets to help each other succeed.

THE LIBRARY

Many people may overlook a priceless resource that can save time and add expertise to any Internet search, and could be a close ally of professional analysts—the library.[5] Whether in a university library, company research unit, government library, county facility, or city library, the librarian has been trained to help the user to find out where to get the answers needed. Intelligence researchers often forget that outside the agency or company, almost any librarian is pledged to provide unbiased, confidential assistance to help any client to find what he or she needs. Libraries not only contain volumes of data on any subject, but today are apt to provide automated indexes of publications, people, entities, and topics that can lead an analyst to the most authoritative and useful content on the topic sought. Because libraries subscribe to fee-based directories, indices, bibliographies, periodicals (including research publications), business profiles, and other sources, they are important sources to consider when planning a project. The Reference and User Services Association of the American Library Association defines reference transactions as "information consultations in which library staff recommend, interpret, evaluate and/or use information resources to help others meet particular information needs."[6] Today's library is likely to provide a Web site accessible to anyone on the Internet for general assistance, and to library patrons with user credentials for specific services, possibly including access to subscription databases.

Certain libraries provide very helpful tutorials to assist in finding references on the Internet. For example, the Library of Congress has posted many excellent resources available over the Web, such as an extensive list of online research resources at http://www.loc.gov/rr/ ElectronicResources/subjects.php?subjectID=69 (which includes search engines). The University of California at Berkeley posted a search engine tutorial at http://www.lib.berkeley.edu/TeachingLib/Guides/Internet/ SearchEngines.html. Currently, the three favorite search engines Berkeley profiles are Google, Yahoo! (which by the time you read this may be another manifestation of Bing), and Exalead. The Humboldt State University Library has posted a tutorial on search strategy at http:// library.humboldt.edu/infoservices/sstrawrksht.htm. Cornell University Library presents search tips at http://www2.etown.edu/vl/starter.html. A few hours' reading of search tips (found by Googling Internet search tips or similar terms) can provide a good primer for new analysts, and can update experienced searchers' skills.

Beginners in Internet searching may not be inclined to think of themselves as fledgling librarians, but in fact they are asked to understand at least where to find the online directories and catalogs they may need to use for any type of search. Having library resources available may save much time and expense. When an investigator is starting the search for a new subject in a new area, the librarian can probably reduce the time needed to plan the collection, by suggesting good places to start. Print and electronic copies of such reference works as telephone and crisscross directories, biographies, lists of publications, business profiles, medical resources, journals, legal references, obituaries (often a source for the living as well as the dead), government databases, and scientific resources are available through the library. The trend in publishing is toward electronic databases from printed reference materials. Once a resource proves useful, the analyst should make a note about where to find it again, and maintain a list of useful sources.

SCOPE NOTES

The most important lesson I learned from over four years of Internet searching is that based on client directions, time, and resource constraints, some of the most critical references to a subject may not be found, which can lead to the false impression that there are no derogatory references. The vast majority of investigations will show only favorable or neutral information about the subject. However, an inadequate search often misses key references. Examples of poor searching include links not reviewed, dependence on one or a few search engines and Web sites, failure to use all available keywords (e.g., name variations), and omitting alternative sources, such as looking only in government records when a news media reference may provide facts about arrests, convictions, and judgments. Constraints imposed on searchers can also impact results, such as when the assignment calls for using only a person's name and work or formal email address, ignoring personal email addresses, nicknames, handles, and similar additional keywords. The client's directives and search unit's policies control the search. Because of lingering uncertainty about the propriety of including off-duty activities in employers' Internet vetting, some inquiries are destined to avoid the very references most likely to produce evidence of online misbehavior or other derogatory results.

Another aspect of scope is how much time and effort to spend looking for information using secondary search terms. Besides a person's name, nicknames, other identifiers, addresses, telephone numbers, email addresses, and handles, references may be found by searching on a spouse, significant other, siblings, parents, children, friends, and associates. The analyst must decide how far into the community of online associations to pursue possible references to the subject. Areas that might be overlooked include photographs, videos, and similar media postings that can be tagged (indexed) to the name of the subject or to a person close to him or her. It is important for the analyst to understand the potential for finding substantive information in seemingly unlikely places. For example, photographs of a foreign trip might raise important issues if a subject is seeking a clearance and has not reported the trip abroad, or apparent associations with foreigners depicted, even if the content of the photos themselves seems benign. Searching images, blogs, and other, more specialized activities may be productive.

In planning the scope of a search, aligning the time allocation and search methods with limitations provided by the client can be critical to success. If the client is to be charged a fee for the search, scope is also vital to pricing, since analyst time in searching, capturing, assessing, and reporting findings must be done at a rate that allows the service to stay within budget (and profit margin). Clients charged by the hour versus a firm fixed price make it easier to scope a search, while short deadlines can complicate the process. At this writing, Internet searching is generally a time-consuming business because it takes awhile to review the references found. Automation can reduce the time spent and expand the scope and accuracy of searching. More on automation appears below.

The starting point for planning the scope of a search is the subject (person, entity, topic) about which information is needed. If the name is all that will be used for searching, the scope will normally be limited to the name and all logical variations. If, in addition, the client's policies and procedures, tasking, and desired results have a broader scope, there are several other search terms and strategies that should be considered, including

- Seek references on all identifiers, including nicknames, user names, email addresses, handles, etc., of not only the subject, but also selected family, friends, associates, fellow employees, classmates, and social networking friends.
- Review records available online for spouse, significant other, and immediate family (which sometimes reveal legal, employment, and behavioral issues that do not appear elsewhere).
- Use crisscross directories, "Whois" lookups (Web site registration data), and search on telephone numbers, IP addresses, Web sites, blogs, photographic, video, and game sites where references to the subject or additional searchable identifiers may be found.
- Use cached or archived pages where older references to the subject on defunct Web pages or Web sites no longer in existence are found.
- Use advanced searches and combinations of search terms to find references that otherwise might be in the usual haystack of search results hiding the needles.
- Review search engine results efficiently, such as by scanning thumbnails to find the most relevant quickly, starting with the first and last pages of results, changing the number of results per

page (e.g., from the default ten to one hundred), and reading the most promising links first, setting aside the others for later.

Besides planning for search engine collection, an analyst should consider the list of more specific and "invisible Web" sites where databases may contain references to the subject. Among these are business, college, association, government, volunteer, court, real estate, and licensing databases (to name a few). Depending on the purpose of the search, consider quering lists posted by government and watchdog groups of people and entities involved in illicit activities, including the Excluded Parties List (government contracting denied), OFAC (Treasury's Office of Foreign Assets Control sanctions), U.S. Customs' online list of adverse rulings, SEC's enforcement actions, State Department's list of foreign terrorist organizations, FDA's debarment list, World Bank's list of ineligible contractors, and POGO's list of federal contractor misconduct, to name a few. A list of these types of Web sites appears later, in Chapter 16.

Collection and analysis in Internet intelligence go hand-in-hand, as initial expectations are revised based on findings, and follow-up searches on hunches provide unexpectedly good data or perhaps wash out. The search plan should be revised as the project progresses, to ensure inclusion of all logical sources of information, within the resource and time constraints available.

Not only is planning essential to achieve efficiency in Internet intelligence production, but it is also critical to lawful, principled, ethical investigation. Having a cogent, consistent approach protects the analyst and the client from possible claims of bias, unfairness, violation of privacy, and illicit conduct. Given the persistent proclivity of some to misbehave, it is likely that they will object and even go to court when their misdeeds are exposed by good online investigations. However, the organized investigator will be able to demonstrate that the search, analysis, and reporting were conducted within all appropriate norms, and the results are a proper depiction of the subject's behavior.

NOTES

1. Hetherington, Cynthia, "Web 2.0 Investigations That Move Beyond Google," ASIS International Webinar, February 17, 2010; Hock, Randolph, *The Extreme Searcher's Internet Handbook* (Medford, NJ: Cyber Age Books, 2004).
2. Intelius, http://www.intelius.com/.
3. U.S. Search, http://www.ussearch.com/consumer/index.jsp.

4. Sherman, Chris, and Price, Gary, *The Invisible Web, Uncovering Information Sources Search Engines Can't See* (Medford, NJ: Information Today, 2001).
5. Cassell, Kay Ann, and Hiremath, Uma, *Reference and Information Services in the 21st Century, An Introduction*, 2nd ed. (New York: Neal-Schuman Publishers, 2009).
6. Ibid.

15

Search Techniques

Professionals looking for intelligence on the Internet find the effort fruitful, if not always easy. The information provided in this and the next two chapters assumes that the reader has some familiarity with personal computers and surfing the Internet. Here, the reader will receive pointers from those who rely on the Internet for open-source information on a daily basis. The bibliography contains reference volumes where a reader can find a complete introduction to the Internet and its exploitation.

INTERNET CONTENT

On the Internet, most Web pages are written in Hypertext Markup Language (HTML),[1] which allows the creation of, and access to, structured documents (including text, pictures, and other content), but many sites also have scripts and features in programming languages such as JavaScript,[2] and effects provided by Flash Player[3] and other plug-ins. Also appearing on the Internet are text in American Standard Code for Information Interchange (ASCII),[4] gateways into databases, and dynamic content pulled into the browser in a combination of static and continuously changing windows. Web sites' displays of stock market updates, news headlines, moving pictures, live videos, and other content are designed to attract and entertain users, call attention to advertising, and communicate in more sophisticated ways than static, two-dimensional documents. The analyst needs to look beyond the flash and find the facts, then capture the Web page contents needed (at least the text containing the facts found).

Fortunately for searchers, expertise in the Internet's structural components is not needed for finding intelligence. However, it is important to remember that the programming behind everything we see on the Web is responsible for how it is displayed, and we should capture content by using appropriate tools, to ensure professional information collection and retention. Because the content of Web sites can change frequently, it is imperative for an analyst/investigator to capture the content properly at the time of the search.

Every Internet page has a Uniform Resource Locator (URL) address (i.e., what you see in the box at the top of the browser), which is translated by a Domain Name System (DNS) server into the correct Internet Protocol (IP) address, to which the browser is directed.[5] Visiting an Internet page allows the browser to pull its content (via a stream of packets) into a computer and onto a screen that the user can peruse. Each link on which the user clicks takes the browser to a new Web page. Before clicking on a link, the user must decide whether it is a likely source of useful information. As Internet information collectors become more familiar with sources, they initially assess the potential authority, accuracy, and reliability of references by the URLs of Web sites found in search tools. Further, it is often necessary to trace the authors and owners of Web sites in order to collect and analyze information and find leads on those hosting and posting on the Internet (more on that in Chapter 16). Therefore, it is important to understand the basics of URLs, IP addresses, and their roles.[6]

The many types of Internet content can be daunting to analysts, as it is necessary to find ways to identify, filter, capture, evaluate, and report the text, photos, videos, audio, and other content about a subject of interest. Generally, the content is in digital format, so it can be copied and filed by the investigator, and digitally signed if necessary to preserve its integrity as evidence.[7] The systems and tools available provide a solid start, but there is still no substitute for a trained, experienced, knowledgeable, and creative analyst, who understands how to look for, find, assess, and report what is needed. Contrary to popular belief, there is no application—not even Google—that can easily find everything you are looking for.

THE BROWSER

Google and other search engines operate on Web sites that interact with the user's browser.[8] Professional investigators should become familiar with the functions of their browser when a search is conducted, and may wish to experiment with browsers to select the one most comfortable to use in searching. Besides Internet Explorer (over 60% market share), Firefox (over 24%), Safari, Chrome, and Opera are popular browsers.[9] Toolbars for browsers allow rapid access to search engines, providing add-on applications that can facilitate searching. Browsers may store URLs visited and cookies (tiny scripts) reflecting an interaction with a Web site. Browsers also may store copies of Web page content (e.g., text and images in HTML), which may reside in temporary computer memory to speed up reloading of a Web page. When investigations are sensitive, analysts may wish to consider whether it is prudent to store vestiges of searches on the computer used, and therefore may wish to adjust the browser's settings. A user can browse in private mode and delete links, cookies, and temporary files created through the browser.

Another key consideration is that a great deal of searching will inevitably produce links to Web sites with malicious code[10] designed to infect a browser or workstation, often with the purpose of making the target computer a "zombie" or stealing financial information, such as credit card account data. Even the most careful analyst clicks on links that pose dangerous risks to the investigative workstation, because innocent Web sites may be attacked and infected. Therefore, some investigators deliberately use an "investigative box," that is, a workstation separate from their normal work or personal computer, to avoid the risks of infection, and to allow rebuilding of the PC's operating system if it should suffer from a catastrophic attack. Any PC used for intelligence collection should be equipped with antivirus, antimalware, and firewall software, but those are not 100% effective. Since browsing Web sites is an indispensible part of investigations, care should be taken to limit potential damage.

THE SEARCH ENGINE

The search engine is a highly useful tool for collecting and analyzing information from the Internet, accessed with a browser. When people consider researching a topic on the Internet, Google is the tool of choice 65% or more of the time. The reason is that the developers of Google have created systems that provide rank-ordered views of references to the search term in very little time (usually in a second or less), gleaned from a much larger storehouse of data than any other search engine offers.[11] Google's tools (robots or bots) are constantly spidering Internet sites (i.e., surveying and recording or caching pages and links found) and indexing those pages, that is, enabling

Google's systems to find references to a search term instantly. Google delivers search results to users in pages listing two-line summaries of references in PageRank order, a patented popularity ranking calculated using an algorithm from over one hundred factors. Clicking on a link returned by a Google search takes the user to the live Web page (not the cached version on Google's server). However, one may find that the term searched is no longer there, for example, if the page is inaccessible, changed, or deleted. If so, the posting that Google indexed is in the cached page that accompanies the Google reference. The cached version may even allow access to a page that otherwise would be inaccessible if registration is required for access to the live version. The combination of these and other technologies and services enables Google to offer searches that no other search engine currently can match for quantity, quality, and usefulness.

Although Google provides very useful search results, it is an advertising company, earning huge profits from providing users with links to advertisers that may relate to the subject of the search. The excellence of Google as a tool is somewhat mitigated by the intent to optimize the ads that might appeal to the user, rather than the specific purpose of the search. However, the more experience a person has with Google, the less the chance that the ads will interfere with success in research. Another factor to remember is that although it provides access to more Internet references than other search engines, Google provides a snapshot of part of the Internet at a time within thirty days or so of when a page was cached; that is, references may not be current, and searches are not conducted against all Internet content. Another way to measure the ability of Google to present Internet information is to use estimates of the number of pages Google has indexed against the total number of Web pages. Google has not published how many pages it has indexed in several years, but reasonable published estimates say over 8 billion. Netcraft estimated the total number of Web sites at 206,675,938 in March 2010, and based on an average of 273 pages per Web site (a 2007 estimate), the number of Web pages in 2010 would be 56,422,531,074.[12] Whatever the accuracy of these estimates, even if Google has 10 billion pages indexed, that would be about 18% of the Web pages available on the Internet. Of course, not all pages are suitable for indexing, such as those with dynamic content.

Inasmuch as Google is the habitual choice of most Internet researchers,[13] it is worthwhile for a user to become familiar with ways to get the best results from Google. Google tips and tricks (sometimes referred to as "Google hacks," meaning specific ways to enter searches) are readily found, easy to understand and use, and greatly improve results.[14] It is a good reminder to any researcher or analyst that it can be very helpful to look at a search as a process in itself, which can be studied and improved to ensure the best results. A few minutes preparing to do the search in a cogent way pays big dividends in results.

Getting to know the general ways in which search engines operate can be helpful in evaluating the results and in further collection. Not all of a search engine's indexed pages may be presented in search returns, because the engine's software may not include pages that are almost never visited. More searching may be required to find items that algorithms rank lower or that are not displayed in results. The subculture of advertising analysts and webmasters, who try to attract potential customers to Web sites and ads, carefully measures success in terms of the number of "hits" on sites, pages, and terms—page popularity. Search engines like Google, Bing, and Yahoo! also measure the popularity of sites, pages, and terms, but may elect not to index or present the least popular in search results. The analyst does not care how often a page was visited, and is focused on finding all the substantively useful references to the subject. Therefore, the analyst should not assume that the search engine is prioritizing results in the most useful way for intelligence collection and analysis.

Following are additional key attributes of Google search: The combination of PageRank order of results and Boolean advanced searching with individual or multiple terms allows Google to deliver the most useful references for investigators. Special tools and features allow a focus on images, videos, maps, news, blogs, and so forth, and country-based searching, as well as topical searches, for example, for businesses in the United States, United Kingdom, or Canada. Translation of foreign language pages is available, although results are quite rough (i.e., ungrammatical and inaccurate in interpretation). Tracking and search preferences allow analysts to use Google as an all-around, personalized intelligence collection platform, updating findings periodically. Cached pages allow access even if a page has recently changed. Google's advanced search page allows a user to formulate single or multiterm search attempts without worrying about the precise Boolean query format.

Besides Google, analysts should consider using other search engines, to find additional references that are presented in a different order and may not appear in the first several hundred Google results. Google, Yahoo!, Bing, and Ask together conduct over 98% of the searches on the Internet.[15] It is useful to know these major engines (by popularity, volume of indexed pages, and potential to assist a searcher):

Yahoo! (yahoo.com) is reputed to have over 4 billion pages indexed and a 16.89% share of searches conducted in March 2010. Because of agreements with Microsoft's Bing, it is unknown at this writing whether a Yahoo! search may actually employ the Bing search engine. Yahoo! Search ranks by keyword density and integrates its directories and other services (which are similar to Google's) well with searching. Boolean search protocols are much like Google's.[16]

Bing, a Microsoft service, has updated its search engine (since June 2009 called a "decision engine") and in midsummer of 2009 agreed to power Yahoo! Search. Bing's market share was 11.7% in March 2010. Bing includes semantic technology from Powerset (purchased in 2008), which reportedly allows results to include related searches to help users find information. Images, video, local, news, and product searches supplement Web-wide searching, and services such as translation and mapping compete with Google's.[17]

Ask.com, which is reputed to have over 2 billion pages indexed and conducted just over 3% of searches in March 2010, ranks results by ExpertRank, the number of the same subject pages that reference a site. Refinement of search results through filters, suggestions, and editorial comments is its unique feature, including an attempt to allow users to phrase questions in "natural language," as well as keywords.[18]

AOL search, which owns MapQuest, enhances Google's search engine results with its own additions. AltaVista is powered by Yahoo!, as is Fast (AlltheWeb.com). Gigablast claims to do "real-time spidering." Netscape search is powered by Google. Snap.com is powered in part by Gigablast, Smarter.com, SimplyHired.com, X1 Technologies, and enhanced by Ask.com.[19] These search engines may not rank highest in number of searches conducted, pages indexed, market share, or elegance of presentation, but all have enjoyed a following because of their success in finding what a large number of people were looking for. At this writing, it is obvious that consolidation has reduced the choices of search engines, legacy offerings are disappearing, and the trend is toward the top four.

The choice of the search engines listed above should not be interpreted as a rejection of others, such as Lycos.com, Mama.com, and Exalead.com (and there are others). These other search engines may not provide any more or better results than the largest ones, but on occasion, they manage to find and rank highest the subject of a particular search. It is not how many references, but which terms and pages a search engine may have indexed, cached, and presented, that will determine its success for an individual search on a specific occasion.

METASEARCH ENGINES

The goal in using multiple search engines is to find more relevant data quickly, so each analyst must decide what added search engines to use and how much time should be spent reviewing results. One approach is to use metasearch engines, which use several different search engines simultaneously to gather sets of results from each and then amalgamate returns into ranked pages of links.[20] The results contain fewer of the component engines' results and present them in a different order. Two of the largest metasearch engines are Dogpile.com and Clusty.com. Dogpile combines Google, Yahoo!, Bing, and Ask. Clusty uses Ask, Open Directory, Gigablast, Yahoo!News, and others, and "clusters" results from the same place, presenting the clusters, sources, and sites in a box alongside results, allowing the searcher to jump to most likely links to the same search term, organization, sources, or sites.[21] The advantage of using metasearch engines in addition to others is that sometimes an analyst can find the attributes of the subject more quickly, and likely lists of Web sites to pursue further information collection.

Companies like Google, Exalead, and Copernic (Mama.com) provide search software to companies for internal use. Enterprise search engines and Copernic are discussed in Chapter 17.

FINDING SEARCH ENGINES

Among the ways to refresh and validate the tools used is to conduct research periodically into search tools and sources themselves. Good places to look include

Library of Congress at http://www.loc.gov/rr/ElectronicResources/
subjects.php?subjectID=69
Genius Find at http://www.geniusfind.com/—a directory of search
engines and databases
Search engine and directory list at http://pandia.com/powersearch/

Yahoo's catalog of search engines and directories at http://dir.yahoo.com/Computers_and_Internet/Internet/World_Wide_Web/Searching_the_Web/Search_Engines_and_Directories/

The eHow Web site has tutorials on many "how-to's," including using Internet resources at http://www.ehow.com/internet/

SEARCH TERMS

Even the best search engines depend on apt choices of search terms, entered in the appropriate manner. The default operation of most search engines is to look for all and each of the words entered in the search box. A search for John Doe in Google produces references to John Doe, John (alone), and Doe (alone). To search an exact word or phrase, a Boolean expression or advanced search must be used. This is important because searches for John Doe and "John Doe" produce different results. For some inquiries, searching both ways is appropriate. Following are some suggestions for search term selection:

- Use variations of names to capture all relevant references. For example, John James Doe can also be searched as John J. Doe, John Doe, Jack Doe, JJ Doe, and Doe, John. It can be helpful to include a discriminator (place, employer, school, activity, date) to find the right John Doe and to yield more useful results, such as John Doe Dallas, John Doe Texas A&M, John Doe Texas Instruments, or John Doe skydiving. Knowing and using such discriminators can be especially helpful when searching a common name and when looking for a particular set of references. If a Boolean operator like AND is the default, as in Google, simply adding the term in the search box works. If not, use the advanced search feature.
- Eliminate references not identifiable with the subject of the search. Perhaps John Doe the Cleveland sports star, who is not identifiable with the subject, has dozens of references in the first few pages of results. By using Boolean queries, one could eliminate the Cleveland Doe (e.g., by using the Boolean NOT query, searching John Doe -Cleveland, or -Indians in Google). The single biggest problem with the search engines is that they provide many references that are not useful, even though the results literally match the search term. Finding ways to help the search engine focus on the subject of interest will provide better results.

182

- Find Internet sites that may have information about the subject not indexed by search engines. If you find a reference to Texas A&M in your John Doe search, try the Texas A&M site, alumni organizations, professional organizations in the subject's field, and the local or campus newspapers, TV channels, and news publications in College Station, Texas. Such Web sites may indeed have data on Doe that has not been accessible to search engines' indexing. Such references may reside in databases that can easily be searched by going to the Web site and using its built-in search engine. Even if that Web site's internal search engine is Google, the data residing on servers accessible through the site may not be available to the Internet Google servers.

When time available for the search is limited, it is important to view results most efficiently. A normal impulse is to use one search term and view only one or two of the thumbnail pages of results (i.e., ten to twenty results), which often limits the effectiveness of the search. The two major hurdles all searchers face are the time consumed in executing searches and the time used to review and analyze results for useful data. In truth, people are so used to getting what they need from a quick question to Google that the accuracy, thoroughness, completeness, and timeliness of the process may suffer. Some strategies that may help include increasing the number of results shown on each page from 10 to 20, 30, 50, or 100; changing filtering options to include "explicit images" (e.g., because involvement in porn could be relevant to the purpose of the search); and including language preferences, especially if the subject is foreign or has spent time abroad. In addition, overseas versions of Google and other search engines can help find links to Web sites abroad. These examples illustrate the advantages of knowing how Google's features work.

Time can be a significant factor in search filtering, such as specifying the year or time frame in conjunction with a search term. Advanced search options allow the user to limit the time frame, and thereby eliminate references irrelevant to the purpose of the search. This is one of the drop-down options in Google advanced searching.

SOCIAL AND COMMERCIAL SEARCHING

Today's Internet features all types of sites supported by advertising and sales that aim to attract users not only as one-time buyers, but also as continual users. Web sites become communities where people carry on a variety of functions, stay logged on, communicate in a variety of modes, and share data in a number of different ways. Certain Web sites are in such common use that they count visitors per minute, hour, day, and month, as well as the registered members who constitute their customer base. Because some references to these sites (e.g., user true names) are indexed and included in search engine results (e.g., MySpace, Facebook, LinkedIn), it is possible that separate searching is unnecessary. However, the variety of activities online carried out over some of these sites suggest that they should be included in separate searches, especially if the purpose is to find anomalous, illicit, or otherwise derogatory behavior. In addition to those listed below, some of the Web sites in this category will be handled in a separate section of Chapter 16.

SOCIAL NETWORKING SITES

Some social networking Web sites have become so large that they must be considered as communities unto themselves, worth a separate search even though they are indexed by search engines. This is because a thorough search should include even the most recent postings (more recent than thirty days) and because content on these sites can change frequently. Rapid growth continued for almost all social sites in 2009–2010, including adoption of mobile versions for cell phone access. Growth in Internet use into 2010 included longer times on social networking sites and a shift from MySpace (the previous favorite) to Facebook (now by far the favorite). Facebook and MySpace together accounted for 96% of the social networking use.[22] The largest social Web sites that should be considered in searching are listed below.[23]

> Facebook has over 400 million registered users and over 60 million status updates posted daily, or 54% of U.S. Internet users, according to comScore in December 2009. Users sign in using an email address and password, and have multiple ways to share and post information, two levels of privacy settings, and a favored group of friends. True name searches can lead to Facebook profiles, whether conducted via Google or the Facebook Web site (because Facebook makes it easy to find and connect with friends, and friends of friends). To see more than the public profile, one must sign into Facebook (membership is free). Facebook also

offers applications and features that facilitate sharing a variety of interests, from short notes to photos to links and other content. Facebook's authorized use policy ("Terms" link at the bottom of the home page) states in part that a user will not employ an automated system to collect other users' information, and will obtain consent from users whose information is collected. An investigator can see the parts of a user's Facebook profile that the user has decided will be displayed to the public (i.e., not limited to exposure only within a chosen circle of friends). Whether it might be considered a violation of the Facebook terms for an investigator to collect posted information without the consent of the user remains an unanswered question. A public profile that can be viewed without logging onto Facebook carries no privacy protection, and a profile accessible when signed on may be available to 400 million people (a number one-third greater than the U.S. population—hardly what could be called "privacy protected").

YouTube (a Google property) hosts videos and currently holds massive numbers of postings, while serving millions of daily users uploading and viewing videos. The size of hosted content can be illustrated by a 2008 court case[24] in which a judge reportedly ordered YouTube to turn over about 12 terabytes of data documenting users' viewing habits to Viacom, which sued YouTube over unauthorized display of copyrighted materials, including 150,000 clips that had been viewed 1.5 billion times. While videos can be an important source of information and documentation of misbehavior, they are currently searched by keyword, title, or poster identity (usually a nickname), and not by matching video content, such as a facial image.

MySpace, formerly the largest social networking site, still hosts about 12 million daily visitors and 27% of 205,709,000 unique U.S. Internet users (according to comScore, December 2009). True name searches will find MySpace hits, but most MySpace users' profiles have nicknames. Nicknames can be handy for finding other Internet postings by the same person (i.e., by searching the nickname), but investigators must be careful, because there are some popular nicknames used by several or even many people. MySpace links users with friends and their profiles, has blogs, photos, and videos, and specializes in music and entertainment choices. Bands, musicians, and performers have MySpace promotional profiles. MySpace privacy and use policies[25] say that both members and visitors may not employ users' content without their permission, whether posted publicly or for a limited audience through privacy filters. However, free membership, most members' choice to display their content publicly, and indexing through search engines all mean that users should have no reasonable privacy expectations.

Twitter is the largest "micro-blogging platform," with over 54 million users, and reportedly sends most of its traffic to users' profiles on MySpace, Google, and Facebook, according to Hitwise. ComScore reported about 75 million worldwide visitors to Twitter's Web site in January 2010, 23.5 million of whom were Americans. As a Web site, Twitter ranks number twelfth, both globally and in the United States, with about 50 million tweets daily.[26] While many members receive tweets and follow others through the service, fewer send out tweets (the average Twitter user has twenty-seven followers).[27] Despite the limitation of 140 characters of text and public nature of tweets, people share some remarkably personal and revealing postings, including unflattering behaviors and statements. The Library of Congress recently decided to archive all public tweets.

LinkedIn, a business networking site, had over 43 million registered users in 170 industries as of the summer of 2009. LinkedIn profiles are written and posted by members (unlike most of those on sites like ZoomInfo.com and Plaxo.com, which harvest links and establish sometimes error-prone profiles using automation, as well as subscriber input). LinkedIn provides a number of services to subscribers, such as sharing contact information and photos of members, displaying resumes, finding marketing and business opportunities, and staying in touch with old colleagues. Analysts should carefully verify details of items that users post, but since they are the best source of their own background information and may depend on LinkedIn to find opportunities, there is logical support for the authoritative nature of profiles. LinkedIn profiles can be useful when little is known about a subject and more education and work history are needed as starting points. Like a resume or application, the LinkedIn profile requires verification.

Professional investigators are well advised to keep up with the less popular social networking sites that may also provide information, including the following:

Flickr (a Yahoo! property), a photo and video hosting site, has over 3.6 billion images. Like other photo display sites, "tagging" (linking a name/nickname to the photo or virtual album posted) allows searching of the images. Intelligence from photos can include establishing activities, associates, and misbehavior of interest.

Bebo is a site used by about 3% of U.S. Internet habitués, who can also use the site to collate postings from other popular sites.

Tagged is another social networking site that claims about 3% of U.S. Internet users.

Friendster.com claims to have 110 million users worldwide.[28]

Live Journal at http://www.LiveJournal.com claims to host 27 million journals and communities and about 162,000 postings daily, which theoretically can be found through search engines.

MyLife.com (formerly Reunion.com) claims 750 million profiles and the ability to help users find other people.

Hi5 claims 50 million monthly visitors and specializes in flirting.

Orkut is an online community owned by Google and popular in Brazil.

PerfSpot specializes in rating, reviewing, and sharing links.

Classmates.com is a fee-based school/military site that settled a deception class-action lawsuit in March 2010.

A separate category of popular Web sites concentrates on finding mates, significant others, dates, and sexual partners. These include eHarmony.com, Match.com, Yahoo! Personals, Chemistry, PerfectMatch, Lavalife, and others. Many different types of dating and friendship Web sites exist for niche groups, including ones based on religion, sexual orientation, ethnicity, national origin, international affairs ("Russian women," "Asian women"), biracial dating, wealth, and activity preferences. The AshleyMadison.com trademark is "Life is short. Have an affair." Most of these sites charge fees, require registration, and some claim to allow only those approved to become members. Many dating sites appear to cater to those seeking PG-rated social experiences, while others offer an X-rated approach. Generally, subjects who subscribe to dating Web sites do not use their true names, and their user names do not appear in search engine results.

As might be expected on the Internet, which still produces high profits for porn sites, there are quite a few Web sites that are focused on sex, porn, and "hookups" between people, both straight and gay. Most of these sites require membership and charge fees, while many generate spam, display false but enticing offers, include explicit content on their pages and in subscriber communications unsuitable for most workplaces, display online porn offers, and even act as hubs for identity theft. The home page of the adult type of site often contains views of nudity, sex acts, alternative lifestyles (e.g., bondage and discipline, fetishes, group sex), and other potentially controversial content. Display of such images and audio could be considered offensive and create a hostile work environment under Title VII of the Civil Rights Act.

Often, porn/adult Web sites seem to have an uncanny ability to see the browser user's location, as they display come-ons and pop-up ads featuring scantily clad or nude people tagged with a town near the user (matched through the IP address from the browser). Some porn sites generate cookies and open new browser windows with explicit content. Among the porn-social sites are AdultFriendFinder.com, XTube.com, Fling.com, WildMatch.com, even some links found on Craigslist.org, and many more. Some claim to be adult sex classified advertising. Some have been widely criticized (e.g., AdultFriendFinder) for fraudulent postings and links. Analysts need to consider whether to use a proxy server in accessing such sites (to shield the origin of the inquiry and protect the analyst's computer from malicious code and advertising from the porn sites). Registered users on adult sites use nicknames and postings that are not generally indexed by search engines unless they are also listed elsewhere online. Since adult sites may be venues for misbehavior, such as violating a company's authorized computer use policy, an investigator may need to sign up in order to search for a subject on a particular site.

Another category of Web site espouses or supports causes, advocacy, protests, and fundraising online, like Care2.com (which claims over 13 million members), Meetup.com (which hosts many different types of sites of affinity groups, causes, and protest groups), and Indymedia.org (which publishes stories and announcements about protesters' causes). Intelligence collectors may need to focus on this type of site if civil disobedience, vandalism, or violence is threatened against a person or entity. Examples of protest groups that have engaged in illicit activities, and have been accused of terrorist, animal rights, or ecoterrorist acts, include animal rights groups (e.g., WAROnline.org, SHAC.net, Animal Liberation Front—animalliberationpressoffice.org, animanliberationfront.com, DirectAction.info, People for the Ethical Treatment of Animals—PETA. org, StopAnimalTests.com) and environmental rights (Earth-Liberation-Front.org, OriginalELF.com, Protest.net). Other activism is focused on such causes as peace, antinuclear weapons/energy, anticorporate/

World Bank/International Monetary Fund, communist, socialist, Maoist, Islamist, Neo-Nazi, White Supremacist, gun rights, militias, and many others. Not all such causes, or their Web sites, espouse illegal activities to achieve their aims. However, planned activities such as demonstrations can include open invitations to individuals or groups that may engage in dangerous and illegal activities threatening business and government.

Some Web sites belong to organizations advocating for rights, such as privacy advocates like Electronic Frontier Foundation (eff.org), Electronic Privacy Information Center (epic.org), and Center for Democracy and Technology (cdt.org). There are many others, of course, including political parties' Web sites and their support groups, as well as think tanks, major nonprofits, and other nongovernmental and nonprofit organizations. While many pages of these sites are indexed, it may be necessary to search them directly, to access documents referring to a subject that appear only in unindexed databases on the sites.

E-COMMERCE SITES

Certain e-commerce (online sales) Web sites have become so popular that they have captured vast audiences of Internet users from print and broadcast media, catalog/telephone sales, and retail outlets. Of course, the major retailers like Wal-Mart, Sears/Kmart/Lands End, Costco, Target, Macy's, Nordstrom, etc., all have useful online sales sites. In addition, some major corporations, particularly high-tech firms, have mastered Internet marketing of their products, such as Cisco, Dell, HP, Microsoft, Intuit (QuickBooks, TurboTax), Adobe, and others, many of which conduct the bulk of their sales online. Some pages of commercial Web sites may be indexed, but in a thorough search, it may be important to include a query on these Web sites:

> eBay and its companion site PayPal are the quintessential classified sales and payment processors on the U.S. Internet. Many businesses have been built around their services, which include a measure of anonymity for users. Nicknames of users may be based on email addresses or user names appearing in other places. Finding an eBay account may allow an analyst to detect activities such as selling items deemed inappropriate (e.g., items apparently from work, like the individual we once found who was selling t-shirts and memorabilia from the TV show where he was a technician,

or the girlfriend of a manufacturing company employee found selling items from her boyfriend's factory that had not yet been placed on sale to the public). While eBay's AUP does not allow illicit sales, it has powerful legal and security staffs who help law enforcement deal with persistent sales of stolen, contraband, and improperly offered merchandise, and sellers who take money without providing products. PayPal has grown to offer commercial and credit card as well as small-scale personal payments. Most PayPal accounts link to a user's credit card or bank account as their foundational funding source. PayPal members can "bill" each other or outsiders with an email that facilitates a transaction over PayPal. Investigators frequently must conduct a transaction to elicit identifying information about an eBay or PayPal user.

Skype, a company founded by Estonian technologists, was bought and subsequently sold off by eBay, and is an example of an Internet service offering communications capabilities to anyone with an Internet connection and host device. Skype is a massive peer-to-peer telecommunications network, offering free software, free computer-to-computer (or even Internet phone) telephone calls, video teleconferencing, instant messaging, and a degree of privacy. The privacy comes from the fact that packets sent from Skype software carrying voice or data travel over the Internet through other Skype users' computers, and the packets themselves are privacy protected. This makes interception of Skype communications through a host's routers difficult if not impossible, and even if the packet stream is intercepted, it may not be comprehensible. Skype users employ nicknames as well as true names for accounts. Skype also offers low-cost telecommunications services, both nationally and internationally, that connect with wire-line and wireless telecommunications carriers. Reverse directories do not usually list the subscribers to Skype telephone numbers. Some spam and automated solicitations slip past Skype's filters. Since the user chooses the area code of a Skype-issued telephone number, it may not be an indication of the subscriber's actual place of residence.

Craigslist is a very large, localized, free classified advertising service that allows postings in a variety of types of listings clustered in regional geographical areas. Many types of resale personal items, notices, and service offerings appear on Craigslist. Like eBay, some illicit activities (such as prostitution and sale of contraband) may be detectable on Craigslist. Users communicate through an anonymizing email relay interface, or post their own email address or telephone number.

Amazon is a large Internet bookstore that has become a one-stop shopping Web site with some social networking features. Using their account logon, patrons can rate a book, publication, or other products, tagging such postings with a true name or nickname. Some users post frequently, providing insight into their views, reading/shopping habits, and personalities. Amazon's Kindle is an example of an electronic reader that has an Internet connection and allows a variety of activities with published materials. Other e-books available from Sony, Apple, Barnes & Noble, etc., enable a variety of reading options and Internet communications, some of which are hosted as well on smart cell phones, as well as larger platforms. Based on the popularity of its iPhone, Apple (and its imitators) offers many types of networking applications on a cell-Internet platform, and the next-generation iPad foreshadows continued evolution in networking. Among these are geolocation-based services that allow users to connect, communicate, or query based on where they are. Fierce competition is ongoing from Google, Microsoft, and cell phone manufacturers. Since multiple types of Internet-based services and social networking are meshed in these platforms, searchers should anticipate that further development of these devices will continue to provide opportunities for intelligence on their users.

DIRECTORIES

Web directories have provided a vital resource for many years, giving an encyclopedic list of topics in every major category and subcategory area, with links to sources. Open Directory Project, a free service (http://www.dmoz.org/), is the prime example of a resource where subject matter experts ("volunteer editors") have listed the best places for a user to find information on the chosen topic. Varieties of commercial directories are also available, such as Yahoo!. In some cases, the sites listed provide a fee to the Web site providing the directory. Perusing the catalog of topics can help put a researcher on the right track toward information of a certain type. In addition, looking at a site like Yahoo! Directory can assist the analyst in finding the major sources on a topic, since presumably the repositories have been screened for their value and quality.

Many Internet users are accustomed to Googling a roughly worded question, almost as an impulse when seeking information. One weakness of this approach is that in order to increase the speed of the process, the user has not surveyed the topic, formulated the question carefully, or found the primary sources of the type of information sought. The user with blind faith in the search engine's algorithms is willing to accept whatever comes up in the first two pages (ten to twenty results) that Google provides. It is a remarkable tribute to search engines that they so often provide answers "close enough" to what the user needs (or thinks he or she needs). When it's the local bicycle shop, restaurant, or product shopping, these quick searches fit the bill. However, they are decidedly insufficient qualitatively or quantitatively for the serious investigator.

The online directory allows a researcher to zoom in on a topic from the atmosphere down to ground level, surveying the landscape from various heights to ensure that key resources will not escape notice. As searchers gain experience and develop rich lists of favorite Web sites, the directory may no longer be as useful. Yet it still pays to know the topic, especially if it is unfamiliar to the analyst.

Online versions of free telephone directories are quite useful for identifying and locating individuals, including PeopleFinders.com, Zabasearch.com, Daplus.us, WhitePages.com, and AnyWho.com. By getting to know what types of name-based and reverse directory information are provided for free, it is often possible for the analyst to verify contact and basic biographical information about a person or description of an entity. Many online directories also link to fee-based services. In general, fee-based services provide data that are potentially useful, but must be verified to avoid errors, and could be relatively costly if the analyst escalates the extent of information requested for progressively higher fees. One annoying aspect of some fee-based directories is that they promise to provide data (e.g., identification of the subscriber to a telephone number, profile of a person) by suggesting that the facts "are in our database." When the user requests the data, they may or may not contain the type or extent of detail promised, and may be inaccurate or dated.

BLOGS

Weblogs or "blogs" have evolved from commercial and personal online publishing and social chat functions. Blog sites encourage readers to comment on postings, write their own publications, follow topics and writers of choice online, and create new expressions of art, knowledge, guidance, commentary, news, formal and informal communications, and interest group notifications (among others). Blogs are so numerous (almost 127 million online, according to Nielsen) that in almost any specialty area, it is difficult to keep up with their comings and goings and the fora influential on the topics discussed. Those writing blogs and commenting often use pseudonyms or nicknames that must be searched in order to find what is published, and must be matched with true identities. Blog sites offer free hosting and help users create essentially their own Web sites, which are sometimes refereed and sometimes unmonitored. Rants, comments, and postings can at times get crude and controversial. Almost any contentious issue will appear in the blogosphere. Finding postings by a subject can reveal strong personal feelings, demonstrate writing ability, and illustrate a subject's maturity, judgment, and discretion (or lack thereof).

Keyword searching for blogs is facilitated by Web sites[29] such as the following:

- BlogSearch.google.com is Google's all-around blog search engine, offering email alerts, a "blog search gadget" for a Google home page, and a blog search feed in Google reader.
- IceRocket at http://www.icerocket.com/ provides blog and Web searching, tracking and other tools, and includes Twitter and MySpace in its searches.
- Technorati.com provides blog searching tools and tracks the top one hundred bloggers.
- BlogPulse at http://www.blogpulse.com/ is a Nielsen property that allows blog searches.

CHAT

Online chat rooms are nothing more than Web sites that allow users to type in text messages, monitor others' exchanges ("lurk"), and follow specific topics, general areas of interest, or whatever users decide to post. Most chat content is not indexed or archived, but users can decide to copy and save dialogues, forward them, and quote them at will. There is no expectation of privacy in chat rooms, but each chat room has its own rules about participation, expected behaviors, and privacy, which are strictest for sites designed for teens and children. Usually, even in the strictest of chat rooms, the only penalty for violating such rules is expulsion. Many chats are monitored (censored), but many are not. Today's chat evolved from Internet Relay Chat (IRC), which developed before the modern Internet as a method for researchers using networked systems to exchange messages and discuss ideas.[30] IRC channels exist among groups of users who consider themselves different from the great mass of Internet users. Among those still using IRC are computer programmers, hackers/crackers, peer-to-peer network relay aficionados, adult/porn sites (e.g., live video with text), gangs and criminal groups, as well as many types of innocent users. Webcams, cell phones, and other devices allow multiple group connections for chats within simultaneous chats. Some chats include voice exchanges, in either large or small groups. It appears that generally, legacy forms of chat are giving way to other methods of online brief communications, including instant messaging (which can spontaneously connect two or more participants), conference calling, and Twitter.

Investigators may find themselves in chat rooms in such circumstances as monitoring adults seeking to lure children into sexual activities or tracing illicit activities involving hardware, software, movies, videos, and music. In such cases, capturing the content of chat is important, and searching for keywords may not be possible outside the Web site. Chat room users may choose an identifier unique to the site, or use an online ID established already (e.g., for Yahoo!, which hosts chat rooms at http://messenger.yahoo.com/features/chatrooms).

Examples of popular chat rooms,[31] some free and some fee based, some requiring software for advanced features, are AOL chat (peopleconnection.aol.com), Babel.com, Talkcity.com, ICQ (mirabilis.com), Teenspot.com, PalTalk.com, ShoutMix.com, and TeenChat.com. Many others specialize in dating, flirting, matchmaking, affinity groups, nationalities, and multiple services like those offered by Yahoo! and AOL.

Additional search tools and strategies appear in the next chapter.

NOTES

1. HTML introduction, http://www.w3schools.com/html/html_intro.asp (accessed June 1, 2010).
2. Java by Sun, now part of Oracle, http://www.java.com/en/ (accessed June 1, 2010).
3. Flash Player by Adobe, http://get.adobe.com/flashplayer/ (accessed June 1, 2010).

4. ASCII, http://www.webopedia.com/TERM/A/ASCII.htm (accessed June 1, 2010).
5. InterNIC Domain Name System tutorial, http://www.internic.net/faqs/authoritative-dns.html (accessed June 1, 2010).
6. IP address tutorial, http://computer.howstuffworks.com/internet/basics/question549.htm (accessed June 1, 2010); network packet structure tutorial, http://computer.howstuffworks.com/question525.htm (accessed June 1, 2010).
7. Digital signature (and digital certificate, public key infrastructure) defined, http://searchsecurity.techtarget.com/sDefinition/0,,sid14_gci211953,00.html (accessed June 1, 2010).
8. Browser definition, http://www.webopedia.com/TERM/B/browser.html (accessed June 1, 2010).
9. Abbas, "Internet Explorer Market Share Will Drop Below 50% by 2011. Chrome Growing Strongly!" February 1, 2010, http://tnerd.com/2010/02/01/internet-explorer-market-share-will-drop-below-50-by-2011-chrome-growing-strongly/ (accessed April 18, 2010).
10. Malicious code (NIST definition), http://csrc.nist.gov/publications/nistir/threats/section3_3.html (accessed June 1, 2010).
11. "How Google Works," http://www.google.com/howgoogleworks/ (accessed June 1, 2010).
12. Boutell.com estimated the number of Web pages in 2007 at about 30 billion, based on an average of 273 pages per site on 70.4 million Web sites. Based on the same average number of pages for the 206,675,938 Web sites counted by Netcraft in March 2010, a reasonable estimate of the number of Web pages in 2010 would be 56,422,531,074; http://www.boutell.com/newfaq/misc/sizeofweb.html and http://news.netcraft.com/archives/web_server_survey.html (both accessed June 1, 2010).
13. Boulton, Clint, "Search Engines: Bing Rallies to 11.7% Search Share as Google Clings to 65%." eWeek.com, based on a comScore report, April 9, 2010, http://www.eweek.com/c/a/Search-Engines/Bing-Rallies-to-117-Search-Share-as-Google-Clings-to-65-688653/.
14. Dornfest, Rael, Bausch, Paul, and Calishain, Tara, *Google Hacks*, 3rd ed. (Sebastopol, CA: O'Reilly Media, 2006).
15. Op. cit.
16. Yahoo! search, http://tools.search.yahoo.com/about/ (accessed August 21, 2010).
17. Briggs, Josh, "How Microsoft Bing Works," http://computer.howstuffworks.com/internet/basics/microsoft-bing.htm (accessed August 21, 2010).
18. About Ask.com, http://about.ask.com/en/docs/about/index.shtml (accessed August 21, 2010).
19. Descriptions are from the search engines themselves. Prescott, Lee Ann, "Social Networking by the Numbers," Principal, Research-Write, December 2009, http://www.slideshare.net/laprescott/social-networking-by-the-numbers-december-2009 (accessed April 10, 2010).

195

20. Sherman, Chris, "Metacrawlers and Metasearch Engines," Search Engine Watch, March 23, 2005, http://searchenginewatch.com/2156241 (accessed June 1, 2010).
21. Op. cit.
22. Pingdom, "Internet 2009 in Numbers," posted January 22, 2010, http://royal.pingdom.com/2010/01/22/internet-2009-in-numbers/ (accessed June 1, 2010).
    Web sites:
      • 234 million—the number of Web sites as of December 2009
      • 47 million—added Web sites in 2009
23. Social and business networking site statistics are those published by the sites themselves, except where other sources are cited. Online social networking is expanding. In December 2009, there were 248 million unique monthly users on the top eight social networking sites (SNSs) in the United States, an increase of 41% from January 2009. Mintel finds that 61% of Internet users have a profile on at least one SNS, up from 41% a year before. Marketing spend on SNS increased 166% from 2007, reaching $2.4 billion in 2009, and is becoming an increasingly important way to reach a young, often hard-to-reach audience; http://www.researchandmarkets.com/product/c49539/social_networking_in_the_united_states_2010 (accessed August 21, 2010). Social networking site reviews were accessed on April 10, 2010 at http://social-networking-websites-review.toptenreviews.com.
24. Helft, Miguel, "Google Told to Turn Over User Data of YouTube," *New York Times*, July 4, 2008.
25. MySpace terms, http://www.myspace.com/index.cfm?fuseaction=misc.terms (accessed April 2, 2010).
26. Wilhelm, Alex, "Twitter Statistics: The Full Picture," February 22, 2010, http://thenextweb.com/socialmedia/2010/02/22/twitter-statistics-full-picture/ (accessed April 10, 2010); Maris, Dagis, "Twitter Statistics of User Engagement," January 29, 2010, http://www.socialtimes.com/2010/01/twitter-statistics-of-user-engagement/?red=rb (accessed April 10, 2010).
27. CNN Money, March 10, 2010: 50 million Twitter user accounts, most of whom follow others rather than posting their own content, http://money.cnn.com/2010/03/10/technology/twitter_users_active/ (accessed September 24, 2010).
28. Friendster is at http://www.friendster.com/info/index.php (accessed April 10, 2010).
29. Descriptions were obtained from the Web sites themselves.
30. IRC descriptions may be found at http://irchelp.org/ and http://www.livinginternet.com/r/r.htm (both accessed June 1, 2010).
31. Ibid.

16

Finding Sources

Thousands of Web sites offer access to government records and other types of public information compiled by agencies, nonprofits, news organizations, and commercial enterprises. Investigators should remember that as with other published materials, verification is necessary before accepting any record as fact, and before assuming that when a record is not found in an online database, it does not exist. In all probability, even a very thorough search will not include absolutely every database that could contain a record of the subject. However, by maintaining an up-to-date, complete list of URLs and searches, the analyst can credibly assert that a search was as thorough as possible. Not all government records are offered online, not all online are offered free, and it is not always possible to obtain identifiable records, because many records offer only a name to match, without other identifying data to verify that it is the same person as the subject.

It is appropriate to spend a moment on disclaimers, which are found with virtually all databases. Disclaimers generally say that the agency or entity hosting the database is not responsible for any errors, and use of the data found is the responsibility and at the risk of the user. Some disclaimers sound like they were written for software (disclaiming liability for any damage or failure to perform as indicated). If the implicit threats we read in this type of disclaimer were true, then the database would have little value, like software that would not work in your computer. Yet we should not depend on data that may contain errors (and have little choice but to trust the software). The solution is to be careful to verify relevant facts found in records, and to understand that even a fairly low percentage of risk in the accuracy of data or functioning of the database must be excluded by hosts that are in the business of government, and not in the business of providing irrefutable information online. When data found online may be the basis for action, the analyst should be careful not only to present the data with any caveats deemed necessary under the relevant laws (e.g., Fair Credit Reporting Act), policies, and guidelines, but also to point to any next steps needed to confirm the data.

The sources cited below are among those that have proven most productive for my practice.

U.S. GOVERNMENT

U.S. government information is increasingly available online because of e-government initiatives of the last several administrations, beginning in Clinton's time (1993–present). After September 11, 2001, access to some online records was modified, to ensure that operational security of the government would not be jeopardized by allowing terrorists to use the records for attacks. Another trend in recent years has been to remove identifiers (date of birth, social security number, address) from records made available online, in an effort to protect people against identity theft and misuse of personal information. However, there are incredible amounts of data in public records still available online, for free. An invaluable resource to find U.S. records is usa. gov, through which many different types of databases can be found.[1]

Among the useful U.S. government sites for finding misbehavior by people and entities are

PACER (http://pacer.uspci.uscourts.gov/) provides access to most federal criminal, civil, and bankruptcy court records. Users must register and pay eight cents per page.

The U.S. Court of Federal claims is accessible at http://www.uscfc. uscourts.gov/.

U.S. Tax Court dockets can be searched at http://www.ustaxcourt. gov/UstcDockInq/asp/SearchPartyOptions.asp.

The Excluded Parties List System (https://www.epls.gov/) allows the user to search for those excluded from government contracts.

The Treasury Department's Office of Foreign Assets Control provides the Specially Designated Nationals and Blocked Persons List of those cited for trade sanctions for economic, national security, and foreign policy reasons, which can be found at http://www.treas.gov/offices/enforcement/ofac/sdn/.

The U.S. Department of Commerce, Bureau of Industry and Security, publishes a Denied Persons List at http://www.bis.doc.gov/dpl/thedeniallist.asp.

The U.S. Customs' Rulings Online Search System is available at http://rulings.cbp.gov/index.asp.

The Securities and Exchange Commission enforcement actions are available at http://www.sec.gov/divisions/enforce/enforceactions.shtml.

The Department of Health and Human Services' excluded individuals and entities search is available at http://exclusions.oig.hhs.gov/, and fraud enforcement at http://oig.hhs.gov/fraud.asp, while Public Health Service and Federal Drug Administration sanctions can be found at http://silk.nih.gov/public/cbz1bje.@www.orilist.html. HHS also lists names of those defaulting on student loans at http://defaulteddocs.dhhs.gov/name.asp.

The State Department posts lists of foreign terrorist organizations at http://www.state.gov/s/ct/rls/other/des/123085.htm, and terrorists excluded from the United States at http://www.state.gov/s/ct/rls/other/des/123086.htm.

The Justice Department has provided a nationwide list of registered sexual offenders that interacts with state and territorial lists at http://www.nsopw.gov/Core/Conditions.aspx?AspxAutoDetectCookieSupport=1.

The Bureau of Federal Prisons has an inmate list available at http://www.bop.gov/inmate_locator/index.jsp.

Other agencies offering online postings of enforcement activities include the Occupational Safety and Health Administration (OSHA) and the National Labor Relations Board (NLRB).

The Patent and Trademark Office offers search options on its site at http://www.uspto.gov/, but often search engines will find references to a patent's inventor recorded by commercial firms.

STATE, COUNTY, AND LOCAL GOVERNMENTS

State, county, and local government information also can be found online, as agencies scan and load records into databases to make operations more efficient, and to comply with open government laws and regulations. It is important to remember that many government agencies struggle with the cost and complexity of compiling and maintaining records, and automation has not gone smoothly at some. Vital records such as births, deaths, marriages, and the like have been transitioned from paper to computers, but agencies hosting such records have relied on fees to offset the costs of maintenance and staffing. Therefore, it is not unusual for agencies to charge users a fee for a search, for records retrieval, and for a certified copy of the record—even though the record must be publicly available by law. Some jurisdictions charge more than others, some require a subscription or account for access, and many opt to provide records through selected contractors or automation providers such as LexisNexis.

A handy Web site for locating online government records is provided by BRB Publications at http://www.brbpub.com/default.asp and http://www.publicrecordsources.com/. Licenses can be found at http://www.verifyprolicense.com/, from the same publisher. Links help the searcher to find the right county for an address, free online public records, and research companies that will retrieve records from a courthouse or government office for a fee, and list publications to help searchers learn about how different types of records are accessed and kept. Each state, county, and municipality may have different standards and access rules, although many states have attempted to allow searches of all county court records through a single state Web portal. It is prudent to spend a few minutes determining what types of online records a state or geographical government may offer, because the records could include the subject of inquiry, more are available online than ever before, and more come online frequently. Reference works such as Heatherington and Sankey's *The Manual to Online Public Records*, which provides a state-by-state listing with URLs, can be helpful, but no sooner do such books go into print than some of the records offered, or the URLs, change.[2] Among the types of records that may be of use when posted are

- Vital records (birth, death, marriage, divorce)
- Criminal and court records (including civil, family, and traffic courts)
- Sexual offender registry
- Corporation, company, and commercial entity registrations
- Uniform Commercial Code (UCC) records
- Real estate property, assessment, and tax records
- Worker's compensation records
- Driver records

- Vehicle and vessel ownership and registration
- Accident reports
- Occupational licensing (usually handled by separate boards for each specialty)
- Prison inmates and incarceration records
- Tax delinquencies and auctions
- Voter registration

Sometimes a local record might surprise you with an unexpected posting. For example, we found a "most wanted" poster displayed online by a small municipal police force, stating that our subject was wanted for fraud. It was interesting to find the posting, and the crime *had* been committed by the subject. We knew that because months before the online posting, the subject had appeared in court and pled guilty to the fraud charges. In fact, the subject had finished serving his sentence by the time the wanted poster was found online. This instance illustrates the fact that an analyst must be careful to weigh all the facts found in postings, and to assess not only their relevance but their timeliness and reliability, before reporting the instance as found. It is also prudent to include analyst comments when there is doubt, uncertainty, or lack of accuracy in any aspect of the findings reported.

OTHER GOVERNMENT-RELATED SOURCES

The World Bank posts a debarment list (disallowed contractors) at http://web.worldbank.org/external/default/main?theSitePK=842 66&contentMDK=64069844&menuPK=116730&pagePK=64148989 &piPK=64148984.

The POGO Web site posts a list of federal contractors alleged to have engaged in misconduct at http://www.contractormisconduct. org/. This database contains some well-known, large companies.

Health Guide USA has links to each state's medical license databases to allow verification for physicians' credentials at http://www. healthguideusa.org/medical_license_lookup.htm.

Guide Star lists nonprofit entities in a searchable database (with registration required for details) at http://www2.guidestar.org/ Home.aspx.

A private company offers to validate social security numbers. When a social security number is entered at http://www.ssnvalidator.

com/, the system verifies that its user is not deceased and provides the approximate date and state of issuance.

Active military and veterans of the armed forces can be found on a variety of Web sites, including http://www.military.com/buddy-finder/, http://www.publicrecordfinder.com/military.html, http://www.military-search.com/, and http://www.searchmil.com/. Some of these sites include ads from fee-based people search services.

A telephone directory of federal employees is online at http://www.info.gov/phone.htm.

The Council on Licensure, Enforcement and Regulation has a directory of professional regulatory boards and colleges online at http://www.clearhq.org/Default.aspx?pageId=481138.

BUSINESS-RELATED SOURCES

A variety of information sources about businesses provide online access to profiles, including corporate filings in the SEC's EDGAR database at http://www.sec.gov/edgar.shtml. For private lists of profiles, Hoover's at http://www.hoovers.com/, Dun & Bradstreet at http://sbs.dnb.com/webapp/wcs/stores/servlet/SmbHome?storeId=10001, and the Better Business Bureau at http://www.bbb.org/us/Find-Business-Reviews/ are good sources. Other options include the http://biznar.com/biznar/ "deep web business search," http://us.kompass.com/, which list millions of businesses, and Yahoo! business directory (which includes company Web sites) at http://dir.yahoo.com/Business_and_Economy/Directories/Companies/. A manifestation of user-provided information on businesses and people is the Web site http://www.corporationwiki.com/, and http://www.wikipedia.org/ is also apt to have information posted on businesses. Caution should be exercised in using a wiki as a primary source of data, because by its nature, a wiki allows collaborative editing and creation of postings by anyone, which can make a wiki's content suspect. The level of review and verification provided for posted materials, including source citations, is primary evidence of credibility.

There are Web sites devoted to messages and forums for those following corporations' stock value and business development, including the message board hosted by Yahoo! at http://messages.finance.yahoo.com/mb/YHOO. Postings are usually by nickname, preserving the anonymity of the writers, and sometimes feature scathing criticism, and even insider revelations (which can bedevil corporations and pose legal risks). Another site with business message boards that can occasionally include vitriolic criticisms of businesses is RagingBull.com, and numerous blogs and chat rooms include business-related commentary. Several Web sites are like a cross between yellow pages and business profile repositories, hosting data that are created from other Web sites (often from the businesses' own Web sites). An example is Manta.com, which claims to list over 22 million U.S. businesses. Details of business profiles that are found through Google searches should be verified, because they may come from the business itself or Internet postings from nonauthoritative sources.

Some Web sites cater to ratings of employers, such as JobVent.com, where employees may praise or pan their workplace, usually using pseudonyms. The Motley Fool (Fool.com) focuses on stocks and users, like those on Yahoo! message boards, entertaining not only straight news items but also commentary (sometimes quite critical) about companies and their leaders.

NEWS

Many current and several-year-old news items are likely to be found by search engines. However, these only scratch the surface of potential news media references to a subject. For many years, news archiving and retrieval services have offered searching by subscription, including Dialog.com, Nexis.com, ThompsonReuters.com, and Factiva.com. Free news references can be found on News.Google.com and News.Yahoo.com. Major newspapers and news Web sites also offer archival searches, many charging a fee for full texts of stories. Current (e.g., last two weeks) stories are usually available for free. Magazines, journals, and other publications increasingly can be retrieved, but possibly through pay-as-you-go sites or by subscription. Some major news sites are searchable by comprehensive, automated search engines like Copernic.com (which now owns Mama.com, a metasearch engine). More on Copernic appears in the next chapter.

A successful strategy for finding references to persons and businesses in smaller communities and suburbs is to search for news media Web sites in the municipality, county, region, and state where the subject is located, and in the subject matter area of the subject's work or hobby. This search should include educational institutions' publications as well as commercial news sites. Events such as newsworthy awards, arrests, achievements, lawsuits, family deaths, graduations, etc., may appear in news media reports and verify or reveal known or new facts about the subject. At http://dir.yahoo.com/news_and_media/ and http://www.dmoz.org/News/, a researcher can find media outlets that should be considered as potential sources of stories that may or may not be indexed by the major search engines.

WEB 2.0

From Wikipedia (a good example of Web 2.0):

> The term "Web 2.0" (2004–present) is commonly associated with web applications that facilitate interactive information sharing, interoperability, user-centered design, and collaboration on the World Wide Web. Examples of Web 2.0 include web-based communities, hosted services, web applications, social networking sites, video-sharing sites, wikis, blogs, mashups, and folksonomies. A Web 2.0 site allows its users to interact with other users or to change Web site content, in contrast to non-interactive Web sites where users are limited to the passive viewing of information that is provided to them.[3]

Mashups are services that combine data or functionality from two or more services, and "folksonomy is a system of classification derived from the practice and method of collaboratively creating and managing tags to annotate and categorize content" (links and footnote removed).[4]

What makes Web 2.0 useful from the investigator's standpoint is that applications, Web sites, and interactive communications (including mobile, instant messaging [IM] and mashups) all not only allow extended networking and communications, but also enable investigators to track subjects in many new ways. Some of the new Web sites offering Web 2.0 features also enable a user to track other users (e.g., Trackle.com, Monitter.com, and Friendfeed.com). When added to the formidable functionality in Google alerts (Google.com/alerts), it is possible to find information about current activities of someone online, especially when the subject actively posts updates on popular Web sites and is "tracked" by others. When an individual poses a threat, is investigated for ongoing criminal activities, or (unfortunately) is stalked by a malevolent person, these applications enable a type of surveillance previously unknown. Two aspects of these rather new Web 2.0 features are that the implications of usage are not known to substantial percentages of users (thus creating vulnerabilities

they are unaware of), and the average user may be divulging information to the public at large that is neither prudent nor well understood.
The popularity of Web 2.0 (exemplified by the hundreds of millions of
users of Facebook, MySpace, and Twitter, to name just three Web sites)[5]
is a primary reason why personnel security must consider employee and
candidate activities online, because so many people define themselves by
online activities.

An intelligence or investigative collector employing Web 2.0 should
find out the "handles" used by subjects of interest for their postings and
communications. Often, these handles also appear in email addresses, profiles, and frequently in Twitter and similar IM services. It is not unusual
for an individual to use the same handle for multiple Web 2.0 services.
It is also normal for several Web sites to list the person's true name in
conjunction with the handle, especially on social networking sites. A key
goal in the initial stages of any Internet investigation is to find all available
virtual identities of the subject, because of the additional data that could
be available, and the possibility that the added information may not be
available without all the subject's handles. While some HR departments
have avoided searching social networking sites on applicants for ethical
reasons (actually, legal doubt), there is a good reason to search them: They
link a true name (which may not appear in their profile, but nevertheless
leads to their profile) with a user name, nickname, or handle seen elsewhere. This type of handle is a virtual alias on the public Internet, and
should be treated as such.

Among the more productive postings from today's Web sites are blogs
and mashed up social networking entries. Today the likelihood that an
individual will be documented in illicit, socially unacceptable, or otherwise derogatory behaviors is much higher due to the proliferation of Web
2.0 services, because the quantity of casual, unguarded content attributable to individuals has increased considerably. On the other hand, the
proclivity for users to engage in joking, exaggeration, jargon, and double
entendre could easily confuse and mislead an observer.

In discussing the value of collaborative tools on the Internet, Navy
Department Chief Information Officer Rob Carey said in a blog post on
March 26, 2010:[6]

> Of course, with access comes the responsibility to ensure that certain
> measures are taken to keep our networks and our people safe. To that
> end, users must protect their information online, be aware of who and
> what they interact with, and abide by existing regulations on ethics,
> operational security and privacy.

CIO Carey recognizes the value of online collaboration for the Navy, and the U.S. Armed Forces have developed several Web 2.0 applications to enable efficiencies within the services. However, he also recognizes that individual users must play a role in the protection of data, secure computing, and privacy protection in order to ensure that the vulnerabilities do not outweigh the strengths of new collaborative tools.

Web 2.0 has become a rather amorphous term for online services enabled to optimize networking. Naturally, searches have followed the path of those desiring to find and connect with their friends and contacts online. In large part, services and searching have migrated from desktops to laptops to handheld computers and cell phones, many of which are enabled with multiple networks, both wired and wireless, photo and video capabilities (transmission enabled), and connected via literally thousands of intermeshed applications to automate the mobile, ever-connected user. What these functions may mean for users, their employers, and their colleagues is a rapidly evolving series of policy, privacy and social/behavioral questions.[7] However, as millions of users flock to the latest services, they create both intelligence collection opportunities and the reasons for such collection.

Following is a list of some Web 2.0 search tools that can provide good results when mastered by the investigator:

Trackle.com (beta) provides social network, blog, and consumer site searching, with alerts, and premium service offers tracking helpful for investigators focused on keeping updated on subjects and keywords as they appear online.

Monitter.com searches and tracks Twitter.

Yoname.com searches email addresses, first and last names, user names, and phone numbers.

Friendfeed.com searches social networking sites, blogs, and other sites.

Yauba.com claims to be a "privacy safe" real-time search engine for the Internet and social sites.

Searching Twitter with http://search.twitter.com/ promises "right now" postings.

Other "real time" searches can be conducted on Oneriot.com, Scoopler.com, Crowdeye.com, Addictomatic.com, and Collecta.com, which include RSS feeds, blog postings, Twitter, Flickr, social networking sites, and news.

An example of the potential value for investigators of correlating social networking postings to identify individuals and discover behaviors is illustrated by a study reported in 2009 by Arvind Narayanan and Dr. Vitaly Shmatikov, from the University of Texas at Austin,[8] who developed an algorithm by which they identified the names and addresses of anonymous Twitter, Flickr, and Live Journal users by looking at relationships between all the members of a social network—not just the immediate friends connected with members. They found that one-third of those who are on both Flickr and Twitter can be identified from the completely anonymous Twitter graph, despite the fact that the overlap of members between the two services is thought to be about 15%. The researchers suggest that the more social network sites are used, the more difficult it will become to remain anonymous.[9]

Many of the Web 2.0 sites above are useful for finding people[10] and major stolen items, monitoring brands, protecting intellectual property, discovering slanderous or otherwise troublesome postings about a company or brand, and many other similar uses. Some can unearth employees in the act of embezzling, theft, and unauthorized disclosures. Law firms often focus before and during trial on the witnesses and evidence to be used (as is appropriate), oblivious to the fact that witnesses, stakeholders, interested parties, and even jurors may be using the Internet to post both relevant and irrelevant items, both appropriate and inappropriate comments, and sometimes postings that may have a material impact on the trial. Preparing to depose or examine a witness on the stand can be strengthened by reviewing what the witness said about the topic or related issues that may well appear online. Posted materials can help impeach testimony or steer a cross-examination away from an area where the witness's likely answers might hurt the attorney's case. If one side in a case reviews Internet postings, but the other does not, there could be an advantage. Public sector witnesses have been blindsided when defense lawyers' searches have found online materials used to question the objectivity of their testimony.[11] Some lawyers who are Internet-savvy scan for postings related to their cases, but this useful practice has yet to catch on with the legal profession as a whole.

LOOKING UP SUBSCRIBERS

Often, an investigator will discover a telephone number, address, Internet Protocol (IP) address (i.e., the string of numbers identifying a Web site), URL, or other identifying information that needs to be connected with the individual or organization of interest. People who post illicit materials online using anonymous virtual identities are pursued by stakeholders, for example. A variety of resources and search strategies exist for the investigator.

Telephone numbers and addresses can be found in crisscross directories. Some of our favorites include

PeopleFinders.com allows searches by name, address, phone, email, social security number, and an advanced (multifacet) search.

Zabasearch.com provides name and telephone number searching, and free results may include the approximate date of birth and date of data capture.

Daplus.us (Info USA) and Whitepages.com provide name, business, address, and telephone number lookups, and sponsors have links offering more data for a fee.

AnyWho.com is AT&T's national white and yellow pages and reverse lookup directory.

Similar services to those listed above can be found on 411locate. com, addresses.com, people.yahoo.com, switchboard.com, and ussearch.com (which offers fee-based added information) and other sites.

When using online white and yellow pages, it is important to remember that misspellings, inaccurate (e.g., outdated) references, and other errors appear in free listings. In addition, unlisted telephone numbers (and the proliferation of unlisted cell phones as primary or sole numbers) have made it more difficult to obtain primary contact information for some subjects. Likewise, rural towns where post office boxes are preferred over residential mailboxes may impede finding or verifying a name-address combination. When crisscross directories like those suggested fail to provide sufficient information, real estate records may be an alternative. Sites like http://www.netronline.com/ may be helpful in finding free online listings provided by counties, some of which can be searched by address, name, etc. For example, an investigator starting with a name or an address could find the mailing address, owners' names, property description, and taxes of many homes in the United States.

Web sites are frequently a focus of Internet intelligence interest. Unfortunately, because of spam, many Web site owners hide their contact information through anonymization services provided by Web site hosts. Large services like GoDaddy.com, ThePlanet.com, 1and1.com, FatCow. com, NetworkSolutions.com, Microsoft, and Yahoo! offer a variety of options for Web site owners, from registration of the domain name to shared or exclusive use of servers, site certificates, sales checkout, credit card merchant services, etc. Design and maintenance of Web site content are often done by outsourced contractors, including the host companies. It is important to know how to look up domain name ownership, IP address, and other Web site attributes, so that those active on the Web can be profiled accurately. This is generally known by the term *Whois* lookup.

Several services offering Whois tracing include

SamSpade.org

http://domains.whois.com/domain.php?action=whois (requires human user)

http://www.betterwhois.com/ (claims to be more accurate)

DomainTools.com (provides current, deleted, and expired domains and other services, including reverse IP lookup and traceroute)

http://www.networksolutions.com/whois/index.jsp and http://network-tools.com/ (which offers multiple services)

L-Soft, which offers a service for lookups for listservs (server-based email broadcast services) across the Internet at http://www.lsoft. com/lists/listref.html

IP2Location, which offers to provide the geographic location of IP addresses at http://www.ip2location.com/1.2.3.4

The Internet Assigned Numbers Authority (IANA) at http://www. iana.org/ provides coordination of the Domain Name System (DNS) and protocols for routing Web traffic to the proper IP address from the URL entered, and manages the global DNS root and the pool of IP numbers, allocating them to the regional Internet registries. It may be necessary to look up registries, registrars, domain name holders, and IP addresses using IANA and Internet registry resources. The Internet Corporation for Assigned Names and Numbers (ICANN) at http://www.icann.org/ coordinates IP addressing across the world. The American Registry for Internet Numbers (ARIN) is responsible for North America and the Caribbean, available at https://www.arin.net/resources/index.html. The Internet is using IPv4 and IPv6 (a larger number of IP addresses coming online) to route network communications. The main thing for an investigator to understand is that just as the packets (bits of data) flowing to and from a computer "know where to go" using the Internet's protocols, it is possible to find out, at least to a limited extent, who is at the other end of Internet connections, by identifying the IP addresses used to route those packets. In the future, IPv6 may allow identification of senders through better authentication built in to the protocol. However, the trend toward protecting users' privacy against spammers harvesting email addresses from the public Internet may offset the investigator's ability to identify users from virtual identities.

EMAIL

Email plays a part in many Internet investigations. Email addresses can sometimes be found using search engines, and both the user name and the entire address should be searched. Email can sometimes be traced on its route from sender to receiver, at least to the extent that the message header is not tampered with, depending on the email service provider. Emails may be sent from an Internet service provider like Yahoo!, Microsoft, or AOL, or through a Web mail service like Google's gmail. Email also may come from a mail server operated by a corporation or an outsourced mail service provider. Email addresses may reflect the Web site of a business owner (e.g., john.doe@company.com) or the email service provider (e.g., jdoe2@verizon.net, bigsam@hotmail.com). Internet investigators will sooner or later confront the need to identify the sender of an email. The prospects of success for identifying "anonymous" emailers are not always high, but at least the initial steps are comparatively simple:

1. Obtain the message header. Ask the recipient of the email to capture the message header and send it to you. Merely forwarding the message will not provide you with the original email's message header. To obtain the message header, that is, the routing information about where the email came from, the recipient should view and print it or copy and paste it from the email program used. With Yahoo! mail, click the link "Full Headers" at the bottom of the page. With Outlook, click "Options," and the routing information appears. In gmail, click on the down arrow next to "Reply" at the top right of the message pane and select "Show Original." In any email program, look in help for "message header" or "full header" for instructions on how to find the routing information.

2. Review and analyze the message header. The header usually displays the sender's email and IP address (which consists of numbers in the format XXX.XXX.XXX.XXX, for example, 123.435.987.654), shown closest to the sender's email address at the bottom of the header. The IP addresses shown between the bottom and the top

(where the recipient's email address appears) are the IP addresses of servers through which the message was routed.

3. Use a reverse IP address lookup service to identify the IP address of the sender. This will usually at least provide the user's ISP, allow placement in a geographical region, and in some cases provide the IP address of the mail server used by the sender. It may not be possible to identify the individual sender from a dynamic IP address unless the mail service provider will agree to determine who used that IP address on a specific date at a specific time (shown on the message—if the time/date stamp is accurate). Most ISPs and mail service providers demand a legal process (subpoena or warrant) for an outside investigator to identify senders by IP address. Law enforcement or court intervention would be needed for that step. With a fixed IP address, the mail host of the sender, and possibly the sender himself or herself can be identified. Internal enterprise investigators may be able to use IT records to identify the sender of an email launched within the enterprise.

4. In attempting to identify the sender of an email, do not overlook analysis of the possible suspects' activities at the time that the email was sent, and include an analysis of the user name, content, and context of the message itself. These often provide clues to the sender's identity. While it is possible for someone to create a free email account just to send one email, it is also possible that the sender used the same "anonymous" email address or handle for many other communications, which may be linked with the sender on the Internet. Some email accounts contain public profiles identifying the user. Some are linked with the user's work or true name email addresses on social sites, business, and other sites.

5. When all else fails, it may be possible to engage the sender of an email in an exchange of messages that could lead to his or her identification. This ploy demands sophisticated manipulation of the communications so as not to tip off the person that someone is trying to identify who he or she is, and also requires that the person answer the email. If the sender is determined to remain anonymous, he or she may never return to the email account used. However, some people are curious to see if there is a response to their provocation.

As an analyst becomes more experienced and comfortable with Internet investigations, it is almost inevitable that she will be asked to find out something that simply is not available on the Internet. There are many types of misbehavior, including malicious and destructive communications, hate speech, bullying, stalking, slander against individuals and organizations, and postings corrosive of morale and civil behavior. Hard economic times sometimes bring out the worst in people, as do extreme political beliefs. Personal disputes and sexual pursuits arise frequently in all groups. Analysts are asked to identify anonymous actors using the Internet to carry out misbehavior. While every assignment may prove possible to accomplish, the ability of users to hide behind virtual identities can erect an impenetrable barrier. When a high degree of difficulty is found, it is important to enlist the help of others, such as IT systems administrators and "white hat" hackers, who may be able to trace activities using their systems security methods, including system logs, firewalls, user monitoring tools, and Web tracing tools. Often, the subject is a person within the organization itself, even if the communications appear to come from outside. The analyst contributes to the identification of the subject and resolution of the case, even if it proves impossible to use conventional Internet investigative methods, because a thorough inquiry explores every possible means (within reason). Collaboration with others with different skill sets has proven to add value to all types of Internet investigations.

While it may appear that the URLs of the suggested sources above comprise a long list, they are only a part of the wide variety of sources available. If an analyst were to use a substantial number of the URLs in manual searches, it could take a long time. Further, searching is step 1; review, filtering, capture, and analysis must still be done. Automating the search process can dramatically improve efficiency, so that is the topic of the next chapter.

NOTES

1. A great site to find government resources is usa.gov at http://www.usa.gov/.
2. Hetherington, Cynthia, and Stankey, Michael L., *The Manual to Online Public Records, The Researcher's Tool to Online Public Records and Public Information*, 6th ed. (Tempe, AZ: BRB Publications, 2008).
3. http://en.wikipedia.org/wiki/Web_2.0 (accessed September 24, 2010).
4. http://en.wikipedia.org/wiki/Folksonomy (accessed September 24, 2010).
5. Web host analysis, http://news.netcraft.com/hosting-analysis (accessed April 16, 2010).
6. Carey, Rob, Navy CIO's blog, http://www.doncio.navy.mil/Blog.aspx (accessed June 10, 2010).

7. Smith, Aaron, "Mobile Access 2010," Pew Internet and American Life Project, July 7, 2010, http://www.pewinternet.org/~/media//Files/Reports/2010/PIP_Mobile_Access_2010.pdf (accessed August 22, 2010), which illustrates rapid growth in wireless Internet use in all types of devices, including the fact that as of May 2010, 59% of adult Americans go online wirelessly, with increases in both laptop and cell Web users.

8. Schneier, Bruce, "Schneier on Security: Identifying People Using Anonymous Social Networking Data," April 6, 2009, http://www.schneier.com/blog/archives/2009/04/identifying_peo.html (accessed April 17, 2010), relating the results of a study by Arvind Narayanan and Dr. Vitaly Shmatikov, from the University of Texas at Austin, in "De-Anonymizing Social Networks," for IEEE Security and Privacy '09, available at http://randomwalker.info/social-networks/.

9. As the above Texas study illustrates, sophisticated computer analysis may be capable of sifting huge quantities of data online to find previously hidden activities of "anonymous" users, meaning that one future possibility includes automated vetting tools that expose prior postings when candidates are cyber vetted.

10. Taub, Eric A., "Going beyond Google to Find a Lost Friend," *New York Times*, March 25, 2010.

11. For example: Dwyer, Tim, "The Officer Who Posted Too Much on MySpace," *New York Times*, March 10, 2009, http://www.nytimes.com/2009/03/11/nyregion/11about.html?_r=2 (accessed August 22, 2010). A man arrested for illegal possession of a gun while on probation, resisting arrest, and using a stolen motorcycle was acquitted of the most serious charges (gun possession) by claiming that the officer's MySpace page, which referred to the film *Training Day* and had other cynical postings, showed that the officer's word could not be trusted, and the defendant's claims of brutality and dishonesty were accepted by the jury.

17

Automation of Searching

Search engines are amazing in their automation of the search process, because they deliver the results of several complex and difficult system functions in less than a second, consistently and with high quality. Like the dial tone always present when we pick up the phone, we take it for granted that in mere seconds we can execute a search and dive into results. Search engines like Google combine the spiders that crawl the Web, applications that capture text and images, many servers that store billions of pages, indexing that allows instant retrieval, and algorithms to serve up references in the order most probably useful to the user. These are all wondrous functions.

However, further automation is required to reduce the time needed for professional analysts to collect and present information quickly and simultaneously from many different search engines and Web sites where references are most likely to be found. When one looks for an automated Internet search tool, not many choices are found besides Internet search engines and intranet database searching systems. Although in the broadest sense, Google is a tool, it is really a Web site offering a search service. Unfortunately, there are still few good options for desktop search software for the use of an investigator.[1]

WHY AUTOMATE SEARCHING?

Given the capabilities of Google, is further automation of searching needed? The answer becomes obvious after only a few hours of searching.

The list of Web sites (URLs) that must be visited to initiate a search on the same subject each time is long. The number of pages returned for the average search is high. The manual, serial searching method is lengthy, repetitious, and exhausting, packed with duplication and false positives. The searcher longs for the capabilities of a super-metasearch engine that can deliver the most relevant, de-duplicated results in the quickest, most painless manner. It is difficult to carry out a thorough, accurate Internet search quickly.

Broken down into its core processes, the automated search needs to

- Enter the same search term or terms into the search boxes in a list of URLs (the user enters a term once, and the system enters the same term as many times as needed)
- Conduct a multithreaded search (i.e., simultaneously visit the URLs designated and retrieve search results) in about the time it normally takes one search engine
- Present the references found to the analyst for review
- Eliminate nonrelevant, duplicate, and nonidentifiable references and broken links (e.g., links returning "404" errors—page not available)

Additional capabilities for an automated search system could include downloading and storing chosen Web pages, facilitating search of new terms found as searching progresses (e.g., a new user name/email address), and extracting data from search results and placing the data into draft reports.

Two of the steps outlined are very time-consuming: executing the searches and reviewing the results. After years of looking for tools (software that is either free or affordable for an individual user), I have found few that are both ideal for the investigator and affordable in cost.

ENTERPRISE SEARCH MIDDLEWARE

A whole branch of applications has been created for corporate data mining, to "know what we know" from massive databases that all large enterprises now have. These intranet applications often can extract data from multiple different types of databases through application programming interfaces that convert a query into the right language for each individual database. As "middleware," the applications then retrieve and "normalize" the data found and present it to the user in a way that is simple and usable, such as converting the information's format for use in a desktop program such as a browser, document, or spreadsheet. Besides in-house shared data storage, one of the databases used for inputs into the middleware can be the Internet.[2] However, the unstructured data formatting and searching dynamics of the Internet are formidable challenges for retrieving identifiable information and integrating it into the mix.

Often, middleware programs help visualize the data, by presenting it in charts, graphs, images, and other renditions that essentially allow the user to look at large amounts of information charted over a timeline, with links, trends, developments, anomalies, and other attributes highlighted, including grouping both identical and similar information. At the high end, the programs optimize a process of decision making, such as pricing new products made from complex components imported from several different places, and predicting when price points, new technologies, competition, or timelines require action or change, process management and logistics, etc. Several programs facilitate data mining for police and corporate security investigators by processing voluminous information in government databases. Enterprise database software tools such as those described can cost from hundreds of thousands to millions of dollars, including several thousand dollars for each user in software, maintenance, and training. Unless the investigator has access to a large agency's customized systems and budget, such tools probably are unsuitable or unaffordable for Internet searching. Those who do use custom systems inevitably get more useful information from their in-house databases than the Internet, because the systems are not optimized for thorough Internet searching.

Investigative analytical and visualization tools are being used by large intelligence and investigative agencies. An example is i2's Analysis Product Line, including Analyst's Notebook, which provides an integrated suite of database software designed for the investigator looking for relationships, patterns, and trends (used by over two thousand organizations worldwide, including government agencies).[3] A competing system is Sentinel Visualizer.[4] These types of systems cost several thousand dollars per user for software, maintenance, appropriate hardware, and training. Many intelligence and investigative agency analysts use these tools successfully, and data captured from the Internet during investigations can be incorporated into the process. However, these systems are neither designed nor optimized for open-source data integration into the applications, because they do not conduct comprehensive Internet searching as an integrated function. One reason is that intelligence and law enforcement agencies do not want to have a system that is integrated with their sensitive and classified internal databases connected directly to the public Internet. Another reason is that the Internet is not just another database, but rather a huge network of disparate types of data sources and program languages. Essentially, professional analytical software for investigative analysts was not designed for Internet searching and costs too much for most individuals and small agencies.

The types of software/middleware designed for law enforcement, court, and jail records management systems allow queries of public records (e.g., driver's licenses, car registrations, telephone directories) and law enforcement databases (e.g., the National Crime Information Center, court and inmate records).[5] Some systems span multiple jurisdictions, merging data from many databases. Unfortunately, these systems are much better at integrating structured data from linked records systems than they are at including Internet data, which are unstructured. Still, continued development of these systems is closing in on the goal of true integration of open-source data into the corporate body of knowledge. Many investigators prefer a tool singularly focused on open-source information from the Internet.

BEST-IN-CLASS DESKTOP TOOL

Currently, an example exists of a commercial-off-the-shelf tool well suited for Internet investigators, known as Copernic Professional, made by a Montreal company (Copernic.com) that also owns the classical meta-search engine Mama.com.[6] Copernic makes a free desktop Internet search tool and a turbo-charged Copernic Agent Professional version for about $80. The professional version allows a user to do customized searching efficiently and facilitates review, filtering, and reporting. In addition, Copernic makes desktop and enterprise search tools that index and search corporate or agency data (again, free for private use, modest fee based for commercial use). Copernic also makes a tool to track Web sites and topics and another tool to extract the essence of text found, to facilitate the reporting process. While Copernic Agent Professional is not the only tool available, its success among private and corporate investigators qualifies it to be the only one mentioned here.

INVESTIGATIVE SEARCH TOOL REQUIREMENTS

The ideal automated search tool is able to access chosen Web sites' search functions in large numbers. Copernic, for example, may query two hundred plus or minus sites and return results in a few seconds. Filtering the results can be more efficient when the application allows the analyst to discard references that are false and select those that need in-depth review quickly and easily. Code that helps identify true references by name resolution (entity resolution) can help the analyst to filter possible references to a subject quickly and home in on those most likely to be identifiable. Much of the postsearch processing still must be the responsibility of the analyst.

Today, massive databases of public and private data are offered to subscribers of services like those provided by LexisNexis (e.g., Acurint).[7] One of LexisNexis's most successful capabilities in delivering records services is the ability to mine huge databases, reportedly carried out by advanced computer systems developed for the purpose.[8] The systems retrieve references to the subject of a query and pull related information into a cohesive report. As remarkable as the Acurint systems are, it is revealing that similar systems are not available to search for, identify references to, filter for accuracy, and compose a report on information available on the Internet. Several government agencies and private companies are trying to develop tools that can deliver such a report from the Internet. As a nonprogrammer, I find it easiest to explain the current situation by reflecting that in the FBI, I always found at least two or more people with the same name when searching FBI indices. The world's billions of people are reflected in Internet data, and one can imagine how many people with the same name appear online. Ensuring that the information found relates to the subject of interest and not someone else is still the art of the analyst.

One way to automate searching would be to have a multistep process, such as

Enter known data into a database →
    Auto-search retrieves terms from database, executes Internet searches →
        Auto-retrieve captures pages (text), places results in database →
            Auto-analyze performs name resolution
            Ranks results by likelihood of relevance
            Selects new search terms from text retrieved
            Sends new terms through auto-search, which executes searches
            Repeats the auto-retrieve and analysis process for second-tier results
            Presents all results to the user →
            User selects items for inclusion →
Auto-report presents a draft report to the user

The above process could include artificial intelligence (AI; a complex set of algorithms to allow the computer system to decide the highest-value retrieved data and place them into a draft report according to criteria programmed into the software). One type of AI might eliminate all confirming facts found (e.g., references that show the subject has the same address and profile already known) and report only conflicting or derogatory findings. AI would allow more processing and less human analysis, but in the end, there is a need for analysts to make decisions about which references are identifiable with the subject, which are usable based on policy and standards of reporting, and which should be followed up with further investigation to determine the facts and resolve any potential discrepancies. The contribution of automation is that the analyst's time is focused on assessment and reporting of results, rather than a manual process of search, review, select, capture, and report. Relieving the analyst of time-consuming, repetitive actions can allow much more efficient exploitation of open-source intelligence and allow processing of more subjects, more quickly and with better results.

A HOMEGROWN SOLUTION

In order to solve the problem of collection online, my company developed our own proprietary tool for analysts to use in conducting searches. It functions much like a group of search engines bound together into a multithreaded search engine. The tool is loaded with URLs that usually produce the best search results (major search engines, alternative search terms such as exact match, and a variety of social networking and selected online search sites). The analyst enters a search term (name, email, IP address, phone, postal address, or up to ten keywords). The predetermined searches are done simultaneously, in a few seconds. The analyst then scans the results from each fruitful search and captures the content from the links. The tool is flexible, allowing the analyst to update the queried URLs as needed, to fit the purpose. It allows hour upon hour of serial, manual searching to be done in minutes.

We are still in the process of building our next-generation search and analysis tool, which we hope will reduce the time required to analyze search results by capturing references in a database from which identifiable information can be scanned, reviewed, and accepted or rejected efficiently, and reports can be generated automatically.

REDUCING ANALYTICAL TIME USING AUTOMATION

As related above, the analyst oversees a multistep process in providing reports of open-source Internet intelligence on any topic, including the search, filtering, analysis, composition, and reporting. Each of the five steps mentioned is actually a serial, multitask process, because the initial search is supplemented by searches of new terms found in results. Here's how we have managed to reduce the time needed for an investigator to report results of an Internet search:

- Do as many searches as possible simultaneously, using available automation. For a new practitioner, we recommend Copernic Agent (free), and Copernic Agent Professional when an $80 commitment is affordable. Use the search and metasearch engines and URLs mentioned in the previous chapters to ensure that the search is comprehensive, accurate, and reliable.
- Review and select results for inclusion in reporting, capturing images of Internet pages deemed to contain substantive information.
- Summarize and provide links to sources of reported items in the report.
- Append images of the Web pages used in the report where appropriate.
- Retain a file with collected items.

For an individual subject, the above process can be accomplished in about two hours by an experienced analyst. However, if the references are extensive and the substance of data found is lengthy, considerable additional time may be required to analyze results, choose the most apt items responsive to the assignment, and compose the report language. The magic of the analyst is exercising the logic and intuition needed to find and report what those requesting the search want to know. Often, the question is whether there is some past behavior by a person or entity that may pose a risk in a future association, such as an employee, contractor, holder of a clearance, witness, suspect, customer, partner, trustee, supplier, or merger acquisition. The successful analyst recognizes and reports precisely the facts that may be of concern or moment in decision making. This is the essence of value-based intelligence.

CACHING AND DATA MINING

Today's collection tools, database programs, and storage capabilities allow even the small agency to identify, capture, and cache data likely to be of investigative use. For example, if the analyst can identify a series of Web sites/URLs that contain postings of potential interest to the client, then they can be collected continuously and placed in storage. At first blush, this may seem to be a daunting task for an analyst who is not a programmer of search tools or databases and does not have the IT skills to be the architect of an enterprise records management system. However, the tools mentioned in this book can be used to construct a low-cost solution that is capable of collecting valuable data on practically any topic. For example, using free Internet search and tracking tools can allow an analyst to find, copy, and store Web pages in HTML or Portable Document Format (PDF) in a free MySQL or Excel database, or simply in an unstructured folder. For $100, the analyst can put the database on a separate hard drive with a terabyte of space. Several search utilities, costing from nothing (i.e., part of a PC operating system) up to about $50, allow the analyst to mine the database in moments to retrieve information on any topic. Now the analyst has a proprietary solution to data collection and exploitation on a topic of special interest.

With programming help and advanced tools, analysts have used the method outlined above to capture information about criminal activities online, copying and storing the computer activities of pirates, fencers, drug dealers, thieves, crackers, credit card fraudsters, and spammers. Once a channel for illicit activities is identified, it can be monitored and recorded for enforcement, intelligence, and security use. This approach could be described as the great equalizer on the largely unpoliced Internet.

THE HUMAN INTERFACE IN INTERNET INVESTIGATIONS

A colleague in law enforcement recently complained privately to me that today's crop of incoming investigators is more apt to expect to find all the answers at the computer screen, and seems reluctant to use interviews, field investigation, and traditional surveillance techniques to gather information. There may be some truth to this idea, but in reality, human interaction must be used to identify the Web sites of greatest interest and to find out the methodology of offenders. With only one or a few infiltrators, complex Internet communications systems can be identified and monitored by intelligence officers. Coordination among officers is critical to build on both human and cyber intelligence to gain and maintain the best surveillance possible. Among the sources used for this type of approach are

- Recently captured, arrested, or convicted individuals knowledgeable about online support for the illicit enterprises
- Data retrieved during computer forensic analysis of systems used in crimes and in lawful intercepts
- Confidences shared with trusted inside sources by those involved in the illicit enterprise
- Online infiltration of an illicit enterprise by an investigator
- Witness reports

To collect intelligence needed on people and entities engaged in misbehavior, it is sometimes necessary for an investigator to assume an undercover role. Care should be taken in such undertakings to ensure that the undercover officer does not commit illegal acts. In addition, both ethical and psychological reviews are needed to keep the undercover person on track and avoid the kinds of activities that could be reprehensible. Recent history has taught both law enforcement and private investigators many lessons about how not to carry out undercover activities. Undercover activities fall under the rubric of "Don't try this at home," requiring professional training and experience in investigations.

Closely related to the undercover role is the concept of "pretexting." Neither undercover investigation nor pretexting is illegal or unethical in and of itself, but if either involves certain types of inducement to commit crimes, illicit deception, or fraud, it can be unlawful. Classical pretexting is for an individual to ask questions as though he or she were entitled to receive the answers, which may involve misleading or misdirecting the subject. Using a too broad definition of pretexting unfortunately led investigators to pretend to be the subjects of their investigations in communications with telephone companies, to obtain copies of the subjects' telephone bills. This constituted wire fraud, a federal crime. When an investigator assumes a role that is not fraudulent and asks questions of a subject or associates, a pretext can remain within legal and ethical boundaries. For example, asking a subject or his family about his welfare and inviting him to an upcoming reunion can result in elicitation of substantive data, including the subject's Internet activities. Another example is when an investigator using a pseudonym makes a request to a subject to be included among customers of an illicit enterprise, such as distribution of pirated movies, music, and software for a fee. When a pretext such as

223

these results in acceptance of the undercover officer, it may be possible to gain access to illegal, ongoing Web communications. Such communications can be captured and cached to facilitate collection of evidence, intelligence, and security protection information.

A persistent question about propriety in background vetting online is whether it is ethical to pose as a fellow alumnus or associate or, without identifying oneself as an investigator, to ask a subject to be included as a friend ("to friend" the subject) with access to privacy-protected data on a subject's social site profile. A subject, upon learning the friend is an investigator, might consider such a ploy to be a violation of privacy. However, there are two issues to consider. One is the reason that the investigator might want to view the data only shown to the subject's "friends." If there is reason to believe that the data could contain substantive information about misbehavior by the subject, there could be a strong reason to attempt the ploy described. Further, if the subject has a wide circle of friends (i.e., a large number), the "privacy" protected may be minimal. The investigator, possibly aided by others in the background investigation, should consider other alternatives, such as interviews of the subject's associates (who could be among the social site's listed friends). The reason that it is ethical to use the pretext is that it provides a type of objective answer to the question about the subject's suspected misbehavior and is actually less intrusive than interviews of the subject's associates.

Another issue relating to Internet investigative ethics is whether viewing a subject's associates' postings is proper. The subject may have been notified and given consent to Internet vetting, but his friends have not. This question concerns the degree to which the privacy of the associates is breached. We have found that it is not unusual for a friend or acquaintance to post information of value about a subject, including seriously illicit behaviors. There are three issues to consider: Is the posting public? Are the data collected about the subject? Can the finding be reported without breaching the associate's privacy? Because the postings are (for the most part) public, there is no legal protection to the information, no matter who posted it. Like a newspaper story that names several people, there is no logical or legal basis for contending that the mention of others, including the author, constitutes a reason for declining to read the story about any one of those named. When the information is substantive, it should properly appear in the report (with or without naming the others, as the investigator considers appropriate). When the information is not relevant, identifiable, or useful, it does not appear in the report, and so it could be argued that no one's privacy is breached. The inclusion of associates' names and other information about them in a report on the subject could be avoided (to protect their privacy), but might need to be included as a list of potential witnesses to corroborate misbehavior.

Internet intelligence is only one component of a whole picture that is needed about people, entities, and topics where strategic and tactical decisions must be made. Even while deeply engaged online, analysts must remember that recognizing the human intelligence opportunities is as important as finding the data targeted.

Combining open-source intelligence from the public Internet, deep Web, cached data, and recent postings calls on the investigator to keep up to date with what is available online, how to find and exploit new sources, and how to assess findings. Those who do this well can make a significant contribution to the knowledge needed by enterprise decision makers.

NOTES

1. Based on the author's company's review of moderately priced desktop software options for comprehensive Internet searching for investigative purposes, 2005–present, few choices were available at the time this book was written.
2. A good depiction and definition of middleware and its functions can be found at http://www.pcmag.com/encyclopedia_term/0,2542,t=middlewa re&i=47013,00.asp (accessed August 22, 2010).
3. Kardell-Lessard, Stacy, and Feneis, Penny, "Determining Entity Relationships in Combating Refund Fraud," Minnesota Department of Revenue, i2 Analyst's Notebook, http://www.taxadmin.org/FTA/Meet/07am_data/ Papers/Tuesday/Technology/RefundFraud.pdf (accessed April 15, 2010). This article includes the assertion that every major FBI investigation uses i2's Analyst's Notebook. i2 is found at http://www.i2group.com/.
4. Sentinel Visualizer is found at http://www.fmsasg.com/.
5. International Association of Crime Analysts (IACA) evaluation of crime analysis software, http://www.iaca.net/Software.asp (accessed April 15, 2010).
6. Copernic is found at http://www.copernic.com/.
7. LexisNexis is found at http://www.lexisnexis.com/, as is Acurint.
8. O'Harrow, Robert, Jr., *No Place to Hide* (New York: Free Press, 2005).

225

18

Internet Intelligence Reporting

Based on current legal and policy standards (or lack thereof) about the use of Internet intelligence, it appears that the highest risk is in the reporting and subsequent use of online data. Merely conducting an online search creates a record in the computer used. Reports may be oral or written, but it is clear that even where formal reports are not written, the activities of the Web searcher are chronicled in one form or another in the computer systems used to access the Internet. Today, many enterprises allow anyone to search any topic, to process any information gained as they wish, and to reach whatever conclusions or decisions they believe are appropriate based on their findings. Major search engines store records of queries not only on the workstation of the researcher, but also on search engine servers, identifying queries with IP addresses. A serial murderer in the Midwest was convicted based in part on evidence of searching and mapping done on his PC. Internet search records could be subpoenaed to show bias or unfair treatment. If a pattern of unfair practices were suspected, for example, bias in hiring, the enterprise's Internet search records could be obtained, for civil or criminal proceedings.

RECORDS

The overall positive effects of using the Internet as a quick reference tool far outweigh the risks of second-guessing the decisions made based on such searches. However, when the decisions made could impact people, significant assets, or information, the enterprise policy should be to create and maintain business records of the process. Among the benefits derived from such documentation are protection of process integrity against liability claims for impropriety, a "paper trail" from which processes can be improved, and records that can be consulted for facts in the future. Since substantive Internet intelligence reporting may be provided to several different recipients or may be summarized for executive use, it is important to have coherent reporting and records retention schemes.

What follows is a series of recommendations about how open-source intelligence and specifically Internet information should be reported.[1] Ultimately, the client decides the best, most efficient way that findings should be conveyed. Experience has shown that when a report is complete but simple and straightforward, it has great value. Further, if it is well written, that is, cleverly worded, holds the attention of the reader, and is grammatical and well organized, it is most effective in communicating the essential facts that decision makers need.

CONTENT

The first principle of good business and government record keeping is to have a file for each case or project, in which a copy is kept of each document, reference, or link that was used in the matter. If the issue does not rise to the level of a case or project, then it is appropriate to keep a copy of any memo, notes, or correspondence in a file on the general topic, indexed for retrieval, should that be necessary in the future. Records routinely kept in this manner can resolve many potential issues that might arise, including refreshing recollections, documenting actions taken, and being available to support a legal claim. Internet searches, in both raw and finished form, should be preserved in files when appropriate.

Basic principles of business and government reporting should be observed, including recording the dates that items are found, the original dates the items were created and their authors (if available), the precise locations, and any other details that identify and describe the data found, who handled them, and how they were preserved. Data should be stored in a manner designed to protect their security and integrity. By observing such routines, analysts will ensure that the reliability of the content is as high as possible, and may be qualified as evidence in a court.

There are several ways to approach report content, based on client needs. One type of report is the report by exception, in which known facts and items developed that are not expected to impact a decision are omitted from the report. Unreported data are still maintained in the file containing the record of the inquiry, in case someone needs to refer to them, but they are not set out in the case report. For example, when the purpose of the report is to ascertain whether there is any information available from an Internet search that could impact a hiring or clearance decision, the investigator could be told to leave out of the report verification of address, employer, telephone number, etc., and even the fact that the subject has MySpace and Facebook profiles. Names of other people not needed for an adjudication could be omitted. Of course, the report should not contain information identifying the subject as a member of a protected class (race, religion, ethnicity, sex, etc.) with very few exceptions. However, if the subject's behavior or documents online show that the subject misbehaved, for example, violated a law, showed bad judgment, mistreated someone, or was dishonest, those items would be placed in a report. If there were no derogatory findings, the subject's name could be placed on a list about whom there was nothing to report, based on the criteria for the Internet search conducted. This approach could be very helpful to those enterprises seeking to include Internet vetting in personnel screening, because although the collection and analysis of Internet data may be resource intensive, the reporting is simplified for efficiency.

Another type of reporting is to capture and present any and all information found. Information is frequently organized under topical headings like those found in an Outlook address book: name, address, telephone numbers, email addresses, employer, position, etc. These headings can be expanded or limited based on findings and client requirements, and can apply to people, entities, and topics. New headings can be created to suit the case, such as arrests, civil suits, online activities, news media reports, etc. When a report is lengthy, it is appropriate to include an executive summary at the beginning, briefly presenting all major results. More significant findings, that is, those deemed material to the client, should be prioritized by inclusion as early as possible in a lengthy report.

ANALYST'S COMMENTS

When reporting items found online that may need explanation, it may be appropriate to include an analyst's comments. The comments should be set off from the factual reporting and clearly indicate their origin and purpose. For example:

[Analyst's note: The author of this posting using a name identical with the subject's does not appear to be identifiable with the subject because his residence is located 354 miles from the subject's residence.]

It is appropriate to include analyst's comments in circumstances such as the following:

- The item reported may not be true, may not be identifiable with the subject, or should be treated skeptically.
- The manner in which the item was found could have a bearing on how it is used.
- Additional information could place the item in a new light.
- Other facts found tend to either confirm or deny the item reported.
- An explanation may be needed for a particular type of Internet activity or language used (e.g., jargon).

In the event that an analyst's experience could contribute to the interpretation of a report but inclusion of opinion in the report itself is inappropriate, a separate report cover page or transmittal communication may be used. This is a tradition in law enforcement and intelligence reporting where commentary or guidance is added to a factual report. In language that clearly separates findings from observations, opinions, and possibly suggested guidance, the analyst can set out helpful comments for the client. A (fictionalized) example might be:

In the attached report, references to "PPXX69's" Facebook and Flickr profiles, with the accompanying photos and text, appear to be a series of spoofs, attempts at humor and teasing (some of which could be viewed as obscene) by more than one person. It was not possible to verify that the subject posted the material, or whether the content of the photos and text refer to, portray, or are attributable to the subject. In the view of experienced Internet analysts, these profiles were not intended to be taken seriously. The subject is linked with the items reported by tagging of the subject's name in several of the photos on Flickr and in the Facebook profile, and the use of a nickname that appears in other profiles of the subject. In order to understand the nature of the postings, the subject's explanation could be sought.

During my career, I have had the privilege of participating in every aspect of intelligence and investigative collection, reporting, high-level executive recommendations, testimony, all-source assessments, critical infrastructure protection, intelligence analytical management, training, and comprehensive project documentation. The most important principle I learned is that decision makers want a report to provide the critical facts as clearly and succinctly as possible. Executives look for a summary at the beginning, substantial evidence presented in clear writing in a well-structured body, and reliable sources for the facts reported. Nonpertinent data may be collected and retained until it is confirmed that they are unneeded, but should not be included in a report. Intelligence reporting may need to include items that appear to contradict the central theme or tenor of the evidence, because not every situation is black and white, and competing versions of the facts may be found. Internet and open-source data may contain items deliberately posted to deceive, and a key purpose of collection and analysis is to find and weigh the credibility of all evidence. In the early twenty-first century, it has unfortunately become the norm for some advocates to exaggerate, prevaricate, and deceive to convince the public. It is good to remember that today, the report of open-source intelligence is competing with many types of media catching the client's attention, so the most effective reports are grammatical, succinct, accurate, convincing, and attention grabbing.

ORGANIZATION AND FORMATTING

In some types of intelligence assessment (usually at a higher management level), it is not only the essential facts that are reported, but also the framework for the decisions to be made. In this type of document, the report is a summary of all the relevant intelligence reporting, and is structured to convey:

- Facts as well as can be known
- Options, with all major choices outlined
- Pros and cons for each option
- Summary of the evidence for the best option
- Recommendation for the option to be chosen

The decision support report type outlined above is similar to the transmittal document, where not only findings, but also opinions, assessments, and recommendations are provided. However, it differs in that it includes intelligence summaries with opinions.

The best format for a report is one that will fit the needs of the client and assist the analyst in organizing the contents in a logical, easy-to-understand order. Outlines for two popular types of reports are included to illustrate the types of headings used for a report where the subject is an individual or a company.

A report on a person may use the following outline (include prior as well as current information if called for):

Executive summary
Name, aliases, and identifying information
Contact information (telephone numbers, addresses, email addresses)
Court records (criminal and civil)
Financial situation, including bankruptcies, liens, and judgments
Other derogatory information (e.g., government sanctions, expelled
    from school, discharged from employment, accusations, conflicts
    of interest)
Spouse, significant other, and family
Property ownership
Education
Employment
Profiles and biographies
Online activities
Associates
News media reports
Photographs

A report on a company or entity may use the following outline (include prior as well as current information if called for):

Executive summary
Name, other "doing business as" names, and identifying information
Contact information (telephone numbers, addresses, email addresses,
    Web sites)
Court records (criminal and civil)
Bankruptcies and credit problems
Liens and judgments
Other derogatory information (e.g., government sanctions, stock-
    holder issues, accusations, disputes)
Conflicts of interest
Recalls, consumer complaints, Better Business Bureau report
Entity ownership and control, including SEC filings
Entity reputation and place in the market
Federal, state, and local charters, licenses, and permits
Property ownership
Business credit report (e.g., Dun & Bradstreet, if not covered above)
History

News media reports

As mentioned above, topical headings can be added or deleted as appropriate. Some individuals and organizations have multiple Web sites, and online activities may or may not be a large portion of the report, depending on such activities.

SOURCE CITATIONS

There are two widely used methods of source citations in open-source intelligence reports, one in which the sources appear directly beneath the item reported, and the other in which footnote or endnote style superscript numbers or letters are appended to the item, referring to a citation appearing in a section at the end of each page or, more often, at the end of the report. Normally, citations are not used in the executive summary.

Sources should be shown wherever possible in the main body, because by the nature of open-source reporting, it is possible that doubt or a dispute could arise over the accuracy of an item's substance. Open-source reporting is unlike that from covert or clandestine sources. Most of the time, it is not only unnecessary to protect sources and methods in Internet investigative reports, but also it is important for the consumer of the report to be able to see the source, to help judge the reliability of each item. Internet citations should include the URL from which the data were collected, allowing the reader to refer to the page. A Portable Document Format (PDF) copy of the Web page should be placed in an appendix to the report, or at least maintained in the case file, in case it becomes necessary to review the original source. Because Web sites may change frequently, the version of the page as found should be preserved.

ATTRIBUTION

In reporting an item found on the Internet, the analyst should take care to examine the basis for attributing the information to the subject. Matching a name may not be a strong identification. Where attribution is crucial to the value of the report, the analyst should not assume that the reader has the same level of conviction that the data are identifiable with the subject. It may be desirable to spell out the factors that led to the identification, especially if they are not readily visible in the text. If the client is very familiar with Internet reports, and likely to reach the same conclusions based on the information presented, the facts found can be laid out without comments. However, if the report may be reviewed by others (e.g., an executive concerned with a no-hire decision or withholding of a security clearance, a decision against a merger or pursuing an intellectual property theft case against a competitor), it may be prudent to point out the basis of the item's attribution. Following is a fictionalized example from an actual case:

> Cornelius McCarthy, using the name Markus Smith, addressed a group of teammates in an Internet presentation preserved in an audio recording and posted online as part of his activities as a leader in the Hundred Years War massively multiplayer online fantasy game. In the audio recording (transcript attached), McCarthy used obscenities, racial epithets, and insults for team members, as part of his role as an army leader. He also urged the team to spend all day and all night, as he does, in pursuing online game objectives.
> Source: http://www.hundredyearswar.com/audio/839021hfnaso_4f

> [Analyst's note: The subject was identified by the tag "Pillager" on the audio file at the above URL, which is a user name the subject also employed on his MySpace and Facebook profiles, as well as revealed in a *Variety* interview of April 1, 2009, in which he asserted that his leadership role in the online game enhances his managerial credentials at XWR Systems, where he is employed as a software security programmer. His true name, user name, and online fantasy war pseudonym are recorded together on all of the above profiles found, as well as in the *Variety* story.]

The analyst should carefully note and record (if not report) all of the indicators used to attribute a finding on the Internet to a particular person or entity. This is a good practice even if there is no question asked or denial on the part of a subject that it is a valid attribution. The analyst will find that there are many ways to link an individual or entity with behavior, and often, it only takes an alert observation to record ample evidence of the connection.

VERIFICATION

Attributing a particular behavior or posting to a subject may reflect a single instance or may be part of a pattern of behavior. While it appears that many Internet users have multiple virtual identities (user names, nicknames, handles), it is not unusual for a person to

- List all or many of his or her different nicknames in a Facebook or other profile
- Reveal and publish his or her true name and nickname in a single communication
- Use Twitter or email to update a group with a link to a true name and nickname together

Finding the virtual identities used by a subject assists the Internet investigator to find all or many of the instances where online behavior is observable and attributable to the subject. It is also an excellent way to add to evidence that the attribution is correct and to verify that the same individual is involved. Verification in this sense includes instances such as:

- An individual with the same true name and nickname(s) is involved in the same types of activities, involving the same group(s) of people, over a period of time in the same place.
- An individual habitually and repeatedly uses the same Internet sites, has the same friends, and uses similar language to describe interests, actions, and choices on different occasions.
- An individual makes multiple references to the same activity or behavior on different occasions, in different places, and in different contexts.
- A friend or acquaintance of the subject records or makes references to acts of the subject.
- An individual maintains different profiles over time that refer to other profiles of the same individual, in which identical or similar postings appear.

Verification may sometimes involve a high degree of certainty that the behavior is attributable to the subject, based on multiple references to the same user (based on name, location, and habits) and repeated instances over time. However, verification may be much less certain when there is little to prove or indicate that the same individual is responsible or is portrayed in the references found. When the investigator finds that the available data offer little or no support to verify that the postings are attributable to the subject, that fact should be reported. Not every substantive report can be verified. For example, a PACER online federal court record of a subject's bankruptcy, based on name-only references, could be verified by an Acurint report from LexisNexis. However, if the Acurint report did not show a bankruptcy, perhaps the only way to verify the reference would be to conduct a physical court records review. As with many open-source intelligence endeavors (including human source reporting), the results may contain strong evidence, compelling and verified references, probably attributable behaviors, and possibly identifiable items, or may raise questions (or generate leads) that need to be resolved through additional investigation.

Verification of Internet intelligence reports ultimately may depend on the subject. There are various ways to use the subject to verify misbehavior or otherwise important issues raised by open-source intelligence collection. Before a "confrontational interview" of the subject (i.e., an interview in which a subject is asked about a possibly troubling or derogatory reference), it may be possible to elicit from the subject sufficient information to confirm or deny the reference in question. Among the methods that could be considered are

- "Friending" the subject on a social networking site or activity Web site where the behavior in question might be a logical topic of discussion. Some believe that this tactic can be unethical, especially if the subject is duped into believing that he or she is dealing with a real friend. Impersonation may run afoul of state or local laws, especially if something of value is sought and obtained from deception. However, if the investigator pretends to be a fellow alumnus or other "friendly stranger" and is accepted by the subject, then any admission made by the subject could be considered freely made. This type of elicitation should be done by those trained in the art, and supervised to prevent crossing an ethical line. Assuming an undercover role on the Internet, as in any instance, should not be done in such a way as to encourage illegal or illicit activity by anyone, but can ethically be done to elicit information from a subject willing to enter a discussion.
- Interviewing an associate or contact of the subject who (based on investigation) appears to be able to shed light on the issue, and who may be in a position to elicit further data from the subject, if that is appropriate in the investigation.
- Asking the subject, prior to a confrontational interview, to provide written or oral information likely to include the topical area where the question arose. For example, asking the subject to list all of the social networking and photo posting sites he or she utilizes online could reveal that the posting in question is one listed, or is omitted. Because the requested list may be part of the application process, where deception constitutes grounds for denial of employment, the answers given would be helpful in any decision.

When the subject is interviewed on an issue that arose due to the results of an Internet investigation, it is important to have ready a document with those results to support the interview. The use of the term *confrontational interview* (twice above and here) is not to suggest that the interview is hostile or aggravated in any way. Rather, it is designed to allow the interviewer to attempt to elicit from the subject the facts and circumstances surrounding the items found during the Internet investigation. Experience has shown that at first, subjects tend to omit potentially embarrassing postings. When given the opportunity—because they are confronted with apparent knowledge on the part of the interviewer—most people will admit and explain the potentially troubling behavior found. If the subject continues to deny any involvement with a derogatory posting, the report can be shown to the subject with a request for an explanation. At this point, as with all of the interview, the subject can elect to tell the truth, deny the truth, or explain why the reported information is not what it seems. In any case, the results should be sufficient to verify or rule out use of the findings in the report or in adjudication.

The Internet is a new frontier to many tens of millions, who have made it a new playground, as well as a place where business and government conduct much of their operations. As users cope with the fact that the Internet does not offer an opportunity to avoid responsibility for behavior that is otherwise illegal, illicit, unethical, or socially unacceptable, employers and investigators will also cope with large-scale fantasy and pranks online. Verifying findings in open-source intelligence will be a challenge no matter what the medium of communications. The opportunities presented by the Internet for discovering and addressing computer-based behaviors potentially destructive to the enterprise should be exploited to ensure that business and government take logical, measured steps to hold authorized users to a high standard.

NOTE

1. Reporting guidelines provided in this chapter are based on the author's over forty-two years of report writing of all types, including news media, investigative and intelligence reporting, analysis, predictions, executive recommendations, and strategic risk/threat analyses.

19

Illicit Web Sites and Illegal Behavior Online

Internet investigations frequently focus on individuals or organizations to determine the nature of their behaviors online. Increasingly, investigations of terrorism, organized crime, fraud, economic espionage, smuggling, and other serious crimes find Web sites used in criminal enterprises. As the growth of e-commerce reflects ($155.2 billion annually in the United States, according to Forrester Research),[1] the Internet is a good venue to advertise, attract customers, direct prospects to sales sites, deceive or convince someone, collaborate online, plan and coordinate activities, order goods, and keep track of enterprises. Digital goods are especially easy to sell online. Unfortunately, digital goods might also include pirated films, videos, music, software, and the like.

CYBERCRIME

Child pornography, unauthorized use of computer systems, and contraband digital assets are three examples of crimes that have moved aggressively online. It is worth taking a moment, because of the frequency that such cybercrimes are found, to outline the difficulties they pose for enterprises, investigators, and the Internet as a venue.

Child Pornography and Internet Porn

Child pornography laws in the United States and most of the world generally define depiction and possession of images of underage sexual activity as illegal.[2] In the United States, federal criminal law in Title 18 U.S. Code Sections 2251–2260 forbids production of child pornography (fifteen- to thirty-year sentence), selling or buying children for sexual exploitation (thirty years to life), possession, distribution, and receipt of child pornography (five- to twenty-year sentence), and importation of child pornography (ten-year sentence). The severity of the sentences alone testifies to the seriousness with which the federal criminal justice system treats child pornography. Yet it is all too easy to encounter what appears to be "kiddie porn" online. One of the reasons is articulated by the Department of Justice: "The Internet allows images and digitized movies to be reproduced and disseminated to tens of thousands of individuals at the click of a button.... The technological ease, lack of expense, and anonymity in obtaining and distributing child pornography has resulted in an explosion in the availability, accessibility, and volume of child pornography."[3] The distribution of child pornography anonymously, worldwide via the Web, has allowed a formerly well-controlled crime to explode from the mid-1980s to the present. Ironically, the digital nature of the images has allowed law enforcement to discover and verify possession of known illegal porn in the computers and media of suspects, facilitating enforcement. However, the wide proliferation of images and mingling with other adult materials have created a large burden for the criminal justice system. As much as half of federal, state, and local law enforcement computer forensic examinations involve kiddie porn.

Child pornography involves explicit photos and videos that can be found in many places, including foreign Web sites offering downloads of images that are illegal to view, possess, or convey in America. From the titles and cover photos, even hotel adult videos available on demand on room TVs seem to involve underage performers, although technically they may be of legal age. Complicating enforcement is the cultivation of adult male taste for "young" females engaging in explicit sexual acts, as illustrated by frequent use of such terms as *coed, schoolgirl, teen,* and *young amateur girls* in porn titles. Appearance and dress or undress can make it virtually impossible to ascertain the age of the participants to a casual viewer, but seeking youth in porn sites online is apt to result in finding illegal materials. Because the statutes forbid possession of child pornography, Internet users must be careful to avoid youthful images. However, the same caution applies to investigators, who can inadvertently download child pornography in the course of a routine investigation. The National Center for Missing and Exploited Children, by an act of Congress, handles reports of child exploitation, including child pornography. Further information is available on their Web site, www.ncmec.org, and specific child exploitation guidance can be found at http://www.ncmec.org/missingkids/servlet/PageServlet?LanguageCountry=en_US&PageId=218.

Pornography is a big business on the Internet, and can constitute a problem in and of itself for employers and investigators, such as by consuming systems/network bandwidth, employee diversion, creating a hostile workplace environment, and malware downloads.[4] "As of June 2008, 36 percent of Internet users visit at least one adult Web site each month, according to comScore (2008)." Some porn Web sites are run by organized criminals who offer other services as well, such as prostitution; commit other crimes, such as credit card fraud; and harvest identity information online for spammers and crackers. The relatively large content and programs associated with photos and videos allow crackers to induce porn users to download malware, including bots that can make a user's computer into a "zombie." Bot nets of zombie computers are used in a number of cybercrimes, including distributed denial of service attacks, spam and phishing (fraudulent spam directing users to fake financial Web sites), and harvesting of financial information from individuals and enterprises. Banks and credit card companies devote a significant amount of resources to securing users' identities and transactions against criminals whose advantage stems from the popularity of online pornography. But employers potentially face the most serious risks from online porn, among which are inappropriate and offensive materials displayed on workplace screens, illegal materials including child pornography captured by and stored on enterprise systems, significant diversion from work time and attention by access to online porn, and malware imported into enterprise systems from porn Web sites. Such malware might be used to access and take high-value intellectual property from the enterprise.

Unauthorized Use of Computer Systems

Federal and state laws forbid unauthorized access to and use of computer systems, which can include acquiring, altering, or deleting proprietary data and misusing or disabling proprietary systems. There is a subculture of Internet users who believe that it is their right, if not legal and ethical, to log on to any system that allows them access (even if they must deceive or dissemble to do so), and to acquire and use as they see fit any information that they find. Title 18, U.S. Code, Sections 1029 and 1030 forbid unauthorized access to or misuse of systems or data. These statutes were enacted at least in part due to the fact that someone can steal data and computer/network services from another merely because he or she can cause the targeted system to let him or her in. Early intruders learned that social manipulation and "dumpster diving" were even more successful than clever computer programming in gaining unauthorized access to systems, by finding out users' passwords through deception and in the trash. Today's headlines about Chinese, Russian, and organized crime "hacking" (actually, cracking) reflect the fact that computer systems can still be induced to allow intruders inside, and nation-states, as well as criminals, have reasons to penetrate enterprise systems. At risk for business and government are invaluable intellectual property, secrets, and personally identifying information.[5]

A large number of computer systems penetrations have resulted in recent years in theft of millions of users' identities, financial information, and sensitive personal data.[6] Many large, market-leading companies have lost computer-hosted hardware, software, research, and development data worth hundreds of billions of dollars. While the loss and recovery costs are high for personal data, they are almost incalculable for data that could lead to the failure of an enterprise due to theft of its most valuable technology. In some intellectual property cases of which I am aware, market leaders became also-rans in less than a year or two, and the losses in jobs, corporate value, and national economic strength totaled many tens of billions of dollars. Competition in the world economy depends on our ability to protect the private enterprise's and government agency's knowledge, skills, and automated operations. Some believe that economic warfare is under way between nations willing to support cyber war against competitors and against nations like the United States, which are as yet incapable of protecting the automated enterprises of the nation and its businesses. In truth, any enterprise or agency depends for its success on the ability to resist internal and external cyber attacks, and to ascertain how best to control its own cyberspace. Since the insiders of each enterprise profoundly contribute to or detract from its cyber security, their role is crucial to protection.

> International organized criminals use cyberspace to target individuals and United States infrastructure, using an endless variety of schemes to steal hundreds of millions of dollars from consumers and the United

States economy. These schemes also jeopardize the security of personal information, the stability of business and government infrastructures, and the security and solvency of financial investment markets.[7]

Among the vital lessons that an Internet intelligence investigator-analyst must remember is the likelihood that malicious code will be encountered in all probability after a certain amount of searching. Further, the role of the analyst might be interesting to a cybercriminal for many reasons, not least of which is if he or she is under investigation. The data in the analyst's possession might be sensitive and could even relate to the cybercriminal. While Internet information is being collected, it is possible for a sophisticated person or group to detect the collection and target the analyst. Among the measures to be considered, therefore, are the use of proxies and separate computer workstations for online searching, strong antivirus and antimalware, and constant vigilance to detect attacks on the analyst. Some types of investigation could use undercover roles (e.g., virtual identities such as email services, social Web site personae, and masked IP addresses) to help avoid detection by subjects of investigation or others who could pose a threat to the analyst. A concerted attack using high-end software designed for penetrating computer systems (e.g., password cracker or malware payloads in ostensibly innocent email) could pose a threat to most computer systems.[8] It is up to the analyst and his or her team to assess the nature of the opponent (subject) they are investigating, and to take adequate measures for self-protection.

Contraband Digital Assets

Besides child pornography, there are several other kinds of digital property that may be illegal to access, take without permission, possess, sell, alter, or delete. Examples include pirated (illegally copied) films, videos, music, video games, and software. The Motion Picture Association of America estimated that the film industry lost $2.3 billion to Internet piracy in 2005.[9] A 2007 study by the Institute for Policy Innovation estimated that each year, copyright piracy from motion pictures, sound recordings, business and entertainment software, and video games costs the U.S. economy $58 billion in total output, 373,375 American jobs, and $16.3 billion in earnings, and costs federal, state, and local governments $2.6 billion in tax revenue.[10] However, copyright piracy losses pale in comparison with the damages from annual thefts of manufacturers' intellectual property (IP), including research and development of new products.

In 2001, a survey of U.S. business firms by ASIS International and PricewaterhouseCoopers found an estimated annual loss of between $53 and $59 billion, and 40% of respondents reported a loss of IP. Various estimates dating from about seven years ago suggested that U.S. losses of IP totaled $250 to $300 billion annually, and U.S. IP has a value of about $5 trillion (about half the U.S. economy).[11] The Open Security Foundation's ten-year data breach breakdown of personally identifying information lost included 8% from fraud, 13% from the Internet, 16% from hacking, 20% from stolen laptops, and 7% from stolen computers (with the rest from miscellaneous losses), and broke down the origins of the loss as 63% from outside the enterprise, 21% from insiders (accidental), 8% from insiders (malicious), 3% from insiders (unknown), and 5% of unknown origin.[12]

Because there are too many intangibles to place much weight on these statistics, the important lesson is that IP theft is a crime with much greater impact than others, benefits a firm or conglomerate and possibly a country at the expense of another, and results in devastating damage to a company that loses its market edge to a competitor. Prolonged and deep losses of IP can mean the end of industries and of a national economy itself, while the 10 million or so Americans that have their identities stolen yearly suffer both financially and in terms of faith in the Internet as a safe medium.

Internet investigations are crucial to brand and IP protection. Early appearances of new products and services based on stolen IP can allow a firm or agency to detect the loss and begin addressing recovery. Today, it may take only weeks for a competitor to integrate designs acquired through corporate espionage into a new product, and the reverse engineering process has been mastered in parts of the world with weak policing of IP (e.g., China, Southeast Asia, parts of the former Soviet Union, and Latin America). While civil and criminal law may help protect U.S. corporations from competing products based on stolen IP within North America, investigation and recovery in the rest of the world can be challenging. Among the many examples[13] of significant losses due to IP economic espionage are

- Major cell phone and personal digital assistant models
- Personal computers
- Automobiles and auto parts
- Purses and leather goods
- Golf clubs
- Electronics manufacturing, control, and testing equipment

- Aeronautics control systems and software
- Biotechnology research, including pharmaceuticals

Periodic reports about knock-offs of high-end watches sold on street corners in major cities and on the Internet illustrate the issue. Whether or not a $39 to $99 "Rolex" is considered the real thing by a buyer, knock-offs do their damage to brands and the sales of legitimate products. Resilient markets for contraband goods allow stolen, counterfeit, and diverted products to be sold through both physical and online outlets. Perhaps the most insidious of these is the Internet market for pharmaceuticals.

Hundreds of Web sites offer prescription drugs online, including major drugstore chains, mail-order pharmacies, and health insurance plan–associated drug providers.[14] Illicit online pharmacies have proliferated in the past few years, offering generic and discount drugs, with and without a prescription, and often pretending to be Canadian pharmacies. American consumers, who seek discount drugs online, can easily be confused about the illicit online pharmacies, because they look and behave much like legitimate mail-order drugstores. Often, the online pharmacies are not in Canada, and drugs they sell are shipped from abroad to U.S. customers. Among many examples encountered over the past few years are

- Large (multihundreds of millions of dollars annually) Indian pharmaceutical manufacturers offering discount brand name prescription drugs through distributors online who pretend to be Canadian pharmacies. Often, these Web sites show photos of brand name prescription drugs but sell India-made generic drugs instead.
- Russian online pharmacies offering drugs without prescriptions, claiming locations and licenses in North America but in fact located abroad, often providing substandard, generic products.
- Drug distributors online located in Canada, England, the Seychelles Islands, and Asia specializing in Viagra and other sex enhancement drugs but offering a wide variety of brand and generic medicines ordered via the Internet and mailed to the customer. Some demand prescriptions and some offer a free prescription from a staff physician who issues a script from an online form without ever seeing the patient.

The most dangerous aspect of the online pharmacies (besides loss of money by customers) is that the actual composition of the drugs received in the mail may be counterfeit (including inactive and even dangerous ingredients), substrength, or generic products that may not medicate the patient as intended. Some customers of Internet pharmacies take harmful knock-off medicines, over- or undermedicating themselves, all because they tried to lower the costs of their prescriptions. Drug companies lose billions of dollars annually from illegal online sales. Investigative efforts by the companies, FDA, FBI, and Customs (to name a few agencies) continually find high-volume illegal activities and overseas operations that are apt to be up and running again quickly when they are shut down by enforcement, either physically or online. The volume of imports makes it difficult to intercept all but a handful of medicines that arrive in overseas mail. The cumulative costs of lost sales, investigations, and brand protection, meanwhile, are passed along to all customers.

Internet investigators may be asked to contribute to efforts against online illegal activities of all kinds. Among the steps to be included are

- Identify the owners and operators of the Web sites, where possible. Even though they are anonymized, Web sites can still be traced to the host network.
- Trace the corporate structure and financing of businesses associated with the Web site. Often, the owner, administrator, and technical and billing contacts are part of the illegal operation. Sometimes, the Web site is maintained by a commercial host that is not involved in illegal acts and would cooperate, rather than be implicated.
- Find associated Web sites, communications channels, and points of contact online.

Because of the proliferation of organized criminal enterprises such as those mentioned above, Internet investigations have become an important part of prevention and response for both law enforcement and private security.

INFORMATION (CYBER) WARFARE

There is also that National Strategy to Secure Cyberspace dating back to 2003; but there is no publicly available cyber war strategy.

—Richard A. Clarke, *Cyber War: The Next Threat to National Security and What to Do About It* (New York: Harper Collins, 2010)

Although any person or organization can engage in offensive information warfare, many of the operations that take place in practice are attributed to a few general classes. These include insiders, hackers, criminals, corporations, governments and terrorists.

—Dorothy E. Denning, *Information Warfare and Security*
(New York: ACM Press, 1999)

As mentioned earlier, because computer networks are a part of the U.S. critical infrastructure, and because (as Chinese Army officers have been saying since 1995 and Al Qaeda leaders since about the same time) the vulnerability of the U.S. information infrastructure (including the Internet) constitutes a "great equalizer" between asymmetric armed forces, cyber warfare has increased as a threat.[15] Chinese military doctrine suggests that information operations are appropriate even when war is not under way.[16] In the past twenty years, several major cyber attacks have illustrated the threat, including intrusions by both state and nonstate actors on Estonia, Korea, Israel, the United States, and large companies like Google. Some of these attacks were suspected or known to have come from (or been allowed by) the authorities in nations hostile to the targets. Besides disruption or destruction, cyber warfare aims include espionage, tracking dissidents, preventing demonstrations, and exerting control over information available to populations.

A key area of concern to Internet investigators is attribution: Who posted what is found? Information warfare activities consist of casing or scouting targets, infiltration, preparation for attack (which might include planting code on computers for use in a later attack), and small-scale attacks to test defenses, detection, tracing, and reactions of the target. These acts may leave evidence in server logs and files. Such evidence must be traced, in order to identify a perpetrator, which inevitably involves Internet searching. The difficult job of proving who conducted a cyber attack, or preparations for one, is a study in digital and network forensics. Internet analysts will engage in inquiries that may involve state actors (e.g., intelligence and military units of foreign nations), terrorists, crackers, and organized criminals, as well as ordinary hackers. Experienced investigators may be able to intuit from experience the nature of the attack and the probable intent—even identity—of the perpetrator, when it is not possible to pinpoint the actor with certainty. Piercing the veil of anonymity is a vital task, whether the misbehavior is a teenage prank or a serious criminal act. Proxies and intermediate network hops help in concealment, but may provide clues to the actors.

Press accounts and literature—both fiction and nonfiction—for over twenty years have profiled "hackers" who are devoted to understanding how computers, networks, and applications work, and how to manipulate them for any purpose. Defeating systems' defenses is a particular specialty of hackers. Today's toolkit includes a substantial amount of software created to help IT systems managers with security and testing, and applications designed to do such esoteric tasks as breaking encryption, creating and finding steganography (images with hidden, embedded data), and guessing passwords.

Journeymen cyber warriors no longer need to program to achieve their goals, because plenty of software is available for their use online. Hackers possess certain attributes, such as persistence, deep knowledge of computer functions, and insatiable curiosity, as well as varying ethical and legal standards. However, the hacker of 2010 wants to distinguish himself or herself from crackers, who apparently live to break into systems owned by others, and are considered cybercriminals. Like many who have been involved with computer experts, programmers, cryptographers, computer forensic analysts, and other expert users, I believe that there are "white hat hackers," who are highly ethical and apt to assist law enforcement and national security practitioners, and "black hat hackers," who are apt to commit crimes with computer systems. Internet investigators will inevitably run into both types of individuals, and should remember that skilled hackers are capable of avoiding detection, impersonating others online, and mastering many networked systems. It's also worth noting that anyone who spends a great deal of time in an activity such as using computers is inevitably going to make mistakes and leave clues and evidence of their activities.

What is similar about the average amateur subject of Internet investigations and the professional cyber warrior is their humanity. Humans are error- and accident-prone. Investigators focused on the most professional and determined adversaries like organized criminals, terrorists, and hackers should not assume that the investigation is impossible or too difficult to accomplish. In over forty years of experience, it has never ceased to amaze me how frequently intelligence officers forget or neglect to follow procedures and, by doing so, allow counterintelligence to discover their activities and minimize their effectiveness. Anyone can make a mistake. A subject may have an overt profile online, as well as undercover activities that are linked. It is the Internet analyst's job to find the mistakes and links, and see how they fit into the subject's portrait.

The most serious threats to business and government computer systems include talented and determined individuals who will be among those investigated online. The Internet analyst should remember that any subject of investigation could be one of them, and be prepared to find his or her tracks online.

NOTES

1. Fowler, Geoffrey A., "E-Commerce Growth Slows, but Still Out-Paces Retail," *Wall Street Journal* blog, March 10, 2010, http://blogs.wsj.com/ digits/2010/03/08/e-commerce-growth-slows-but-still-out-paces-retail/ tab/article/ (accessed May 5, 2010).
2. Child Exploitation and Obscenity Section, U.S. Department of Justice, http://www.justice.gov/criminal/ceos/childporn_stats.html (accessed May 5, 2010). Also http://www.justice.gov/criminal/ceos/childporn.html (accessed May 5, 2010).
3. Ibid.
4. Edelman, Benjamin, "Markets—Red Light States: Who Buys Online Adult Entertainment?" *Journal of Economic Perspectives*, 23(1), 2009, which discusses the economic aspects of adult porn online and the demographics of those accessing online porn; see http://people.hbs.edu/bedelman/papers/ redlightstates.pdf (accessed May 5, 2010). Also http://www.cybercrime. gov/cclaws.html#fedcode (accessed May 5, 2010).
5. In FBI congressional testimony and results of the annual Computer Security Institute–FBI computer crime survey, the toll on businesses and agencies from cybercrime has been outlined for over ten years. For example, Mueller, Robert S., III, Director, FBI, prepared testimony on FBI's fiscal 2011 budget, before the House Committee on Appropriations, March 17, 2010, http:// www.mainjustice.com/2010/03/17/mueller-prepared-testimony-on-fbis-fiscal-2011-budget/ (accessed May 5, 2010).
6. The Open Security Foundation's DataLossDB gathers information about events involving the loss, theft, or exposure of personally identifiable information (PII). See http://datalossdb.org/statistics (accessed May 10, 2010). Identity theft resources and information: http://www.ftc.gov/bcp/edu/ microsites/idtheft/ (accessed June 1, 2010).
7. Op. cit.
8. Hacking tools are described on http://sectools.org/ (accessed June 1, 2010).
9. Motion Picture Association of America (MPAA) statistics on piracy, http:// www.mpaa.org/USPiracyFactSheet.pdf (accessed May 5, 2010).
10. Siwek, Stephen E., *The True Cost of Copyright Industry Piracy to the U.S. Economy*, Institute for Policy Innovation, IPI Center for Technology Freedom, October 2007.
11. PricewaterhouseCoopers, *Trends in Proprietary Information Loss*, a study co-sponsored by ASIS International and the U.S. Chamber of Commerce, Survey Report, September 2002.

12. Almeling, David, Snyder, Darin, Sapoznikow, Michael, McCollum, Whitney, and Weader, Jill, "United States: A Statistical Analysis of Trade Secret Litigation in Federal Courts," *Gonzaga Law Review*, March 2010, http://www.mondaq.com/unitedstates/article.asp?articleid=97150 (accessed May 5, 2010); Yager, Loren, Director of International Affairs and Trade, GAO, "Intellectual Property, Risk and Enforcement Challenges," testimony before the House Judiciary Subcommittee on Courts, the Internet, and Intellectual Property, October 18, 2007, http://www.gao.gov/new.items/d08177t.pdf (accessed June 1, 2010).
13. Products identified as involved in IP theft are from cases known to the author.
14. Internet pharmacies offering drugs to U.S. customers illegally have been tracked by the author. FBI's online pharmacy advice: http://www.fbi.gov/page2/march09/pharmacy_030309.html (accessed June 1, 2010).
15. "Chinese Academics' Paper on Cyberwar Sets Off Alarms in U.S.," *New York Times*, March 21, 2010, http://celebrifi.com/gossip/Chinese-Academics-Paper-on-Cyberwar-Sets-Off-Alarms-in-US-1912782.html (accessed May 8, 2010).
16. Liang, Qiao, and Xiangsui, Wang, *Unrestricted Warfare, Senior Colonels, Chinese Peoples Liberation Army* (Beijing: PLA Literature and Arts Publishing House, 1999). The book asserts that warfare is no longer strictly a military operation, that the battlefield no longer has boundaries, and information warfare provides asymmetric advantages to China; Ventre, Daniel, "Chinese Information and Cyber Warfare," April 13, 2010, http://www.e-ir.info/?p=3845 (accessed May 8, 2010), which noted

> In 1995 the General Wang Pufeng, considered as the "father" of Chinese doctrine of Information Warfare, said that
>
> - The goal of Information Warfare is no longer the conquest of territories or the destruction of enemy troops, but the destruction of the enemy's will to resist.
> - Information Warfare is a war in which the ability to see, to know and to strike more accurately and before the adversary, is as important as firepower.
>
> In 1997, Colonel Baocun Wang added that
>
> - Information Warfare can be conducted in times of peace, crisis and war;
> - Information Warfare consists of offensive and defensive operations;
> - The main components of Information Warfare are C2 (Command and Control), Intelligence, Electronic Warfare, Psychological Warfare, Hackers Warfare and Economic warfare.

Wortzel, Larry M., Commissioner, U.S.-China Economic and Security Review Commission, "China's Approach to Cyber Operations: Implications for the United States," testimony before the Committee on Foreign Affairs, U.S. House of Representatives Hearing on "The Google Predicament: Transforming U.S. Cyberspace Policy to Advance Democracy, Security, and Trade," March 10, 2010:

> Lieutenant General Liu Jixian, of the PLA Academy of Military Science, writes that the PLA must develop asymmetrical capabilities including space-based information support, and networked-focused "soft attack," against potential enemies.

Xu Rongsheng, Chief Scientist at the Cyber Security Lab of the Institute for High Energy Physics of the Chinese Academy of Sciences, told a Chinese news reporter that:

> Cyber warfare may be carried out in two ways. In wartimes, disrupt and damage the networks of infrastructure facilities, such as power systems, telecommunications systems, and education systems, in a country; or in military engagements, the cyber technology of the military forces can be turned into combat capabilities.

Liu Jixian, "Innovation and Development in the Research of Basic Issues of Joint Operations," *China Military Science*, March 2009, in Open Source Center CPP20090928563001; *Dongfang Zaobao*, July 10, 2009, in Open Source Center CPP20090710045002; see http://www.internationalrelations.house. gov/111/wor031010.pdf (accessed May 8, 2010).

20

Model Internet Investigative Standards

Internet investigations are not limited to background investigations on applicants for jobs or clearances, but the issues surrounding Internet vetting are significant and deserving of specific attention. The principles for cyber vetting may apply to other types of Internet inquiries. What follows is a generic model standard, designed as a starting point for a government agency or business entity and adaptable for the use of any enterprise. Since national, state, and local laws, regulations, and ethics vary where the Internet and privacy are concerned, this standard is intended to comply with most current laws in North America and Europe, but not necessarily all of them. Legal review and customization should be a part of adapting the strategy, policy, and procedures modeled here.[1]

ENTERPRISE STRATEGY

Prior to adoption of standards for Internet use in investigations, including background vetting, an enterprise should have an established policy (see Chapter 21). A good place to start is with the enterprise's authorized use policy (AUP), which provides direction to those with authorized access to enterprise computer systems. The norms for protecting IT systems, as expressed in the AUP, should be consistent with those for Internet searching. Today, many businesses and government agencies have a *de facto* policy of allowing any employee to use Internet searching as they see fit in their roles, and to judge a person who is the subject of a search based on information obtained online in making decisions for any purpose. Unfortunately, there are several reasons why this unrestrictive approach can be a bad idea, including that employees may

- Choose to conduct Internet searches on some persons and not others, raising issues of discrimination, fairness, and equal treatment
- Conduct Internet searches in a casual, incomplete, and unskilled manner, or vary search methods/protocols for different subjects, thus raising the same issues as above and possibly missing critical information readily available to a competent searcher
- Judge Internet search results in a subjective way, overlooking some issues, focusing on postings that may not relate to the subject, and reaching invalid conclusions about findings without proper attribution or verifying findings with other investigation
- Act on Internet findings without adequate documentation of the basis for a decision, thus leaving the enterprise without a defense in case of a complaint or lawsuit

In both government and private sector discussions of Internet vetting, it is not unusual to find misunderstanding of the key reasons for Internet searching of persons, which include seeking indications of prior (un) trustworthiness in computer use (a job- and AUP-related factor for most employers and employees); ascertaining behaviors from Internet postings that relate to an individual's eligibility and qualifications for employment, including good judgment (i.e., finding facts online that prior to the Internet were found offline); and finding facts, intelligence, leads, and background information relevant to an investigation. It seems that the freedom to use the Internet as one wishes is somehow limited in some people's minds if the employer exercises its freedom to use the Internet to learn what might be revealed about a person. Provided that logical and legal approaches are taken by both employee and employer, there is no reason that both cannot be free to use the Internet as they wish. The existence and use of the Internet do not entitle anyone to act in an illicit or antisocial manner.

It is useful to reiterate the reason for Internet vetting, even if an applicant has logged on and shown a prospective employer the contents of Web sites, social networking profiles, and other online sites (as some law enforcement and intelligence agencies require). How else will an agency verify that the applicant has displayed all the sites, all the content, and all the past postings that may be relevant to an offer of employment? When an agency decides to ask a candidate to display his or her postings, it is an acknowledgment that review of the data is important, yet it is equally important to verify the applicant's honesty and candor, and see if there is more online (including items posted by others relevant to the subject).

MODEL INTERNET SEARCH GUIDELINES

These Internet search guidelines shall be applied when an Internet search is conducted for an investigative purpose, including searches for gathering background information to support hiring, promotion, and access to protected data, conducting investigations for due diligence, to protect or resolve security issues with information systems, to gather evidence of illegal activities, and for investigations and intelligence operations conducted at the direction of the legal, human resources, IT, and security departments.

Internet searches will be conducted in a thorough, professional manner to achieve optimal results either in house or through an authorized vendor to ensure that they are conducted:

- By trained and experienced personnel using approved systems
- In substantially the same manner for all individuals of the same type
- In accordance with legal, ethical, and enterprise requirements

Internet searches will be conducted, to the extent possible:

- Efficiently, within the time, information systems, client requirements and up-to-date methodology available
- Thoroughly, accessing and retrieving data from as comprehensive an array of resources as possible
- Accurately, using precise search terms, logical variations, and sound methods to find and ascribe information correctly
- To meet the stated needs of the client within enterprise policy

Results of Internet searches will be analyzed and reported in accordance with the following criteria:

- Attribution of information to individual(s) will be supported with evidence, including images of Web pages found and references verifying attribution, along with any indication of conflicting attribution.
- Information that could tend to mitigate, refute, or shed doubt on behavior attributed to an individual will be reported along with that which is attributed.

255

- Verifying data will be reported along with substantive information that could be described as derogatory in nature, conflicts with other information about the subject, or might lead to an adverse decision concerning the subject.
- Sources (links, URLs) and images of pages (captured in PDF or HTML format) with full dates of each item will be reported as appropriate, and collected data will be maintained as long as the report is retained.
- Ultimately, verification of data found online may depend on information received from other sources and directly from the subject, who may be asked to explain findings, and to whom results of investigation may be shown in accordance with regulations and policies.
- Findings not included in the report (e.g., items deemed not identifiable with the subject) will be retained in a file on the search conducted.
- Reports will be formatted to meet the requirements of the investigation, such as:
  - Include all items found on the subject
  - Include only those items that are needed for a specific purpose, "reporting by exception" (such as including only derogatory or complimentary items and omitting known or routine data that do not have a bearing on the outcome of the process)
- Combine Internet findings with other findings, or report Internet findings separately

Analysts tasked with reporting the results of Internet searches must be careful to assess whether findings include false references (e.g., same name, another person), false information (posted in error or on purpose as an attack or as a "joke"), or a disclosure of information about a protected class (race, religion) or about a highly sensitive and potentially embarrassing situation not meant for disclosure. In some instances, an investigator may gain the impression from postings relating to a subject's circle of acquaintances that items about the subject are hazing or harassment, possibly untrue, and would require verification and explanation for a full understanding of their meaning. In some instances, findings could include attributes and activities that may not, under Equal Employment Opportunity law or regulation, be considered for employment.[2] Reports must properly include facts and findings relevant to the investigation, and not those considered irrelevant or prohibited under the law.

Internet searches conducted as part of a background investigation for employment, promotion, or access to protected information are to verify that the person is eligible and qualified for the job, he or she provided true information about his or her background, and to discover any information that appears to call a candidacy into question. All misbehavior should be reported. Minor incidents of juvenile misbehavior online will not be grounds for adverse action, provided that the individual demonstrates the intent to meet enterprise standards.

Prior to final adjudication of a candidacy with substantial Internet search results that could cause an adverse finding, results should be reviewed by a designated management unit and subjects should be provided an opportunity to address the issues raised; verify, explain, or deny the items reported; and furnish facts or mitigation. In appropriate instances, a person should be given the opportunity to express an intent to adhere to all applicable requirements. This process will be followed when a group of candidates deemed otherwise equally qualified for a position includes one or more with derogatory Internet search findings. The process will be carried out by trained staff and address issues raised to determine the

- Facts and circumstances (mitigating or otherwise)
- Seriousness of and culpability for any misbehavior
- Dates of occurrence
- Likelihood of recurrence
- Subject's determination to avoid similar misbehavior in the future

A decision should be made on the subject's eligibility based on the findings from the review.

All personally identifying information involved in an Internet search and review should be properly secured against unauthorized disclosure using approved enterprise processes. When the Internet search and personally identifying materials are no longer needed, they should be destroyed and destruction documented in accordance with enterprise process.

AUTHORIZED INTERNET SEARCH PERSONNEL

Those conducting Internet searches under the guidelines must be trained, must demonstrate a capability with the proper systems, methods, and judgment needed, and should be experienced in Internet investigation. If in-house, the unit should be trained, equipped, and audited to ensure fairness and efficiency. If Internet searching is outsourced, the provider should be contracted to meet the client's standards, and the provider's reports and methods should be reviewed periodically for accuracy, timeliness, and adherence to requirements.

Among the attributes necessary for Internet analysts are strong ethics; an understanding of the types of information found online, major search engines, tools and techniques, the legal and regulatory issues that might arise from certain findings, report writing, and investigative documentation; discretion; and familiarity with security principles. Analysts should be trained in using automated search tools. Less experienced analysts should be supervised and mentored to ensure that their results meet guidelines. Reports on Internet searches should be approved by supervisors prior to presentation to the client.

Since reliability, credibility, attribution, and verification are particularly important in Internet investigations, analysts and supervisors of reporting should pay particular attention to

- Data apparently attributable to the subject without verification
- Comparison of data attributed to the subject with known facts
- Nature of sources linking subject with derogatory information
- Certainty that derogatory information refers to subject and not someone else
- Credibility of the Web sites and postings involved
- Potential sources of verification of information derived from postings
- Indicators of accuracy or inaccuracy in postings
- Mitigating circumstances relevant to analysis of findings

During a review of adverse findings based on Internet search results, it may be appropriate to consider alternatives to actions such as discharge, denial of an employment opportunity, or denial of a clearance, in favor of rehabilitation, probation, monitoring, and training, particularly when the individual is new or unfamiliar with AUP standards and the behavior found is unacceptable in the workplace but relatively commonplace on the Internet. The purpose of the process is to assess whether the subject's documented past behavior indicates that future behavior can reasonably be expected to be of a similar, unacceptable nature, or will meet employer standards.

DEFINITIONS TO CONSIDER

Below are definitions that should be considered when establishing policy, procedures, and guidelines for Internet searching:

Consent is an individual's documented acknowledgment or acceptance of specified conditions.

The Internet is a worldwide network of interconnected computers.

Internet posting is placing information online to make it accessible over the Internet.

Internet searching is a process of locating and retrieving data available on the Internet.

Notice is documented communication to individual(s) of specified conditions.

Verification is the process of confirming facts and evidence, such as obtaining corroboration from different sources or determining direct authorship of a posting.

Vetting is collection, examination, and evaluation of information for acceptance, such as a background investigation on an individual who is a candidate for hire, promotion, or granting or maintaining a security clearance.

Enterprise policies and guidelines for Internet investigations benefit when knowledgeable and experienced personnel participate in their formulation, just as the inquiries themselves are more effective and efficient when carried out by a group that has specialized in them.

NOTES

1. Precursors to the Internet investigative standards and guidelines presented here were developed in research studies by the author as a first draft of potential guidelines for use by the U.S. Department of Defense, working through the Defense Personnel Security Research Center (PERSEREC) under a Northrop Grumman contract. The suggested guidelines presented here reflect the author's views alone.
2. Federal job discrimination laws summary, http://www.eeoc.gov/facts/qanda.html (accessed June 1, 2010).

21

A Model Internet Investigation Policy

A business or government agency must confront the risks and opportunities presented by the Internet. Significant security and personnel suitability issues are created when individuals engage in illegal, illicit, and unethical behaviors online. Such behaviors include

- Unauthorized release of sensitive, proprietary information, either inadvertent or malicious
- Prohibited acts on work or personal computer systems that impact the enterprise, including criminal and antisocial behavior
- Time and attention-intensive personal pursuits that substantially distract individuals from their duties, may expose systems to malicious code, and may usurp IT resources, including computer cycles and network bandwidth using the enterprise network

In addition, large quantities of data posted on the Internet may contain references to applicants, employees, contractors, partners, customers, a merger/acquisition entity, or other individuals who have a relationship with the enterprise. Such references may include information with a material bearing on decision making or that may have a negative impact, such as unauthorized disclosure of proprietary information. The enterprise therefore should create a policy for dealing with Internet investigations where results must meet all applicable laws and regulations and withstand possible outside scrutiny.[1] These standards do not preclude accessing open-source information, including Internet searching, for authorized purposes other than investigations.

Following is a generic enterprise policy for Internet searches:

Enterprise Internet search standards and guidelines shall be followed when Internet searches are conducted on an individual or entity for an investigative purpose, such as part of a background investigation on any candidate for employment, promotion, or access to valuable assets, including information systems. Enterprise Internet search guidelines prescribe authorized searchers, procedures, and adjudication protocols. Executive approval and documentation are required for any exceptions to this policy, which will be in effect until changed in writing.

KEY CONSIDERATIONS

Following are key considerations for every enterprise regarding the inclusion of Internet searching in investigations:

- Some individuals may not realize that material posted online is almost all available publicly.
- Internet activities include fantasy, games, humor, exaggeration, lies, and other content that could create a misimpression of a person's behavior, character, or intent.
- Some postings may be intended for private use only, and not for broader access.
- Some information may concern an individual's protected class, including race, sex, national origin, or ethnicity, which are not to be considered in employment actions under Title VII of the Equal Opportunity Employment Act and related laws.[2]
- More than one individual may use the same email address or user ID online, thus complicating the identification of the person who posted specific materials.
- While a person is accountable for his or her misbehavior, mitigating factors regarding Internet postings should be evaluated (e.g., humorous items).

HIGHER-RISK CANDIDATES

Certain categories of individuals may be considered to represent a higher likelihood of having relevant Internet materials that could impact enterprise decisions, or justify cyber vetting because they will occupy a more sensitive position, including

- Information technology professionals and systems administrators
- Web site designers, software authors, and programmers
- Persons with access to the highest levels of sensitive data, including executives and managers and those in a position to compromise devices or networks, based on their assignments
- Sworn personnel of law enforcement, intelligence, military, security, executive, and similarly demanding positions
- Those with a prior history of extensive computer/Internet use
- Those with a prior history of computer systems abuse or online misbehavior
- Anyone about whom indications of improper Internet use arise from disclosures during application processing or from investigation

APPLICATION PROCEDURES AND FORMS

Internet investigations for background vetting should be supported by application procedures and forms that strengthen and document the notice and consent process for candidates, elicit information to be used in Internet searches, and protect the privacy of individual applicants by limiting the data required (e.g., no logon passwords for Web sites or systems should be requested). An employer may wish to include a policy statement about Internet vetting, such as that a hiring decision about an applicant's Internet references will not be taken prior to an interview concerning any questionable items. The forms (integrated into those used already for applicants) should include

- Notice that the background investigation will include Internet vetting
- Signed consent form acknowledging the above
- Internet-related questions as part of the application form, which should ask for:
  - Email addresses, user names, and nicknames used online
  - Web sites, blogs, online communities, and profiles used frequently, including social networking sites
  - Existing or past postings that might be considered offensive or illicit
  - Instances of disciplinary action or sanction for misuse of an information system
- Other questions deemed appropriate for the computing environment of the enterprise

The current state of the law at all levels makes the issue of prior notice and consent for Internet vetting debatable. Currently used notice and consent forms authorizing a background investigation may be sufficient for many enterprises. Most application forms ask for all the names used by the applicant, but often employers do not require a listing of all of the candidate's email addresses and user names, which in fact are virtual identities and aliases online. Explicit prior notice of Internet vetting is preferable to its inclusion without notice, but many attorneys believe that the current process can include cyber vetting at the discretion of the employer. They argue that when the applicant understands that prior employers, references, associates, and records will be consulted to verify his or her qualifications and eligibility for the position, addition of public Internet records is no more intrusive than the rest of the background investigation. Those arguing against searching without notice point out that some of the posted materials were not intended for viewing by prospective employers. No case law appears to back up this argument to date.

LEGAL ISSUES

In the absence of legislation, litigation, and a history of Internet vetting, every enterprise properly should consider measures to handle those few instances (3 to 6% of those vetted, in our experience) where derogatory information from Internet investigation could result in an adverse finding. Despite the low percentages, even one or a few individuals can represent a significant risk of large-scale loss. Background investigations including Internet vetting are often conducted only after a conditional offer of employment. In such instances, an adverse decision must be documented and the candidate may be legally entitled to an explanation under the Fair Credit Reporting Act and related federal laws and regulations. The subject is the person in the best position to verify findings, including attribution of postings, and explain the behaviors involved. An interview is most often appropriate for this purpose, and should be a part of enterprise procedures.

Interviews conducted during the background investigation process are a part of the investigation, especially when they concern verification and clarification of information discovered online. The honesty of a candidate in providing information to an employer is critical. However, for those heavily involved in Internet use, including email, instant messaging, Web sites, profiles, social networking, etc., it may be difficult to remember all the details of activities over the past seven years or more. For example, email addresses no longer used by an individual may be forgotten, and failure to list a forgotten email address on an application form may not be dishonest (any more than forgetting a street address). One reason for an interview about Internet activities might be to refresh a candidate's recollection about dated postings, virtual identities, or online activities not included on a form but found during an Internet search.

When an Internet investigation and subject interview leave an enterprise with unresolved issues, there are options short of rejection of a candidacy that may be appropriate. Some government agencies have asked a candidate for a high-level clearance or law enforcement position to demonstrate on his or her personal computer the nature and extent of online activities. In the case of a Bozeman, Montana, city requirement for applicants to provide passwords for access to their online accounts, a firestorm erupted in June 2009 at this intrusion into private activities.[3] However, if illegal or prohibited activities or derogatory postings are suspected, the best option for the candidate and the employer may be to have the candidate show the investigator the postings in question. Several chiefs of police have stated that Internet data are too important in judging the trustworthiness of candidate police officers not to require them all to log in and show an investigator their online profiles. This approach avoids violation of user agreements that prohibit sharing passwords to accounts, while allowing the candidate to provide a guided tour that demonstrates and explains postings.

Illegal activities may be detected by Internet searching. A common crime is copyright violation by collecting films, music, and software via file-sharing groups online, rather than authorized retailers. It is important for an employer to consider questions concerning such activities prior to adjudicating a candidacy, because common misdemeanors and misbehavior are likely to be encountered, and some standard is better than none. Examples include

- Frequent, high-volume illicit file sharing in which a candidate engaged
- Underage drinking and illicit drug use
- Inflated claims of education and prior employment experience (possible fraud)
- Use of work resources (e.g., computers, time, and materials) for personal rather than professional purposes (possible theft)
- Unauthorized access to, taking, disclosure, alteration, or deletion of proprietary data

CONFIDENTIALITY

It is very important to the integrity of the Internet investigative process that the confidentiality of the inquiry and any data with personally identifying information be maintained. Security measures should be carried out, documented, and audited periodically, in conjunction with related enterprise systems. When no longer needed, confidential, personally identifying data should be permanently deleted.

ETHICS IN INVESTIGATIONS

It is important to set limits on methods used during Internet vetting to avoid those that could be considered unethical or illegal. Examples of ethical principles include

- Search methods must not violate laws or regulations.
- Internet investigators must not impersonate a subject of inquiry.
- Internet investigators should abide by authorized use policies of Web sites to the extent possible.

DISCIPLINARY ACTION

Employers should include provisions in enterprise disciplinary policy relating to use of the Internet in violation of the employee handbook, ethical standards, industry standards of behavior, and government regulations. The employer's AUP should reflect the same provisions.

Because of the commonality of activities online that could be viewed as illicit or potentially damaging to an enterprise, employers should consider establishing programs to orient, train, supervise, and monitor authorized users who have a history of Internet behaviors that are not allowed at work. Examples include such activities as using file-sharing software for film and music sharing, connecting unauthorized external modems to the workplace network, participation in massively multiplayer online fantasy games or other online games at work, using pornographic materials or other data unsuitable for the workplace, sharing passwords for access to sensitive data or systems, making unauthorized copies of employer data, and storing large personal files improperly (especially illicit copyrighted materials) on workplace servers. The seriousness, frequency, and

266

likelihood of recurrence of such misbehavior should be considered in disciplinary or rehabilitative measures taken under enterprise policy.

MODEL FORMS FOR CANDIDATES

Following are model forms or instructions incorporating the elements needed for Internet vetting that can be used in addition to traditional (existing) forms to integrate Internet searches into applicant processing:

Notice

Information systems are critical to the success of the enterprise, and misuse of enterprise systems, networks, and data is regarded as serious and costly misbehavior. Employees must adhere to enterprise authorized use policies, which state that information systems are for official use only and online misbehavior that may cause harm to the enterprise is prohibited on any computer system. Therefore, enterprise background investigations include an Internet search (Internet vetting), that is, a review of information online that may relate to a candidate's eligibility and qualifications. Information from Internet vetting that could by itself lead to an adverse decision will be reviewed by the enterprise with the candidate, who will be given an opportunity to explain or comment on the information before a final decision is made.

As a part of Internet vetting, candidates will be asked to provide information about their use of computer systems and the Internet. Failure to provide complete and accurate information could be grounds for denial of the position or dismissal.

Consent

I authorize the inclusion of Internet vetting in a background investigation to determine or verify eligibility and qualifications for the position sought.

_____

(Signature)

Questionnaire

Candidates should provide answers to the following questions:

List all online communities in which you are an active member.

List any email addresses that you have used in the past seven years. Remember to include college, military, and Internet service provider (ISP) email addresses. Include all personal, work, school, organizational, military, cell phone, and instant messaging email addresses. List the type, and whether it is current or shared by another user.

List any screen names, handles, or nicknames used online not listed above.

267

List your own Web sites, blogs, or other personal profiles that are online (e.g., MySpace, Facebook, www.yourname.com).

List anyone who shared the use of an email address, or access to the same computer with you, including your spouse or significant other(s), family, roommates, etc. Explain.

Have you ever been disciplined or penalized by an ISP or information systems owner for failure to abide by an authorized use policy? If so, explain.

Have you ever been denied Internet or other information systems services? If so, explain.

Have you ever knowingly violated laws, regulations, or the rules or authorized use policies of an information system provider, including work or home Internet service?

Have you created computer programs, configured or managed information systems, or otherwise participated in computer systems administration? If so, briefly describe.

Have you ever been accused of or been responsible for an information systems outage, failure, intrusion, or security incident? If so, describe.

Have you ever participated in unauthorized file sharing, unauthorized access to digital content (e.g., software, music, movies, files), or similar unauthorized systems activities? If so, explain.

Have you ever connected unauthorized devices (including memory media, modems, personal digital assistants, wireless Internet, cell phones, music pods) to an information system belonging to an employer or someone else? If so, explain.

Please make any comment or statement you would like to add about your history of computer systems and Internet use.

The above suggested forms are not intended to provide all-inclusive, legally vetted wording for all businesses and government agencies, but they are a starting point from which policies and procedures can be instituted.

NOTES

1. The Internet investigation policy presented here was developed in the course of consulting for business, government, and academic clients by the author over the past five years.
2. Federal job discrimination laws summary, http://www.eeoc.gov/facts/qanda.html (accessed June 1, 2010).

3. McCullagh, Declan, "Want a Job? Give Bozeman your Facebook, Google Passwords," CNET News, June 18, 2009, http://news.cnet.com/8301-13578_3-10268282-38.html (accessed May 17, 2010).

22

A Model Internet Posting Policy

Government agencies, businesses, and other organizations should consider adding instructions on Internet posting to their authorized use policy, employee handbook, confidentiality agreements, and disciplinary procedures. Employees, contractors, and other authorized users can post to the Internet from work and from home, and items online can be destructive to the enterprise, if they are untrue, unauthorized, or illicit. Anonymous slander of businesses and agencies is relatively common online, posing challenges including identification of the perpetrator and a response to contain the potential damage. Following is a succinct statement of a model posting policy:[1]

> The Internet is important to us as individuals and to our enterprise, because so many people communicate and rely on information they find online. False, inaccurate, slanderous, or illicit postings can be damaging to the enterprise, our suppliers, partners, and our customers. We depend on our communications, marketing, and human resources departments to post enterprise messages online, including on our Web site and on other Web sites. Because of the risk of mixed messages, miscommunication, and damaging data online, all employees and contractors are required to adhere to the following:
>
> - Enterprise email addresses and official titles are not to be used in Internet postings or communications except as part of approved business functions.
> - Internet postings should not include references to the enterprise without prior coordination with and approval from the appropriate department and your manager.

- Employees and contractors shall not post items on the Internet that depict in text, photos, videos, etc., enterprise functions, data, uniforms, events, or plans unless they are approved in advance by the appropriate manager.
- Employees and contractors shall not post items on the Internet that are illegal, illicit, antisocial, offensive, or could discredit or reflect badly on the enterprise.
- Employees and contractors who find Internet postings believed to discredit the enterprise should bring them to the attention of management and the security department.
- In the event that an employee or contractor is found responsible for a posting or communication that is at odds with enterprise policy or is damaging to the interests of the enterprise, appropriate discipline will be taken, up to and including dismissal.

Besides a stated policy, organizations should consider additional awareness and training measures to deal with the fact that large numbers of employees and contractors are active online, with social networking and other profiles and activities. It is impossible and counterproductive to prevent employees and contractors from posting their employment details online. Recruiting, marketing, and a host of other business functions benefit from the public face of the enterprise on the Internet. However, it is important to have the support of all insiders in protecting the organization from negative postings.

A common problem for employers is postings by employees that are considered illicit or antisocial. Such postings can reflect badly on an enterprise when it is easy to see from Internet profiles that the misbehaving individual is an employee or contractor. Even when there is no direct liability or attribution to the enterprise, the disrepute caused can extend beyond the poster to the employer. Proper Internet posting etiquette should be promoted in training and briefings.

Contractual obligations with suppliers, customers, partners, and others can be impacted by postings of employees, contractors, and their associates, especially when they refer to inside information or reveal proprietary materials. Enterprise reputation and security could be at stake. Awareness and training for employees and contractors should include reminders to protect proprietary data belonging to the enterprise and all of its contractor/partner organizations.

Among the considerations to be included when addressing Internet activities are the confidentiality agreement used by many businesses and government agencies and the approach to employees who are undergoing disciplinary procedures, punishments, considered for layoff, in a dispute, or pending dismissal. Disgruntled employees may vent online either in their own name or anonymously. The personnel and security departments should formulate an approach that anticipates and mitigates the risk that a disgruntled employee could use the Internet to attack the enterprise. Case law supports the enforcement of confidentiality agreements in such cases.

Employees and contractors have a First Amendment right to express themselves as they wish, and experience has shown that references to employers online are overwhelmingly positive. Authorized Internet postings should be encouraged, including professional business Web sites likely to cast the enterprise and the employee in a positive light. Nevertheless, there should be sufficient direction in behavioral standards to discourage misbehavior involving Internet postings.

NOTE

1. The Internet posting policy presented here was developed in the course of consulting for business, government, and academic clients by the author over the past five years.

23

Internet Intelligence Issues

This book will not solve all the issues surrounding Internet investigations and intelligence, but it will allow any practitioner or organization to establish the foundation for sound methodology. The urgency of the need to address Internet behaviors and data available online is illustrated above, but perhaps a bit more evidence is needed for both investigations and ethics.

PRIVACY

Discussing Internet searching with an executive officer of a law enforcement, intelligence, or security function elicits the view that their agencies are free to use the Internet to collect public information about an individual without question. The same discussion with corporate clients and attorneys for the past four plus years has elicited different views, as have the relatively few published legal opinions. Uncertainty over what privacy means on the Internet has paralyzed individuals and organizations who understand the issue of Web postings' threat to an enterprise's well-being, and that paralysis means that there are no Internet search standards. Despite the favorable view in the courts (see Chapter 7) that public postings are not protected, doubt persists. Internet searching as an area of professional practice has probably suffered due to this uncertainty.

At this writing, the International Association of Chiefs of Police, in conjunction with the Department of Defense Personnel Security Research Center (PERSEREC), is conducting a study to determine appropriate standards for cyber vetting and Internet posting policy. Hopefully, the result will be balanced guidelines based on input and consensus from all stakeholders and authorities.[1]

The Privacy Act of 1974, as amended (5 U.S.C. 552a) does not contain a definition of privacy, and the act itself restricts federal government maintenance and disclosure of information about individuals, and permits people to access and correct records about themselves. Generally, federal and state laws recognize a "right to be left alone" and to have a "reasonable expectation of privacy" in one's home and certain other nonpublic places.[2] Computers, networks, and the Internet create additional venues where it is necessary to gauge the extent to which an individual has a reasonable expectation of privacy.

A working definition of "Internet privacy" is the ability to control the information revealed about oneself on the Internet, which implies that a person has the right to post items in a restricted manner, without fear that those items will be used in a way that the person did not intend. This concept, however, confronts the physical world's legal standard of "plain view," since anyone, including government authorities, has a right to collect and act on what can be seen in plain view. Regardless of the intentions of the poster, if the posting is placed in plain view, there is no reasonable expectation of privacy. At least two layers of plain view exist, in the author's opinion: items that a poster intends for a number of other persons to see, and items that are protected from display to all but a very few persons (or only their proprietor). In either case, when privacy is invoked by the requirement to use authentication for access (e.g., a user name and password), then there is an expectation of some degree of privacy.

One could argue that on Facebook, for instance, there is no expectation of privacy on a public profile—it is in plain view. On a profile visible to all 400 million Facebook users, again, there is no reasonable expectation of privacy. On a profile visible to a large number of "friends" (e.g., thirty or more people), it would be difficult to argue that the poster has effectively kept the materials to himself or herself. Only if the posted items are restricted to a small group could the poster expect that they are private, although anyone of the group viewing the items could theoretically reveal them to others, for example, by copying and posting them in a public forum. For all such postings, the objective test of privacy is whether the public or other people have free access to them. While the intent of the poster is important, if the materials are visible to others, they are not private. They are in plain view.

The plain view description above is complicated by the unintended consequences of posting on a site where programs may make items visible, or actively disseminate them, to other viewers. For instance, Facebook has introduced several site changes (and rescinded some under user pressure) that caused a person's postings to appear on his or her friends' profiles. Another example is updates on contacts in LinkedIn, which creates a thumbnail in a user's home page whenever a contact does certain things, like update his or her photo or profile. The attempt to market through social and business networking sites also makes users' data available to businesses affiliated with them. All of the above fly in the face of privacy, and the user's ability to control the dissemination of the data posted.

It is useful to consider the mechanism used to protect the privacy of the information stored on a Web site in assessing whether it is in plain view. Since the same method (user name and password) is employed to protect one's banking and credit transactions, society has come to accept this form of authentication as a protective barrier, behind which data remain private. You log on to the bank Web site. You log on to Facebook, MySpace, or whatever social site. However, there are at least two modes of protection when logon credentials are needed: information exposed to all or a substantial number of members who can also log on, and that to which access is denied except by express permission of the user. Just because the authentication is similar, that does not mean that Facebook is like your online banking. Clearly, items posted on social sites do not enjoy protection from those in the inner circle of the profile, and from any programming designed to share data by pushing it to others online. It is the nature of the exposure allowed by the poster, within the access allowed by the Web site, that determines the degree of privacy reasonably expected for data placed online.

For investigators, the plain view approach to privacy is both ethical and fair. If a user is naïve or unlucky or ignorant enough to broadcast—actually publish in words—data that are of use to an inquiry, then it is appropriate for the investigator to find and collect them. Users overwhelmingly choose little or no protections for postings, and therefore have no claim to privacy of their published data in plain view.

SMOKING GUNS

Some agencies and companies have made an effort to discover the types of materials posted that could pose a danger or problem for them as an employer.

In every instance, it has been possible to find publicly visible, outrageous behavior online. Examples of the kinds of problems that arise include:

- As recounted in the May 2010 issue of *Police Chief* magazine,[3] issues are increasingly arising for law enforcement as the public and defense attorneys find provocative postings, such as:
  - An Indiana state trooper posted a photo of himself pointing a handgun at his head, recounting heavy beer drinking, updating work activities while on duty, and making violent and derogatory statements about homeless people. Press reports led to an internal affairs investigation.
  - A New York officer on the stand in a gun possession case was confronted by the defense attorney with the officer's MySpace and Facebook postings, which included his mood as "devious" and described "watching *Training Day* to brush up on proper police procedures." The defendant had claimed the police beat him and planted a gun and ammo on him. The jury acquitted the defendant of the most serious charges, convicting on resisting arrest, apparently because the officer repeatedly expressed an attitude of violent hostility toward suspects in Internet postings, which reduced his credibility.
  - A New Bedford, Massachusetts, officer was under internal investigation for uploading a crime scene photograph of a deceased person to her Facebook page.
- A Hackensack, New Jersey, police officer elected president of the local Policemen's Benevolent Association union was accused of pretending to be the head of the department's internal affairs division in a popular online forum, but denied the charges and claimed his wife posted the materials out of frustration.[4]
- A Fort Lewis, Washington, soldier was arrested on espionage charges after a sting for trying to help Al Qaeda just prior to his deployment to Iraq. The soldier had reached out to Muslims and eventually to Al Qaeda with Internet postings and emails.[5]
- A forty-year-old male New Jersey teacher was arrested after lewd photos were found on an Atlantic County, New Jersey, school computer that he used to make the photos.[6]
- Cameron Moore, an Agilent Technologies employee, sent a series of anonymous (as "crack_smoking_jesus" and "dr_dweezil") emails and bulletin board postings from his work computer over the Internet, threatening physical harm to Michelangelo Delfino

and Mary E. Day, supposedly in retaliation for their previous online misbehavior. The FBI traced the postings to Moore, who later pled guilty to sending them. Agilent was exonerated in a civil suit brought by Delfino and Day under the Communications Decency Act, 47 U.S.C. Section 230(c), on the grounds that Agilent was unaware and disapproved of his actions, and only furnished the computer systems used by Moore.[7]

Employers are already dealing with complaints about, and accidental discovery of, individuals' misbehavior online, including facts found on the Internet that would have resulted in no-hire or termination decisions had they been known. In a conversation with a vice president of HR for a Fortune 500 corporation, I asked if their high-level background investigations included Internet searches. We were discussing an individual they hired into a prominent position whom we just confirmed as unqualified for the position based on an Internet search (after tens of thousands of dollars' recruitment and vetting costs). After a few moments of silence, of course, the answer was no. I was never able to ascertain why this and so many corporations with positions of such momentous responsibilities ignore Internet data, especially when so high a price is paid for a failure to find essential information. The case we were discussing is the ultimate smoking gun: A government database did not contain what it should have, but Internet postings of government sanctions identified the subject's fatal flaw and serious misbehavior. Just when it seems that the most important information on the Internet is the peccadilloes of netizens, it may be that a query of ordinary government records now is incomplete without a double-check online.

Most serious online misbehavior detected results in administrative sanctions against employees (e.g., firing or discipline), so most does not appear in public. For medium to large enterprises, Internet issues are a daily or at least weekly occurrence. The Internet and people's uses of it are evolving much faster than organizations' measures to address emerging security problems.

COMPLETENESS OF INTERNET SEARCHING

The vastness of the Internet and wide variety of activities raise a question about what constitutes a thorough search. Some personnel departments during background investigations arbitrarily combine a Google search with queries of Facebook and MySpace, ignoring hundreds or thousands of other approaches. Each enterprise should define what constitutes sufficiency of Internet searching for its purposes, based on a risk assessment and cost-benefit analysis of vetting requirements and methods. Complicating this calculation is the fact that there are thousands of Web sites that promote and host illicit activities, from extramarital affairs, to exchange of copyrighted works without permission, to sale and purchase of stolen property. Most illicit sites are part of the "dark Web"; that is, they are not indexed by Google and will not appear in casual Internet search results. Many users of the illicit Web sites will engage in illegal activities without ever being brought to justice. Frequently, the pseudonyms (handles) used in illegal transactions are also found in postings that allow identification of the individuals using them. By correlating the results of astute searches with identifying information on hand, analysts can identify those involved in online misbehavior, especially if they are sloppy and prolific posters.

In addressing the issue of what would constitute a comprehensive view of the Internet, an enterprise may wish to consider what illicit Web sites may pose a threat. Habitual users of such Web sites would probably represent an unacceptable risk. For example, an individual in the habit of sharing digital films or music outside of copyright restrictions would be a high-risk hire for a movie or recording studio. An animal rights protester would be a risky new employee at a pharmaceutical research firm. A bank would not want to hire someone who bought and sold stolen credit card information online. As part of its own security protection, an employer may wish to analyze those Web sites posing the greatest threat, and document, to the extent possible, those individuals known to use the sites. There are Internet intelligence firms that offer the capability of searching the virtual identities of candidates against data captured from the deep Web. Intelligence of this type can be crucial in background vetting.

As Internet investigations mature, there are at least several types of due diligence that will be added to those routinely conducted today:

- A thorough, automated search of Internet-accessible sites and databases for references to a subject's true name, virtual identities, activities, and associates
- A search of captured data from illicit Web sites continuously maintained by Internet intelligence service providers (probably private, not government)

- A defensive scan of Internet activities by employers (or their out-sourced service providers) to find postings potentially dangerous to the enterprise. This is done today for such purposes as brand protection, market assessment, and stock monitoring

It is likely that services such as those described will be provided by the same large data vendors that today furnish government and business with intelligence from large files on people and businesses. Small service providers will include private investigators and researchers.

ADJUDICATION

All investigative and intelligence work requires a customized, actionable product, presented in a timely fashion to a decision maker. The Internet age has made the intelligence process easier, yet complicated the process with a glut of data, some of which is decidedly less trustworthy than traditional sources. When I was privileged in the 1980s to take a course in the literature of intelligence from the great Walter Pforzheimer, the CIA's first legislative counsel,[8] at the Defense Intelligence College, I was struck by his insight into the difference between published accounts of spy stories and the cases themselves (as they appear in government files and the recollections of participants). Having participated with another great man, Tom Troy, in researching the history of the FBI and CIA (for his authoritative books on Bill Donovan and the CIA),[9] I had learned that historical fact and fiction are often intertwined. These lessons had been learned as well in seeing the difference between news accounts of FBI cases that I investigated, supervised, and managed, and what J. Edgar Hoover was apt to call "true facts." What other kind of facts are there? Apparently, Internet facts!

It takes more than a healthy dose of skepticism to judge the results of Internet investigations, and to make the resulting intelligence trustworthy. Making fair and factually supported decisions about people and organizations requires cogent review of all the relevant information available, assessing accurately that which is most reliable. The Internet is full of plausible but untrue data, and yet the quantity of factual information far outweighs the falsehoods. Careful evaluation can and does produce a very worthwhile product. The investigator, supervisor, and adjudicator must understand how to make valid judgments based on Internet data that are integrated with all other source information.

In addition, a process for balance in weighing the value of the information found is available in the guidelines used for adjudicating eligibility for access to classified information. Its principled approach allows the kind of judgments that will withstand scrutiny and tests of fairness. In my experience, routinely discussing findings with a subject and using a team of senior managers to make decisions that can be adverse are necessities in today's litigious society. Enterprises need people—all of us flawed—who can be oriented, trained, and mentored to succeed. When a relatively minor past mistake is found, that should not be the only reason for an adverse decision. In the national security arena, it is vital that trustworthy people be hired and granted clearances. In law enforcement, only the most reliable should be issued a badge and a gun. In granting access to computer systems as a trusted user, especially in the nation's critical infrastructures—largely private enterprises—only those worthy should be selected.

CONCLUSION

Internet searching has become a vital part of the investigative and intelligence processes. Vetting now depends on it. Despite the gap that exists in current law and the hesitation of some, Internet-sourced information should become an integrated part of findings for government, the private sector, and anyone involved in the information business. The notion that privacy or morale are impediments seem laughable at this time in history. Applicants and even students who are preparing to be candidates for business and government positions expect that their postings will be found and reviewed as part of the vetting process. The public would be horrified to think that someone could engage in notorious behavior captured online that is ignored by an employer. Litigation is likely for some who will be punished for their blatant Internet misbehavior, but there is no basis in law for their claims. Fair and ethical vetting will produce much better background investigations, and people have already learned that what one puts online can get a person in trouble.

During five years of learning how to conduct Internet intelligence collection and reporting, I have been indebted to Dr. Roberta Griffith, Tiffany King, Tracey Kropff, and Elizabeth Renzette, as well as my friend Jim Emerson, for what our team has been able to do. They taught me that there is a professional, right, and ethical way to do what is described in this book, and the quality of the intelligence results reflects the quality of these exceptional people.

NOTES

1. Mikkelson, Katherine, "Cybervetting and Monitoring Employees' Online Activities: Assessing the Legal Risks for Employers," *The Public Lawyer*, 18(2), 2010. This article provides an excellent overview of recent case law on the topic of cyber vetting. Entities announcing their participation in the PERSEREC cyber vetting focus groups include IPAT (http://www.ipat.com/news/Pages/Panel_Reviewing_Cyber_Vetting_Policies.aspx) and ASIS International's Law Enforcement Liaison Council (http://www.asisonline.org/councils/documents/DefenseandIntelligence CouncilNewsletterApril10.pdf) (both accessed June 1, 2010).
2. Privacy Act of 1974, as amended, http://www.justice.gov/opcl/privstat.htm. In *Griswold v. Connecticut* (381 U.S. 479) the Supreme Court overturned convictions of the director of Planned Parenthood and a doctor at Yale Medical School for dispersing contraceptive-related information, instruction, and medical advice to married persons, asserting the right to protect one's individual interest in independence in making certain important and personal decisions about one's family, life, and lifestyle.
3. Daigle, Eric P., "Social Networking Policies: Just Another Policy?" in "Chief's Counsel," *Police Chief* magazine, May 2010, p. 12.
4. Bonamo, Mark J., "Fireworks Erupt at Officer Anthony Ferraioli's Hearing," *Hackensack Chronicle*, December 18, 2009, http://www.northjersey.com/news/Fireworks_at_embattled_officers_hearing.html (accessed June 1, 2010).
5. Shukovsky, Paul, and Heckman, Candace, "Soldier Accused of Trying to Aid Al-Qaida, Sting Operation Leads to His Arrest at Fort Lewis," *Seattle Post-Intelligencer*, February 13, 2004, http://www.seattlepi.com/local/160510_guard13.html (accessed June 1, 2010).
6. Staff, "Teacher Accused of Taking Lewd Photographs of Himself Using Computer at Atlantic County Special Services School," May 11, 2010, http://www.pressofatlanticcity.com/news/press/atlantic/article_4a96d9ca-5c7e-11df-b747-001cc4c03286.html?mode=print (accessed June 1, 2010).
7. Samson, Martin, "*Michelangelo Delfino v. Agilent Technologies, Inc.*, 52 Cal. Rptr., 3d 376 (Cal. Crt. App., December 14, 2006)," http://www.internetlibrary.com/cases/lib_case457.cfm (accessed June 1, 2010).
8. Walter Pforzheimer died at age eighty-eight in 2003.
9. Troy, Thomas F., *Donovan and the CIA: A History of the Establishment of the Central Intelligence Agency* (Frederick, MD: University Publications of America, 1981).

BIBLIOGRAPHY

Berners-Lee, Tim, *Weaving the Web.* New York: HarperCollins, 1999.

Cassell, Kay Ann, and Hiremath, Uma, *Reference and Information Services in the 21st Century, An Introduction,* 2nd ed. New York: Neal-Schuman Publishers, 2009.

Clarke, Richard A., *Cyber War: The Next Threat to National Security and What to Do About It.* New York: HarperCollins, 2010.

Computer Science and Telecommunications Board, National Research Council, *The Digital Dilemma, Intellectual Property in the Information Age.* Washington, DC: The National Academies Press, 2000.

Dam, Kenneth W., and Lin, Herbert S., eds., *Cryptography's Role in Securing the Information Society* (Washington, DC: National Research Council, The National Academies Press, 1996.

Denning, Dorothy E., *Information Warfare and Security.* New York: ACM Press, 1999.

Fialka, John J., *War by Other Means, Economic Espionage in America.* New York: W. W. Norton & Co., 1997.

Hall, George M., *The Age of Automation.* New York: Praeger Publishers, 1995.

Hetherington, Cynthia, and Stankey, Michael L., *The Manual to Online Public Records, The Researcher's Tool to Online Public Records and Public Information,* 6th ed. Tempe, AZ: BRB Publications, 2008.

Hock, Randolph, *The Extreme Searcher's Internet Handbook.* Medford, NJ: Cyber Age Books, 2004.

Joint Security Commission, *Redefining Security,* a report to the secretary of defense and the director of central intelligence, February 1994.

Lewis, James A., *Securing Cyberspace for the 44th Presidency, A Report of the CSIS Commission on Cybersecurity for the 44th Presidency.* Washington, DC: Center for Strategic and International Studies, 2008.

McKee, Heidi A., and Porter, James E., *The Ethics of Internet Research, A Rhetorical Case-Based Process.* New York: Peter Lang Pub., 2009.

Nixon, W. Barry, and Kerr, Kim M., *Background Screening and Investigations, Managing Risk from HR and Security Perspectives.* Burlington, MA: Elsevier, 2008.

O'Harrow, Robert, Jr., *No Place to Hide.* New York: Free Press, 2005.

Rubin, Aviel D., Geer, Daniel, and Ranum, Marcus J., *Web Security Sourcebook.* New York: John Wiley & Sons, 1997.

Schlein, Alan M., *Find It Online, The Complete Guide to Online Research,* 2nd ed. Tempe, AZ: Facts on Demand Press, 2001.

Schneider, Fred B., ed., *Trust in Cyberspace.* Washington, DC: National Research Council, The National Academies Press, 1999.

Shaw, Maura D., *Mastering Online Research, A Comprehensive Guide.* Cincinnati, OH: Writer's Digest Books, 2007.

Sherman, Chris, and Price, Gary, *The Invisible Web, Uncovering Information Sources Search Engines Can't See.* Medford, NJ: Information Today, 2001.

Troy, Thomas F., *Donovan and the CIA: A History of the Establishment of the Central Intelligence Agency.* Frederick, MD: University Publications of America, 1981.

Wise, David, *Spy, The Inside Story of How the FBI's Robert Hanssen Betrayed America.* New York: Random House, 2002.

INDEX

For Product Safety Concerns and Information please contact our EU
representative GPSR@taylorandfrancis.com Taylor & Francis Verlag GmbH,
Kaufingerstraße 24, 80331 München, Germany

Printed and bound by CPI Group (UK) Ltd, Croydon, CR0 4YY
08/05/2025
01864475-0001